Yours Truly

Marieke Hardy is a writer, broadcaster, columnist and television producer. She is a regular panellist on ABC's *First Tuesday Book Club*, an award-winning blogger and the creator of the acclaimed comedy series *Laid*. Her first collection of essays, *You'll Be Sorry When I'm Dead*, was published in 2011.

Michaela McGuire's first book, *Apply Within: Stories of Career Sabotage*, was published in 2009. She writes a weekly blog for *The Monthly* called Twirling Towards Freedom, and her Penguin Special *A Story of Grief* was published in 2013.

womenofletters.com.au

Letters are love.

Edgar's Mission is a not-for-profit sanctuary for neglected, abused and discarded farmed animals.

Edgar's Mission's Farm Sanctuary, located in the foothills of the Great Dividing Range at Willowmavin, via Kilmore, Victoria, is currently home to over 250 animal residents. As an animal sanctuary, the mission has a policy to 'Rescue, Rehabilitate and Rehome' wherever possible. Edgar's Mission also runs adoption programs for people willing and able to provide permanent homes for rescued animals.

For the sake of the animals that could not be saved, public outreach is also a big part of everyday life at the sanctuary. With farm tours, school visits and appearances at markets and community events around the state, Edgar's Mission aims to inform and educate the public as well as expand their circle of compassion to include all animals. Feeling the warmth of a farmed animal can clear the mind and inspire change in people's attitudes and actions. After all, the ongoing decision to choose kindness is the greatest contribution a person can make to ending animal suffering.

And it all started with a pig. Edgar's Mission was founded by Pam Ahern and named after her first rescued pig, Edgar. Edgar Alan Pig, aka 'the pig who started it all', sadly passed away shortly after his seventh birthday party in April 2010. Edgar, a gentle giant, touched so many people and was an amazing ambassador for pigs and farmed animals everywhere. He is missed beyond words – but his mission will continue.

edgarsmission.org.au

curated by
MARIEKE HARDY and MICHAELA McGUIRE

Yours Truly

CATHARTIC CONFESSIONS, PASSIONATE DECLARATIONS and VIVID RECOLLECTIONS from

Women of Letters

VIKING
an imprint of
PENGUIN BOOKS

VIKING

Published by the Penguin Group
Penguin Group (Australia)
707 Collins Street, Melbourne, Victoria 3008, Australia
(a division of Penguin Australia Pty Ltd)
Penguin Group (USA) Inc.
375 Hudson Street, New York, New York 10014, USA
Penguin Group (Canada)
90 Eglinton Avenue East, Suite 700, Toronto, Canada ON M4P 2Y3
(a division of Penguin Canada Books Inc.)
Penguin Books Ltd
80 Strand, London WC2R 0RL England
Penguin Ireland
25 St Stephen's Green, Dublin 2, Ireland
(a division of Penguin Books Ltd)
Penguin Books India Pvt Ltd
11 Community Centre, Panchsheel Park, New Delhi 110 017, India
Penguin Group (NZ)
67 Apollo Drive, Rosedale, Auckland 0632, New Zealand
(a division of Penguin New Zealand Pty Ltd)
Penguin Books (South Africa) (Pty) Ltd
Rosebank Office Park, Block D, 181 Jan Smuts Avenue, Parktown North,
Johannesburg 2196, South Africa
Penguin (Beijing) Ltd
7F, Tower B, Jiaming Center, 27 East Third Ring Road North, Chaoyang
District, Beijing 100020, China

Penguin Books Ltd, Registered Offices: 80 Strand, London WC2R 0RL, England

First published by Penguin Group (Australia), 2013

3 5 7 9 10 8 6 4 2

Cover design by Laura Thomas © Penguin Group (Australia)
Based on an original concept © Tara Nielsen
Text design © Penguin Group (Australia)
Typeset in Tribute
Printed and bound in Australia by McPherson's Printing Group,
Maryborough, Victoria

National Library of Australia
Cataloguing-in-Publication data:

Yours Truly / Marieke Hardy, Michaela McGuire
9780670077298 (pbk.)
Australian letters. Australian literature.

826.408

penguin.com.au

MIX
Paper from
responsible sources
FSC® C001695

For Tara Nielsen, with love

CONTENTS

Introduction

Three years after its inception, the little literary salon that could has travelled further than anyone, especially its two slightly dumbstruck creators, ever imagined. In our third year we packed hundreds of postcards and pens into our carry-on luggage and staged shows right across the country. We held our first show in Canberra, in a musty auditorium underneath the National Library. We did so many festival shows – from Perth, to Darwin, to Byron Bay, to Brisbane – that we can't reasonably contain all of those letters between the covers of this book! Those festival letters will appear in 2014 in ebook form.

Although we still stage more traditional shows featuring five women than any other iteration, we've tinkered with the format a little more. As well as our annual east-coast run of Men of Letters shows, we've added something new – a 'People of Letters' event, wherein five pairs of people write a letter to their other half. Women of Letters began as a very simple concept, inviting women of note to pen a letter to a given topic and read it aloud to an audience. While playing with the rules of the format has been an ongoing delight, at their hearts the events remain constant – stories, memories and at times very emotional recollections from some of the nation's most creative minds.

The letters themselves have also spread far and wide, leaving our stage to be turned into books, feature articles and plays, as is the wont of their authors. We feel like proud parents, watching our children grow up and discover new career paths.

It's become something of a tradition that each show features at least one letter that has the entire audience in tears, and we're forever grateful that our letter writers have chosen our stage as the safe space from where they can tell their stories. Backstage, we've become experts in the arts of hand-holding, tissue deployment and the administering of wine. We know that reading these letters to a room full of strangers isn't an easy task, and sometimes worry about whether the writer gets the same emotional payoff that the audience does. We stopped wondering about this after one of our favourite participants wrote a letter to us a couple of months after her second Women of Letters performance:

'The truth is, standing up there and reading my letters has made me believe, for a tiny moment, that I'm not as terrible as I think I am. When I think I can't do something, I remember reading my letters. I remember doing that. And it fills me with happiness and hope that everything will be all right.'

It's our wish that reading these letters will fill our readers with that same happiness and hope.

Yours truly,
Marieke and Michaela

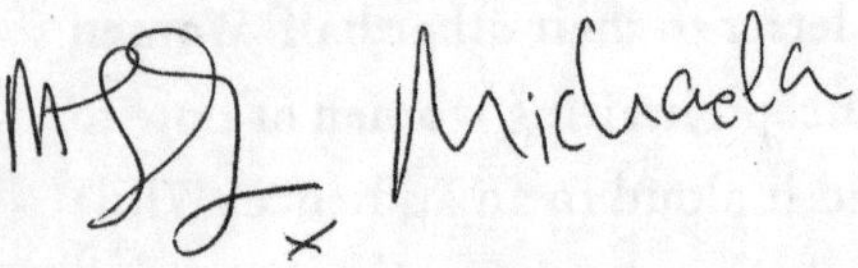

To a secret

CORINNE GRANT

Dear secret,

I don't know when you started. There's no distinct moment tucked away inside me when I remember thinking, 'Holy crap, I don't think God exists. Shit. Okay, don't tell anyone. Especially not the kids in your Sunday School class.'

It was the tail end of the eighties, and even now I can see that bunch of six year olds sitting at their little desks, with their little pencils and little pads, earnestly drawing pictures of Palm Sunday. Here was Jesus riding into Jerusalem on the back of a donkey. Here was everyone singing, 'Blessed is he who comes in the name of the Lord.' Here was the crowd waving palm fronds in celebration. Here was a time before vuvuzelas.

All the children were carefully tracing images of donkeys and temples, trees and people; all except Alison Shepherd, who finished her picture in thirty seconds flat. Alison took her pencil, traced both her hands on the paper and proclaimed loudly, 'There! Palms Sunday!'

If it hadn't been for my God-shaped existential crisis, I probably would have laughed in her little face.

I was sixteen years old at the time and a year before the misery of loneliness had claimed me. I had friends at school, but I didn't really fit in. I was a nerd. I'd never had a boyfriend. I'd only been kissed once, and that was by Peter and he was so drunk it's conceivable he thought I was someone else. Like his girlfriend. But at church, everyone liked me. At church I was a good girl. I *liked* being a good girl. And I liked belonging.

Every Sunday, my mother, my grandmother, my sister and I went to All Saints Anglican. Our town was so small, we could almost wait until we heard the bell in its rickety old tower clanging out the beginning of service before driving over.

I loved our church. I loved its tininess. I loved its red bricks. I loved the deep blue carpet, the stained-glass windows, the wooden pews and the handmade cushions we knelt on to pray. I loved the old version of the Lord's Prayer, because when everybody said '. . . and forgive us our trespasses as we forgive those who trespass against us,' it sounded like snakes were gliding up the aisle.

At church, I felt at home. I felt safe.

Well, I did, until I fucked it all up by questioning my belief in the dude I was supposed to be worshipping.

I can see now that this wasn't my fault. It truly wasn't. It was the Baptists. *It's always the Baptists.* (I refer you to the movie *Footloose* as evidence.)

It all happened in 1989 when a group of city kids – *Baptists* – rolled into town, took over the Girl Guides Hall and started a coffee club. Corryong had a population of just over 1100 people. Every shop, cafe or pizza parlour owner was either your relative, your dad's best friend, the town gossip, or all three. There was nowhere for us kids to hang out unobserved. Until the city Baptists turned up. They laid out tables and chairs and served up cinnamon toast in an adult-free environment. It was the coolest thing our town had ever seen.

And they let everyone in: the Catholics, the Anglicans, the atheists, the Presbyterians – they even let in the O'Donnells, and no one let in the O'Donnells. And their church was so different to ours. They ate real bits of bread for communion (not those weird wafer things) and, shockingly, they wore jeans to church. How hip.

My sister and I would go to the coffee club every Friday night, wasting the day in anticipation until the sun started to set and the doors to paradise would open. There was no indoctrination (we weren't forced to sit in a corner and watch a video about the horrors of premarital sex or catching 'the gay'), we just hung out. In fact, I don't recall anyone talking about Jesus at all. What I do recall was fitting in.

Sometimes we'd have campfires, or progressive dinners, or video nights. There was always something to do and someone to welcome us. Church was nice, but here were people my own age, welcoming me unquestioningly. Baptist Youth Group was where I had my first drink, where I heard all about sex and drugs. Of course I didn't *do* sex and drugs, I was Anglican, but I at least learned the right words to use in impolite conversation. It was where I learned the worst of the swear words and the best of belonging.

The believing in Jesus bit? I never thought about it. I believed in the group. When the summer ended and the Baptists went back to Melbourne, I went back to being a dork. After getting a taste of the joy of being part of something, the hole left when it was taken away again needed filling more than ever.

So when the Sunday School teacher retired, I offered to take the gig. It made me feel like those city kids: earnest, dedicated, selfless. I taught the children Bible stories, and we sang songs and put on plays. At Christmas time we dragged out the same papier-mâché donkey heads and three wise men costumes I'd worn when I was a child. Life had meaning. It had solidity.

I tried so hard to keep those city kids close. I'd write to them and tell them what I was doing and they'd write back full of support and acceptance. But at some point, I don't know when, I realised I wasn't like them. They really believed. Like, really, truly, actually believed. They sent me photos and you could see it in their eyes. And in the clothes they wore. And their haircuts. But mostly in their eyes. It wasn't in me like that at all. I didn't want to believe in Jesus, I just wanted to be loved.

I quit teaching Sunday School when I was seventeen, using the start of year twelve as an excuse. The main reason, though, was that I was afraid of being caught out. I needed to keep my crisis of faith a secret if I wanted to remain everyone's good girl.

I was at university, 600 kilometres away from my town and my church, when I first dipped my toe into the rip-tide of atheism. Frightened, I pulled it out again almost immediately and instead told myself a safer story: it wasn't that I didn't believe in God, I just didn't believe in organised religion. Then I got a little braver, saying that I believed in something, I just wasn't sure what that something was. But deep inside I was still praying: 'That "something" could be you, God – just tell me I'm right. Please drown out the doubt.'

To this day I have never said out loud or to myself that I don't believe in God. I will only go as far as saying, 'I don't *think* I believe.' The other is too big. It's too bereft.

And that's the secret within the secret: I'm not afraid of not belonging – I'm afraid that if there is nothing, no god, no higher power, no something-bigger-than-us-all, then I'm alone. We're all alone. All I have to do is say the words and I'm shot out into space where I'll float silently in the big, bad black for ever and ever and ever.

If I don't search into myself, there's still hope. Dear secret, the only reason I know you exist is because the thought of finding you out frightens me so much it sets my blood to fizzing.

It should never have got to this point. It was the Baptists. The bloody Baptists. If they hadn't shown me what believing really looked like, I could have gone on fooling myself forever. I could have remained blissfully ignorant of the non-belief I am petrified is lurking within me.

So, dear secret, I'm going to keep keeping you from myself. But I'll do you a deal: you forgive me my trespasses, and I'll forgive the Baptists who trespassed against me.

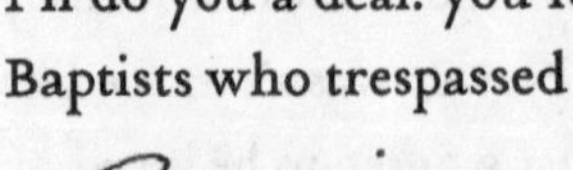

EMILIE ZOEY BAKER

I have, at last, realised that I must confess our affair – and end it. It has gone on too long, carried out in the shadows. Despite the pleasures I've enjoyed with you, you've forced me to lie to my loved ones' faces, to betray my principles. I can no longer live with you, my secret love: processed cheese.

Yes, processed cheese. The really fake kind, the kind that doesn't even go in the fridge: it doesn't need to. It can sit on the shelf in rip-roaring heat and it remains tasty and unspoiled. It's the kind of cheese that you keep in your zombie emergency pack for twenty-five years, and it's still noms. It's smooth and chemical-y and a faded yellow, like a sick lemon. It comes in squares, tubes and triangles, and I freakin' love it.

I buy a little wheel and hide in the car so my partner doesn't see me peeling open the back of a silver triangle and squeezing out the pale ooze onto my tongue. It breaks up in my mouth like a teenage relationship, all messy and short-lived.

I think, for me, it's what people call 'comfort food'. Although I don't really take comfort from it. I'm a massive food snob, I only eat organic-free-range-locally-grown-biodynamic everything – so it's more like a guilty-pleasure licking festival, experienced slunk low, sucking on a tube, alone, with the windows wound up. There's nothing comforting about that.

Processed cheese, you've been a secret I've had to carry through life.

I completely blame my Italian family.

It's ironic. You'd think having an Italian family would mean enjoying an enviable culinary legacy: the ability to make a delicious sauce from any three ingredients in the world, to whip up bruschetta for a light snack, to squeeze my own olive oil, to roll gnocchi with one hand while riding a horse. I *should* be having a sordid affair with antipasta, or scampi. A sexy tryst, just me and a cannoli. Admittedly, it would be harder to secretly eat a soup alla canavese in the car – you can't hide that shit in the glove box. But Italians would find a way.

They're not my actual blood relatives (surprise). They're my stepfather's side, and my brother's blood line. Italian blood. I loved visits to my grandparents' place when I was little. Their house would be filled with the glorious smells of my Nana's cooking, and I adored her. She was brilliant. She'd wake up at 4 a.m., cook scones for the whole family, go to work for a few hours cleaning the hospital, then return as we awoke, ready with breakfast. I loved her solidly. Her hands always smelt of onions and she held me like I meant something, like I was precious, worth protecting.

My brother and I used to mortify poor Nana by speaking our own made-up lingo we called 'Teddy Language', which was some bastardised version of the Italian we'd hear around the house. We'd speak it loudly on the bus, waving our hands in the air and slamming imaginary doors.

Makolacalankatoukolis! Coulo!

It often ended in a resounding *coulo!*, which I think means 'arse'.

Nana's arms were strong from years of cooking, preparing, cleaning, doing and fighting. Fighting with Nono.

My Nono didn't like me at all. He used to swear at me in Greek so no one would believe me. 'No, an Italian doesn't use Greek words,' they'd say. I'd see his eyes shine, knowing I knew he knew that I knew.

Nana and Nono hated my mother, she who married their perfect Italian Son . . . in a vintage green frock and sandals! While he wore . . . an open shirt! He had a big afro haircut and one of my earliest memories is him sitting at the table with pasta dripping down his black fuzzy hair. It was a proper Italian operatic cliché mega-moment – my mother had poured it on his head after a fight in which he'd declared her pasta wasn't as good as his mama's. I remember the spaghetti sliding comically down his head, flattening his afro so he looked like he was wearing a cork hat of dangling pasta. But there was nothing funny about his face. It was set with the blackest expression I'd ever seen. His eyes were as dark as a switched-off TV.

Nana and Nono hired a Sicilian witch to try and get rid of my mother – a fucking *Sicilian witch*. That's shit you don't wanna mess with. That's ancient, deep-dried hen's-feet, bull's-blood, under-the-fingernails kinda stuff right there. And it worked. She got inexplicably very, very sick and they divorced soon after. Well, it was either that or a bolognese in the face.

Yes, it was proper Italian madness in our house. Pasta, antipasta; love, anti-love. That's amore, that's enough. The stuff of life. Italians.

But here's the thing. While between her jobs Nana turned out impeccable, simple-yet-elegant cuisine in the kitchen at home, Nono worked in the Kraft cheese factory. He'd come home every day with some kind of sample and throw it in the fridge. Minutes later, my brother and I would devour whatever exciting geometric cheesy wonder had been stored there.

We weren't allowed to eat such marvels in our hippie home. I was the kid who was sent to school with peanut butter and bean sprout sandwiches, or 'pubes and poo' as my classmates so elegantly described them. I wasn't allowed anything packaged in bright colours, or featuring cartoon characters having fun. Food in a wrapper, all uniformly shaped, uniformly flavoured, organised like little soldiers of culinary normality, was so appealing to a hippie child. Food that was on TV. Kraft cheese was on TV – convenient, easy to eat, modular, factory-made. Clean and normal. What was not to like?

The Singles were the best, tucked into their plastic bed sheets. We'd nudge them awake and unravel them carefully so as not to rip the sides, then fold them and fold them until we had a leaning tower of tiny squares which we'd eat one by one, infuriating our Nono, who'd say, 'Just munch it!' But my chemical romance was something I savoured. To make that off-yellow tower of pleasure last as long as possible was key to its enjoyment.

And it all came from my Italian Nono. He wasn't a grey-haired cherub, ladling homemade sauce from giant pots, smiling like a Dolmio ad, teaching me a hundred things to do with a tomato. He gave me fake cheese. And he didn't even really do it for me. My brother, Nono's true grandchild, was the one he was interested in, the one he'd interact with. I'd listen in while he sat with my brother, running his fingers across kitschy pictures of children being guided by angels. He'd point to the boy in the pictures, and say, 'That's you.' He'd tell my brother stories of men at sea, talking fish and mermen. These used to fascinate me too and I'd lock into his face, seeing it as kind and warm, full of wisdom and delight. My eyes would trace over his long fine wrinkles, which ran from his eyes to his chin like guitar strings that would strum whenever he laughed. Which wasn't very often. (Unless he was wearing his apron that said 'Save water, drink wine', which seemed to crack everyone up.)

As a child, I was a kaleidoscope of love. It was unlimited and unconditional. I didn't know about family scandals and illegitimate children, about God-fearers and unbelievers, about secrets and dramas. I didn't know why Nono didn't love me – I didn't know you could *not*. It wasn't until much later that I knew about the witches and the affairs and the open-shirted dramas. I was only six, and my kaleidoscope heart had over a million colours, a million possibilities. And had he forgiven me for being my wretched self, I would've shared each and every one of them with him, and sailed on the deep green sea of his imagination, offering him new mermaids and opera-singing fish. I would have run my finger across the angel and pointed out that it was *him*.

But after my Nana died, he got meaner as he, and we, grew older. He kicked me and my brother out of his house, ripped out my frangipani tree and threw it over the back fence.

He had dementia, the mean kind. Not the kind where you wander out with a distant grin wearing ladies' undies. The kind where you write everyone out of the will.

It got worse and worse, until he was hospitalised. I was with the family and we watched him die. I blessed his soul, 'cause I figured it was around somewhere, floating like a Kraft Single in the ocean. He looked like a turtle breathing through his mouth. His expression was still. I held his hand: his skin was dry and crunchy, like old rosemary. Then, just like that, I saw life peel away from his face like Glad Wrap off a plate of scones.

I can now, as an adult, look back and say that I loved my Nono. It's an unconditional love, a despite-everything love, the optimistically kaleidoscopic kind of love that I hope will always be with me, no matter what. *That* love can remain, even as everything else changes as you move through life. Life isn't uniform or quality-controlled. It doesn't sit on the shelf forever, unaltered by time and experience.

And that's the problem with you, processed cheese. I've changed over the years, but, horribly, you haven't. You're the same as you ever were, preserved, identical to the day you were squirted into the packet. And the way I've clung to you is a kind of toxic love, a plastic attraction, a guilty fling, which needs to be faced up to and let go.

And so, processed cheese, my spongy industrial secret, I'll never forget the fun times we had. But for my heart, for my health, even for my love of Italy, I must now bid you . . . *arrivederci*.

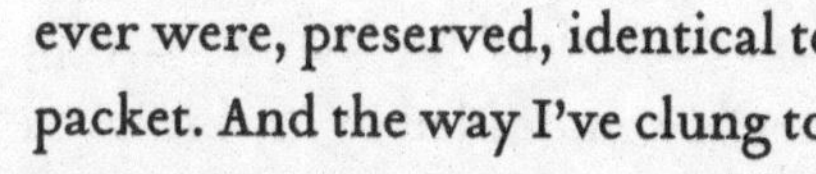

ANNABEL CRABB

My dear Marieke,

Thank you for your email of 4 January, in which you invited me to compose this letter, which is to consist – all being well, and assuming the spoken-word rate standard to a fluent English speaker of no more than moderate blood alcohol level and negligible recent narcotic consumption – of up to 1500 words, concerning a secret of my choice.

I begin by thanking you for the email, Marieke, but you cannot know the guilt and inadequacy that it roused in me the second I browsed its contents.

Let's deal with the inadequacy first.

For pity's sake, Marieke, I have just read your own memoir. Certain passages – the generous elaboration on your feelings for Bob Ellis, the mental image of your dog wiping its arse on the Ellis lawn and the unbridled lechery of the romantic object's own written response – are now indelibly and horribly embedded in my brain, as impossible to remove as crude oil from a Gulf of Mexico cormorant.

Secrets? Having just recovered from your own electrifying recollections of summoning a prostitute with your own boyfriend, and cowering in your wardrobe upon her subsequent arrival, what on Earth could I competitively dredge from my own not-especially-interesting amorous history?

Even upon that well-trammelled field, the ill-advised juvenile crush, I am hopelessly outclassed by you. Sure, I had a private youthful certainty that I would marry Kenneth Williams, the super-camp one from the Carry On movies. I maintained this conviction for several years, during which time history records that Williams remained celibate, though not so much because he was waiting for me to attain the menarche as because he was waiting for Joe Orton to become available.

But you, Marieke: You had a crush on *Young Talent Time*'s Joey Dee, and you *stalked him to his house!*

You understand my position. I feel like I've been asked to play air guitar for Bruce Springsteen.

Desperately, I have combed through my own stock of grubby moments.

What about the time I stole money? My friend Wendy and I were working as waitresses at a hotel in Adelaide's north. The dining room offered a buffet all-you-can-eat dinner and live entertainment from an elderly vaudeville star called Phyl Skinner. Phyl's show-stopping joke was delivered at the front of the stage in her spangled leotard and tights. (She was pushing seventy, Phyl, but she still had spectacular pins.) 'Ladieeeeezzzzz and gennlemun! My right leg is insured for fifty thousand dollars!' she'd holler, and kick the leg high into the air, to a cymbally punctuation from her band (which always, inexplicably, featured a one-legged guitarist wearing an Elvis outfit).

'My left leg . . . is insured for one hundred thousand dollars!' Boom-tish. High kick.

'And between them, I have an uninsured liability!'

It was excellent. On the night that I remember, Wendy and I were roving drinks waiters for what seemed like hundreds of boneheads who were celebrating the end of their amateur footy season. Phyl hadn't even come on stage yet and already Wendy had had her arse grabbed (Wendy's a bit of all right) and I'd had a schooner of beer thrown at me, the owner of the beer's fond intention being to see if my shirt would go see-through when wet.

We met by the bain-marie and agreed on a plan. For the rest of the night, we waited politely on tables and ferried jug after jug to the frothing blokes. The thirstiest tables were a forest of groping hands and proffered twenties, and in the confusion it was easy to charge for three Scotch and Cokes instead of two. Or give change from a twenty for two jugs, instead of one. By the end of the night, Wendy and I were drenched, weary and heavily pawed, but we had one hundred and sixty dollars, which we spent the following day on a spectacular lunch at Jolley's Boathouse, on the banks of the Torrens.

Oh dear, Marieke. It's not working. No matter how I tizz up my secrets with tales of Phyl Skinner's legs or her guitarist's lack of them, I can't disguise my unease.

The truth is I do carry a secret, and it's about you. When I read your email, I felt a deep, visceral lurch of guilt. I did something terrible to you once, and I feel very badly about it.

So I'm just going to come right out and confess.

Do you remember the night you came to my house for dinner? It was the night of the shit ARIAS, in 2010, the one on the steps of the Sydney Opera House when all you saw were close shots of slack-jawed nobodies necking flutes of champagne, or prolonged studies of the feather in Angus Stone's hair.

I remembered that you are a vegan. Not hard, I thought. After all, I myself don't eat meat. Some sort of eggplant couscous-y thing is what I decided to cook, preceded by a bowl of clear tomato broth, a recipe adapted from one I have by Gordon Ramsay. This broth is exactly right, I thought happily as I pottered about preparing it in the late afternoon. Vitamise fresh tomatoes. Fry them for a bit with shallots, then add water and some sundried tomatoes and basil, simmer for a while, then cool. Whizz the lot with an egg white then bring back to the boil. Strain it twice through muslin, and you're left with the most aromatic, tomatoey deliciousness imaginable. And it's as clear as the Mediterranean.

Fuck. Fuckity fuckity fuck. Egg white.

Oh, Marieke. What can I say in my defence? That all the eggy stuff was strained out, and thus I didn't really, properly offend your dietary requirements? That I only used the white, and that I sent the yolk away to live on a nice farm? (I am partial to that deception, myself. We once had a sheep dog that was intolerably vicious and used to bite us on the walk home from the school bus. One day when we came home, the dog was gone. 'Ginger's gone to live on a nice farm,' my dad said. It wasn't 'til about seven years later that the penny dropped. *We* lived on a farm.)

Nothing can be said in my defence, especially given what happened next. I fretted to Jeremy. Fuck! Egg white! He looked at me with the practised ennui of a person who lives with an idiot. 'Throw it out then. There's plenty of food.'

But I, in my foolish pride (it really is a very, very good soup), persisted. It's not like there's any egg actually in it, I reasoned. And she'll never know.

Can you imagine my horror when you looked me straight in the eye and said, 'Dare I ask how you got the soup so clear?' And can you imagine my self-loathing when I discovered – within seconds – that I am not only the sort of person who would crack an egg into a vegan's food, but also the sort of person who will then lie about it?

'Oh,' I gabbled, 'you know – run it through some muslin hundreds of times, simple really . . . Criminy! Is that a piece of spinach in Jessica Mauboy's teeth?'

'Well,' said Jeremy, after you'd left, having charmed the whole household, especially my transfixed four-year-old daughter who now wants to be you. 'Not much doubt about that. She was *totally* on to you.'

Please do not think, Marieke, that I have not punished myself in the months since. When my friend Amy became a vegan, I made her a peach and ginger cobbler using rice milk and Nuttelex, a substance so vile that the only way I can possibly extract pleasure from it is to imagine Kyle Sandilands forced to live eternally in Hell, eating nothing else.

I confessed everything to Amy, hoping perhaps for proxy absolution from a fellow yolk-dodger. Her eyes widened, then narrowed in a way that didn't look good. 'Wow,' she said. 'That's truly appalling.'

Now I, personally, think that her disapproval lost a little of its punch about thirty seconds later when she loaded up a cracker with Stilton and scoffed it. ('I'm really struggling with cheese,' she confessed, indistinctly.) But I certainly wouldn't allow one vegan's fecklessness to derogate from the perfectly righteous outrage of another.

So there it is, Ms Hardy. Having typed these words and reviewed them, I feel – not more at home with the fact of my own monstrosity, exactly, but at least a little better about having told you.

I hope, in time, you might come for dinner again. And I will serve you naturally-fallen fruits and berries, encased tenderly in a Nuttelex-shortened pastry and warmed gently by the radiant heat of my own shame.

With love and apologies,
Annabel

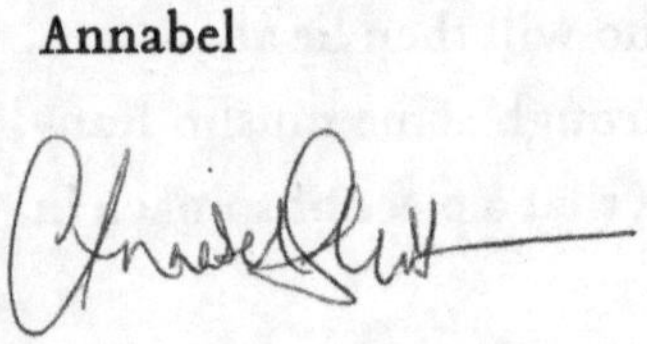

To the history I'd like to rewrite

MELANIE TAIT

Dear Troy,

Do you remember how we met?

Nah, me neither.

Dear Troy,

Here are the ways in which we were different:

1. You were born in 1974; I was born in 1980.
2. Your hair was as curly as the most delicious fried onion ring; my hair was as straight as the side of a calculator.
3. You looked like a good-looking version of Luke Perry; I looked like Lucy from *The Lion, the Witch and the Wardrobe* – the BBC series, not the Hollywood movie.
4. My dad owned the local pub; your dad was barred for life from the local pub. My dad barred him because he thew a glass of beer in Debby McLean's face. Not just the beer – the glass with all the beer in it.

Dear Troy,

Here are the ways in which we were the same:

1. We both had blue eyes.
2. I don't think there is a number two. I think that's it. I don't think we were the same in any other way.

Dear Troy,

I don't think I ever told you this, but I was scared shitless of you at school. Those blue eyes? They seemed mean to me. They seemed like the eyes of someone who'd tease anyone who was different, and I was different because I was the only fat kid in the whole of Robertson Primary.

So if I saw you riding down the street on your beat-up BMX, with your black parker, your flared nostrils and your mean-arse eyes, I'd go the other way.

Dear Troy,

When I was twelve, I convinced Mum and Dad to send me as far away from Robertson as I could get. I loved that place, but I never felt like I fit in there. Did you feel like you fit in there? I'm not sure you did.

The furthest place I could get was Glenfield, two hours on the dot away from Robbo. It was a co-ed boarding school. Did you hear that? A co-ed boarding school.

Which meant I spent an entire year lovesick for Andrew Clegg. Setting him up with my friends, pretending I was into cows, exhausting myself trying to be funny when all he wanted was hot.

Then, guess what? I got 36 per cent in my maths exam. But you knew that, didn't you?

Dear Troy,

Of course, Mum ripped me away from Hurlstone and co-ed boarding and Andrew Clegg.

There were tears and tantrums and my baby brother's toy trucks being flung at walls, but the teen drama of being dragged back to Robertson wasn't complete until she announced: 'Troy Stanton's going to be your maths tutor.'

'No way he is. I hate him. He has mean eyes.'

'He's a nice boy.'

'I don't need a maths tutor and Troy Stanton sure as shit isn't going to teach me anything.'

'Jesus Christ! Where did you get that language?'

I stormed off to my bedroom, full of the rage I'd copied from Brenda in *Beverly Hills, 90210*, and put on Judy Garland at full blast.

Later, Mum came to my door. Even though you lived about 2 kilometres away over two almighty hills, she whispered: 'Troy's a really nice kid, Mellie. He's trying to do something different with his life. He's the first person to do his HSC in his family, and did you know he got 92 per cent in the HSC maths exam? 92 per cent! At Moss Vale High! He hasn't been given any of the same things you have and look how well he's done. He's going to do accountancy at Wollongong Uni and needs the extra money for his petrol each day.'

'He called me fat when I was a kid.'

'When?'

'I dunno.'

'Just give him a chance. If you don't like him, we'll get someone else. I promise, Mellie, he's a really, really nice boy. And he's very good looking.'

'Gross. No, he's not.'

And Troy? That's how my mum decided you'd become part of my life.

Dear Troy,

Do you remember the first night you came over for tutoring?

I was so nervous I'd eaten three Milo bars, four Vita-Weat sandwiches, dinner and two bowls of ice cream. I'd taken the belt off my school uniform, my face was full of pimples and my attitude was just as volatile and pussy as my face.

And there you were. After ringing the doorbell, standing nervously on the porch under the dimming January light, swatting mozzies.

I stood behind Mum and took you in while she welcomed you. Your curly hair was short and still wet from the shower. You had your best Brisbane Broncos jersey on and it was perfectly ironed and tucked into the jeans that were belted tightly around your slim waist.

As you walked in, man, you smelled just like the David Jones men's aftershave counter. You smiled awkwardly at me. And your eyes? They weren't mean eyes at all. They were as blue as my favourite-coloured jelly beans.

Dear Troy,

Here's what we did during maths tutoring:

1. Talked about Judy Garland and John Denver and how if I kept listening to them I'd probably never get a boyfriend. Or if I did get a boyfriend who liked Judy Garland or John Denver, chances are the boyfriend would have a boyfriend of his own at some stage.
2. You'd sit next to me smelling all fantastic, and I'd try not to get caught breathing you in like the loser character in a romantic comedy.
3. Your maths problems:
   A prostitute has a busy, busy night walking up and down the streets of Kings Cross. In one night, the prostitute administers

> three hand jobs at $20 a pop, two head jobs at $50 a pop and one all-the-way session at $100. The prostitute's pimp takes 26 per cent of the prostitute's earnings. What does the prostitute get in his or her paypacket?
> *$192.40*

Or

> Year eight at Oxley College has 160 students. Of those 160 students, 110 kids want to go see Nirvana in concert. Fifty-nine want to go see Michael Jackson. One wants to go see John Denver. What percentage of year eight students at Oxley College will never have a boyfriend?
> *(I can't remember the answer to this one)*

Dear Troy,

Do you remember what I got in the final year maths exam that year? Seventy-two per cent. My marks actually doubled.

I got into the not-dumbest class for maths and a parental decision was made that I didn't need you any more.

A few years went past and you were right: I never stopped listening to John Denver and I never had a boyfriend in high school.

Sometimes you'd come into Mum's shop and we'd chat for half an hour or so. You'd wait by the counter and tell me what was going on in your life and needle me about Judy Garland, and you know what? I can't remember anything that was going on in your life. I only remember your eyes and how nice you smelled and how sweet you were and how even though we were both different to everyone else in town we were somehow the same as each other, somehow.

Dear Troy,

Do you remember that night at the pub?

I do. Like it happened twenty minutes ago.

You were in the bar. You'd given up accounting at Wollongong Uni and you had a job locally as a labourer. Your beautiful curly hair was wild and lighter and had the dust of the day's work in it. You were wearing a blue Bonds singlet, frayed and faded by time and sun and carting bricks. You were glassy-eyed, stoned and on your third beer of the night.

I was in the bistro with two of my girlfriends on a study break. Three private-school girls dressed in designer jeans and matching Esprit jumpers, each with private-school knots in our private-school hair. Eating fancy steak and being drama central about what we'd possibly do if we didn't get over 90 in the HSC.

And then, through the glass doors separating the pub and the bistro, you and I happened to be looking at each other at the exact same time.

We both pulled our attention away from the conversations we were having with our friends and waved. Was it really as slowly as I remember? That wave? And we smiled at each other. I know that was a long smile. I know it was. A wave and a smile.

And it was warm and it was loving and I know we both wished for just a second we were back at my desk yapping about prostitutes and John Denver.

I went back to my steak; you went back to your beer.

Dear Troy,

Here's the history I wish I could change:

a. That there's a public holiday for Good Friday. Why should there be? The whole country doesn't celebrate some dude on a cross.

And if there wasn't a public holiday on Good Friday, then in all probability – note the use of a mathematical word, Troy – Jimmy Baxter wouldn't have had a party on that Thursday night.

b. We're never going to be able to do anything about Good Friday, so let's go to the party. In the history I'd change, I would have gone to the party. If I had gone to the party, we would have got wasted together and sat outside in the crumbling gazebo and chatted all night about maths and shitty music.

c. I didn't go to the party so the history I would change here is that you would have called me to come and pick you up and drop you home. Then you wouldn't have tried to walk home. And you wouldn't have tried to cross the railway line off your chops, not realising there was a train coming. And you wouldn't have looked the driver in the eye and turned back in fright and been finished by it. And your mum and dad and fifteen-year-old brother and three-year-old sister wouldn't have been devastated. And your mates wouldn't carry your memory around with them for every time they get a new job, start a Facebook page, see the Broncos win a game, go to a wedding, have another child or do anything they can do that you can't.

Dear Troy,

The day after you died, your maths teacher came into the shop and said to Mum, 'How are we going to live without seeing those blue eyes again?'

I'd change history so we could.

Multiples and multiples of my love,
Melanie

Melanie Tait

JULIE POSETTI

Dear Julie,

You don't know me yet, but I know you intimately. I know your past, your future and your present.

I can see you now, squatting, huddled with your little sister on the floor of your cluttered wardrobe. You're trying to stem her sobs as the sounds of doors slamming, screaming voices and smashing glass pierce the quiet suburban night. You're worried your stepfather will hear your little sister as you try to stop her hyperventilating tears.

You show your sister only your strong face. You whisper comforting words. But you want to scream at the injustice and stare down the violent man who turns your book-bound nights into horror stories.

I wish I could reach into your present and rescue you from that cupboard. Transport you to a safe place. But I have no time-turner. All I have are these words.

You are strong, Julie. Stronger than you know. You are brave and resilient. And you already know the power of perseverance, at the age of fifteen.

The police will answer your neighbour's call tonight, but they will not see the covered bruises. You'll have to watch them walk away. And he will never change.

I wish I could tell you that you will get out of the house tonight, fall into the safety of Grandma's bed and never have to return to this dark place. I cannot. Not yet. But I can tell you that you *will* survive.

You will escape this place. Your mother will finally break free. Your sister will be protected. You will find a home to which you can return in the evenings without fear. From which you will not be forced to flee in the middle of the night.

You will meet men who prefer the power of words to speaking with their fists. You will even find a few who are tender and reliable.

Your brave, generous heart will know love, selfless love, and great friendship.

But a caution: I know you like to wear that bruised heart on your sleeve, and I so admire that about you – but be careful with it. Exposed hearts are more vulnerable to abuse.

And something else you should know: that wit you're so proud of, that dimpled smile that masks pain, the laugh that mocks adversity, the scaffolding you've built – they will not fool everyone. And they cannot protect you from heartache and heartbreak. You will know them both.

Why am I telling you all this? Why don't I just write down winning lotto numbers and the name of the man you'll marry and sign off now?

Because what you survive and how you survive it will be your history. You will trip and fall – sometimes painfully – but it will be living through trials and triumphs in which your identity will be formed. Know that you will never fail to get back up when you are knocked down.

You are smart, girl. And terribly outspoken. Those books piled on the floor and that fast tongue are your keys to an interesting life. Use them both wisely.

People will ask you, 'Don't you ever wish you'd just kept your mouth shut?' Well, at times you probably will, but you should never be cowed by the many bullies you'll encounter who want to keep the truth hidden or misrepresent it to the world.

What you're enduring now is cementing in you a heart for social justice, a commitment to freedom of expression, a determination to speak truth to power, a refusal to sacrifice your integrity. If you can soften those quests with an ability to listen and an appreciation of silent moments; if you can accept that betrayal, pain, disappointment and grief are inevitable human experiences; if you can figure out how to avoid fearing regret – your life will be rich, interesting and balanced.

I need to go now, but I want to leave you with one promise for the future: you will know the love of your own child. I'm looking at her now. And every day she reminds me more of you.

With love from the future,
x Julie

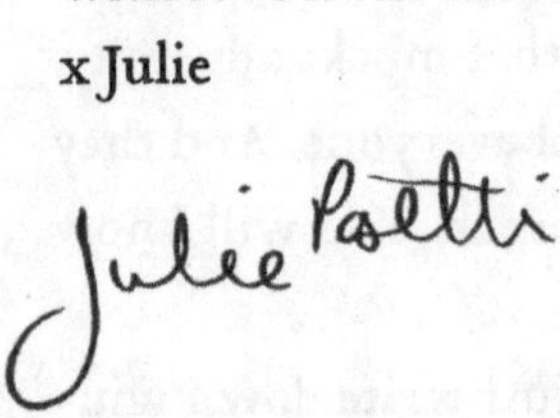

PS Oh, one more thing: remember this – a poodle perm is *never* a good idea!

PPS And another thing: the internet will be big.

LORELEI VASHTI

1.

I have the second-worst problem a writer could have. The first-worst problem is not being Joan Didion, and I have that too. But the second-worst problem for a writer is not being able to bear reading back over your own writing once it's published. I really struggle with this: once something of mine is out in the world, if I re-read it I always get a sick, churning feeling in my stomach. All I can see are the flaws, the weak bits. I see all the things I could have done better.

All writing is rewriting: this is something writers hear all the time. But I also worry that a big part of writing is in the re-reading. If you can't stand to re-read something you've written, you can't learn from it, you can't properly read it as the audience reads it, and you can't improve for next time.

Still, I really can't do it. Whenever I dare to re-read a piece once it appears in the world, I hate it and mentally keep rewriting it forever.

2.

At the University of Queensland they're doing the world's longest continuously running laboratory experiment, called the Pitch Drop Experiment. It started in 1927, when a professor poured some hot pitch into a glass funnel, let it cool, and then waited. His aim was to show that substances that seem solid at room temperature, like pitch or bitumen, are actually deceptively fluid. It took eight years for the first drop to fall, and since then there've been only eight other drops. No one has ever actually seen a drop fall.

The professor who is in charge of the experiment at the moment said this to the *New Yorker*: 'I've been around long enough that I just see time before and time after. It's only when the drop has happened that what has gone before makes sense in the flow of time. That is, I don't become aware of what is going on just before the drop until the drop occurs.'

3.

About four years ago, when I was living in Brisbane not far from the University of Queensland and the Pitch Drop Experiment, I opened up an email. It was a Facebook notification email, which is usually an invitation to an art opening or a clothes swap or a going-away party. When you click on one of those things, you don't usually expect bad news. So when that's what it is, you're not prepared. You click and then, boom: a mouse-activated bomb.

I had fled back to my hometown after a number of things hadn't worked out in Melbourne. Alone, rehabilitating, I was starting to feel stronger again after what felt like years of being lost, and my ex-boyfriend called to say he was coming to town and asked if he could visit. He would be arriving in an hour. We'd been talking regularly on the phone again, but it would be the first time in a year that we'd seen each other and, maybe because I was lost, or bored, or truly in love with him again, I decided I wanted to get back together with him. I'd had a year to think about it, and I hadn't been so sure of anything in a long time. Tonight, I was going to pitch the idea to him and I saw no reason why he wouldn't agree.

I planned a beautiful dinner. I bought flowers and vacuumed. He was going to stay the night, and then we would obviously get married and have babies and live happily ever after.

And then, just before he was expected to arrive, I checked my email. The Facebook notification was from an old friend who was now living in London. I opened it. A click and then, boom. The email told me that a mutual friend had died the night before in Melbourne.

The friend who died was a girl I'd lived with for a short time. We'd brushed our teeth together at night in the hallway, made each other cups of tea in the mornings. Not close-close, but close enough that when I read that email I felt my newly found solidity, the certainty and confidence I had fostered and nurtured for the past year, turn to liquid. My legs buckled. My body tried to burrow itself into the whistle-clean floorboards. I heard the cab pull up and my ex-boyfriend knocked on the door.

For the rest of the day and night, I was too discombobulated, too distressed by the unexpected news to launch into the big speech I'd been planning, the one that went – I think I'm back in love with you; wanna try again? We ate dinner in almost silence and went to sleep coldly beside each other. When he tried to hug me I felt my body go stiff and soon I pushed him away.

He left the next morning and then I let all my heartache out. I didn't know if I was weeping for my friend or for my selfish self, mourning all my lost expectations and hopes. That email was the unexpected drop of pitch. Before it, I had a sense of the future; a confidence that (having finally made a decision after years of avoiding one) things would turn out the way I wanted. Immediately after, everything was different. The hope in my heart was sucked up and away, like a letter in those pneumatic mail systems you see in forties screwball office comedies.

In the months following my ex's visit, I kicked myself. Said a lot of 'if only's. Rewrote the history of that day over and over in different ways. Rewrote it so that I didn't find out about my friend's death until the day after. Rewrote it so that when I did find out, it was by phone call, from a closer friend, someone who could break it to me slowly, gently, prepare me for it. Rewrote it so I didn't find out about it on fucking Facebook.

Later, as more time passed, I would rewrite it in my mind so that I didn't react so hysterically, like a wailing woman, in phone calls to him in the weeks after he told me he had a new girlfriend. I would rewrite it so I behaved better when I didn't get what I thought I wanted; rewrite it so that I acted more elegantly. Rewrite it so that those liquid drops I was crying were for my friend, and not for myself, for my hollowness and sadness. I would rewrite it so that I had truly been mourning her death, not my life.

4.

All writing is rewriting, and if I never had any deadlines I would rewrite forever, aiming eternally for the perfect sentence. But recently I happened upon some pieces I wrote that year, during the months I was pulling myself up and trying to get things published seriously for the first time, and I find myself re-reading them with pleasant surprise. Oh! It's not so terrible after all! I think. This girl is okay! I can see the work is not perfect, but I can also see what she's trying to do. I have a kindness and generosity towards her that I don't have towards myself in the here and now. After years have passed, the urge to rewrite those pieces disappears because the distance has already rewritten them for me. I've changed, so the words don't need to.

Lorelei

EVA COX

To Arthur Augustus Calwell, Minister for Immigration (the first one!),

This is my second start at a letter that I was asked to write to someone to whom I wanted to tell something. So I decided to write to you because a decision you made was responsible for my arrival in Australia as a refugee child. I wanted to write to tell you that I thought your policy was admirable, and that I was pleased that there had once been an immigration minister who had the courage to make ethical decisions. I wanted to ask you whether you could influence your successors to make similar decisions . . . But I have since realised it was not so.

This is how my first version started:

> I was once a ten-year-old who arrived in Australia in 1948 on a charter plane filled with displaced persons, chartered by the Jewish Joint Committee. With me was a cousin from Theresienstadt concentration camp and both our mothers. We came here to join some family members who had made it before the war, thanks to sponsorship by an Australian dentist who met my grandmother at an auction in Vienna.
>
> You let us come in 1948 despite the Gallup poll the previous year that said most Australians were opposed to allowing Jewish refugees to settle here. You are remembered

for saying, 'Two Wongs don't make a white', but, in this case, you did the right thing by letting us in.

Could you write to members of the current government and Opposition and explain the importance of ethical political leadership, over just responding to public opinion . . .?

But then I paused, as one does when writing on the computer, and googled some history of the time, and I was shocked to find more facts. I found we were among the lucky few who made it here post-war, as even then your government placed restrictions on the numbers of displaced European Jews who could be resettled here.

Sadly, the government then was affected by very similar power plays to those currently operating. Then, as now, perceived public opinion – rather than ethical leadership – was used to justify limiting the entry of an out-group.

So this second draft has a different purpose. Now it is more generally about writing letters to politicians. I can't use the process of writing letters to past people to influence the present if you were just as bad!

I wonder whether letter writing was a serious part of earlier political processes. Maybe in those days a letter to an MP was read by someone in their office, and maybe even at high levels. Now there is a whole system set up to collect letters, particularly those to Ministers, so they never see the actual correspondence from voters and constituents, unless perhaps the writer is somebody important.

Letters are now categorised for boilerplate responses by very junior staff: 'Thank you for your letter . . .' The formalised response indicates no serious action will be taken, except maybe the letter being passed on to somebody else.

Did letters have more effect in the past? Many would have been handwritten, or maybe typed and carbon-copied to keep as a record, and often they had some element of the sender in them. There may have been blots and corrections, and even the odd spot of tears, sweat or food to show the paper had been touched by human hands. Maybe the quality of the writing, the ability to shape the words clearly, or the spelling and grammar gave clues as to who had written the missive.

How did you react to letters, Mr Calwell? Did you ever raise questions at party meetings or in Cabinet about what your correspondents said?

What does cause politicians to take notice of an issue raised by the public? Do pleas from individuals ever influence change? Does a letter to a politician (past or present) still have some value? Have such letters ever contributed to political changes? People do still write them these days, even if few are now posted since most are sent electronically. How can we compare handwritten missives with temporary online blurtings?

My earliest political missives would have used pen on paper, at least for the initial drafts. These would have needed corrections, with crossed-out words overwritten at a later stage with white-out. I had a portable typewriter but was not a good typist, as I refused to learn to touch type for fear that I would become a copy typist. Because carbon sheets slipped, copies were often retyped to make sure there was a record of the communication that could be kept and filed, and I hated the thought of spending my time making those copies.

Handwritten or typed? Even then there were discussions about what was best. I had bad handwriting, the consequence of being taught different styles in England and Rome before arriving here, which spoiled my capacity to do the local copperplate required. I was always in trouble because my handwriting wasn't neat. So technology was welcome, as writing up my views used to be messy and hard. I'm glad I don't have to worry any more about whether my writing can be read – but writing this piece has made me rethink!

So back to you, the ghost of AA Caldwell, who I hoped could show the current ALP that bringing in unpopular immigrants is not a problem. Instead, though, I now realise it was ever thus: only some asylum seekers make it into the limited quotas. Then it was assumed that Jews would not 'assimilate' but would retain their own customs; now there are similar anxieties about Muslims in general and boat people in particular. Neither group is ever seen by the majority as 'people like us'!

Maybe if I, as a ten year old at Bondi Beach Public, had written to thank you for allowing us to come in 1948, and had asked you to extend the number of places, you would have actually seen my letter and read it. It might have tweaked your conscience about the very limited numbers you were allowing in, and made you think about those you did not allow to make it here.

Maybe your views would have changed if some of the adults and children who couldn't come had also written to you. In that case I could have used your example to ask the present lot not to use boat people as political pawns in a game of 'who has the nastiest policies'.

My other concern is that, as the nature of letters is changing, they will now be even easier to ignore. No longer do letters show some of the difficulties of putting down the words, or have a distinctive feel or smell. The differences in scripts are likely to be choices of sans or cum serifs with the blandness of the laser printer as handwriting disappears. Stationery and the quality of the paper were once factors that could enhance the content. A nice linen weave, a hint of colour and some distinctive ink were ways to make a contribution stand out from other missives. There is now little difference in paper because we all use bland copy paper, even if we post the letter rather than sending it electronically. They are easier to read, but very impersonal.

Personalising our viewpoints when we are not face to face is becoming much harder as technology mediates our contact. Letters are quickly becoming emails, tweets and other formats. Content is quicker, but blander. That might be why social media often involves visuals like photos, but this is not usual in serious political spheres.

Maybe we need to reconsider the use of images, which, interestingly, have been raised as a problem in lobbying for 'boat people' refugees. The government has banned their being photographed as it is easier to hide their humanity by just focusing on the numbers on a boat. The claim is that this is to protect their privacy, but it conveniently avoids the possibility of our seeing the faces of those we reject!

Would sending a pile of box brownie snapshots with my mythical 1948 letter to a Minister have made a difference? Putting the letter with some photos in an envelope could be the same as adding photos to an email, but we rarely include visuals in political missives. Maybe we need to start using images as well as words. The refusal to photograph boat people, which denies the humanity of their stories, is a good example of the importance of emphasising (or de-emphasising) the personal in the political.

How does all this relate to this letter to history? Am I just being sentimental and nostalgic in assuming that snail mail left a unique trail from senders to recipients? We know that new media can make instant multiple contacts and spread messages – but maybe we should think about how to personalise our political efforts again. Can we still use the letter format effectively to communicate our political messages? Any ideas?

Yours sincerely,
Eva Hauser (now disguised as Anglo Cox)

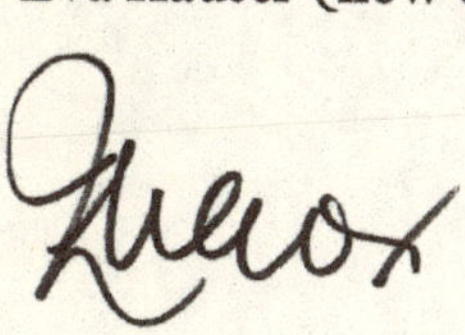

To the person who told me the truth

GEORGIA FIELDS

Dear Isobel,

By the time you read this, I'm not sure if you'll know who I am any more. I hope you will, I hope it with all my heart. But there's every chance I might be just a fuzzy memory. So let me introduce myself again, via this spooky 'time capsule' letter. My name is Georgia Fields. I met you in 2009 when you were six months old, and I have been your nanny for the first three years of your life here on Planet Earth.

Today it is Sunday, 19 February 2012, and I am reading this letter aloud before a gathering of correspondence enthusiasts. The event is called 'Women of Letters' and I've been invited to speak on the panel. My assignment was to write a letter 'to the person who told me the truth'.

When this task reached my inbox (do people still use email inboxes in the future?), I was mute with medium-level dread. Not full-blown dread, like for an upcoming pap smear – medium-level dread. The kind of dread you might experience if you were asked to riffle through the filing cabinet of your memories and pick out a time when someone courageously ripped a bandaid of blissful, comfortable ignorance from your hairy metaphorical knee, exposing you to the harsh and comparatively cruel reality of Truth. The kind of medium-level dread associated with having to articulately compose a witty and graceful account of such a traumatic encounter with

Truth and then to share the whole disturbing thing with a room full of strangers. Medium-level dread.

And so I started to wrack my brains. (Do people still wrack brains in the future? Or do we have a commonly shared brain-cloud of information we can plug into wirelessly with our minds, so no one ever has to ask, 'Who's that guy, I saw him in something recently' when we're at the movies?)

Anyway, I asked myself: which truth-teller should I write this letter to? The girl from my year five class who very truthfully pointed out '*you have a monobrow*' from across the school oval?

Should I write a letter to the person who explained to me that ponies are not baby horses?

Should I write a letter to the reviewer who, rather truthfully, informed the readership of one Melbourne magazine that my music made her 'ashamed to be a woman'? (On a side note, Isobel, I must say that it is very sad that this reviewer's gender identity and sense of worthiness as a woman were able to be so deeply shaken by something as simple as an independent music release.)

In my twenty-eight years on Earth thus far, there has been no shortage of people willing to tell me the truth. And it has been useful in some cases; for example, I have been plucking my eyebrows since I was ten. So when I re-read my assignment – 'to the person who told me the truth' – I interpreted a subtext of 'debunking falsehood'. Of *reverting* to truth, from a state of un-truth. Coming clean, or shattering a paradigm. Which got me thinking. Is there anyone in my life who has been utterly truthful, right from the start?

And so, dear Isobel, I thought of you. Because truthfulness is your default setting, and although it's often frank and occasionally unwarranted, it's always very beautiful, and one of my favourite things about being your friend.

Issy, when you learned how to talk, you said many number of adorable things. Your first word was 'more', after I took away the avocado lunch you were smooshing around in your baby claws. Your tiny vocabulary soon expanded and you went on to question the world around you with a very active and astounding sense of wonder. One morning last year, you enquired, 'What's wrong to your face?' and I, with the patient and graceful air of a professional nanny, calmly explained, 'Isobel, the correct way to ask is, "What's wrong *with* your face?" And it's a pimple. They're pimples.' You very truthfully replied, 'Oh. Looks bad.' But I won't hold that against you. They *did* look pretty bad.

Much earlier, long before you could talk, you spoke to me with your little baby hand. It was about 7.30 on a winter morning, you would have been about nine months old, and we were engaged in our regular pre-breakfast activity of looking out the window and naming things we could see passing by in the pre-dawn shimmer of the wet city street. Perhaps my quiet tone and few words gave away my exhaustion. You leaned deeper into my cuddle and your little baby hand, not too different in size to a chicken McNugget, patted my shoulder as if to say, 'You'll be right, champ.'

When we were travelling in the UK recently, some rather aggressive ducks at the park were honking and flapping and harassing us for our cucumber sandwiches. Slightly terrified, but determined not to let them see that they were getting to you, you yelled, 'Go away, ducks! Get on with your lives!' Okay, so it's kind of a stretch to include that anecdote under the banner of truth-telling, but I couldn't leave it out, 'cause you were totally bad-arse taking on those British ducks.

You delivered another fantastic spurt of truthfulness one morning when I had left the room you were playing in to fix a cup of tea in the kitchen. Suddenly you went quiet, and I, suspecting tomfoolery and/or monkey business, called out, 'Isobel, what are you up to in there?', to which you replied, 'Mischief. I'm always up to mischief.'

You have even taken your truth-telling into the realm of song. I recently bought you a ukulele as a prize for learning to use the potty, and you have started writing songs about your experiences in the world. My current favourite is your song about nuts. You always beg to eat my almonds, even though you don't like them at all. Your almond song goes, 'Sometimes, you eat a nut, and it's yummy . . . Sometimes, you eat a nut and it's not yummy, so you have to go "pppttthhhhffffffff", and spit it out.'

One day at the beach, I tried to hide the truth from you, but you wouldn't let me get away with it. I was doing my best to be upbeat, but my partner and I had just separated and I was heartbroken. I had my sunglasses on to mask some errant, leaky tears and I was using my 'happy voice'. I thought I was doing an excellent job of fooling a toddler *and* building a totally radical sandcastle. But you saw through me like I was covered in Windex and said, 'I'm going to take your sad face.' Then you leaned over, extracted my sad face, took a few running steps towards the water's edge with your chunky toddler legs and threw the sad face into the ocean. *'Don't come back, sad face!'* you yelled. And, of course, I wept, but they were tears of joy, because you had so perfectly and innocently reminded me that sadness is an emotion that passes, like the waves, and sometimes it is something you can take off, like a mask. I smiled more broadly and honestly and wholeheartedly than I had in months. And we went on to build a really cool sandcastle.

Isobel, I wonder about the person you will become when you're old enough to read this letter. It will be the future, we will have jetpacks, and I will be an old but fabulously rich pop star with many grand pianos. Look me up! In the meantime, what life will you have made for yourself? Who was the first boy you kissed? Have you tried falafel? Did you ever get to liking almonds, or do you still spit them out? Are you happy with the path that you're walking?

Sometimes being around you makes me so clucky I think my ovaries will explode. I try and talk myself out of it, saying, 'Georgia, relax, enjoy being in your late twenties. Enjoy getting to sleep in, enjoy your pre-baby body before childbirth turns your vagina into something that resembles a plastic bag caught in a storm drain.' But if I'm honest right now, I really, *really* hope that Future Georgia has her own children. I really hope that we're still friends, and that Future Isobel is happy, that she's maintained her default setting of truthfulness, and that she has a promising career as a pirate/princess/pygmy marmoset (these were your chief interests as a three year old).

Isobel, along with performing and music making, your friendship has been one of the true joys in my life. In the three years I have known you so far, you have met the world with unflinching honesty. Whether you were calling the unnecessarily grumpy lady at the post office 'a meanie' or declaring your unbridled love of yoghurt, truthfulness is your default setting, and I'm so grateful for it.

Thank you for being my friend.

Much love all the way from 2012,
Past Georgia

Georgia Fields

AMANDA PALMER

Dear Anthony,

It's been a long time since I wrote you a letter in the mail mail. I used to type you long, long tomes from Regensburg; I used to sit in bars and cafes and, instead of writing in my journal, I figured it was better to just write to you because what the fuck use is the shit in the journal anyway. And these letters were words I could put into the bank of our friendship, which made my confessions and stupid thoughts a real-er kind of currency – whereas my journal is only satisfying while imagining that *someday*, if I'm famous and dead enough, someone will meticulously pore over every angsty and mediocre entry, finding deep, hidden meaning in any passage.

Then we stopped writing. Now we email, but even the long emails, while infrequent, lack what used to come out of those long, meandering, time-killing bar letters. Here's the truth: maybe it was just because I had the time to kill back then – for those years I was a drunk, email-free time-murderer. Now I can't write you a letter without making a reason like this reason.

I'll be honest . . . I'm sitting in a cafe in Melbourne and writing you this letter to read to a group of people tomorrow who in turn are going to write letters to people who have 'told them the truth'. It's an event. So this letter is a letter but I can't write it as just a letter because I know it's a performance. I could have not told you. I could've tried to take the credit and make myself look like a fantastic friend. I told Michael today I had to write a letter on a theme for reading out loud and sending.

'What's the theme?'

'Someone who told you the truth.'

And then he asked: 'How is Anthony doing anyway?'

He knows me.

Here's the thing: there are two, three, four, five levels of the truth – and you taught me from way early on that they don't stack up in a vertical pile, with a winner on top.

I used to demand the truth as if it was something you could give me, as if anyone could; as if it existed, out there, outside of our heads. Brutal honesty – it used to be my religion, and I was so proud of it. I figured if the truth hurt, it was probably all the more worth saying. Such a typical teenage thing, to point your machine gun at the world, loaded with truth bullets, convinced you'll fix and heal everything. Mostly, though, a teenager just wants to show off their gun. Brutal honesty, you've told me, my friend, can be the opposite of compassion.

But I am saying less now, I swear. I think I always saw reticence as some sign of weakness, but I'm noticing that the older I get, the more attracted I am to people who don't talk as much. Maybe it's because I am fantasising in the gaps, but mostly it's because I'm learning for the first time, really, the *power* of a little sprinkling of truth on a pile of silence. I've never felt so powerful as I have in recent decisions I've made to say less – with Brian, with Neil, with the fanbase. Perfect timing for going into making a record, hopefully. Shut up, and maybe something good will happen.

When you texted me in Africa that you were going to die, that they'd given you six months, I went into a weird, quiet state of shock.

I knew I couldn't say anything to anybody – no one would get this. The next day at the airport, rushing home on the plane, I stopped in the bookshop and bought a blank journal and, to avoid thinking about you dying, I started writing everything you'd ever told me. I put pen to paper and I didn't stop the ink flowing, like I was cleaning out one entire building in my memory. Every room, every last corner, every joke, every memory, everything. And when I lifted my pen to look out the plane window, I would cry, and when I put the pen back on the paper, I would stop crying. And for the first time, I understood what Neil had been going through all his life (not Neil, the husband who I feel like I know, but Neil Gaiman, the writer who I feel like I don't). Writing to escape feeling the pain, feeling anything. And not stopping and going into my head to survive. Not my style. But now I know.

I remember when I got my voice surgery; I don't remember if I told you the details. You were around town and I was at home but we – obviously – weren't talking much, and I can't remember whether I emailed you while I was in my two weeks of silence. It was the best two weeks of my life, not being allowed to talk or whisper. I mention it to people and they assume it must have been a nightmare, but it was *paradise*. It was so incredible that I lied to everyone and tacked on an extra period at the end of the two weeks, like a three-day snooze button. I just didn't want it to end. When it did, I vowed I'd take a silence day every week, to return to paradise. I haven't done it. Not once. But I still haven't forgotten how it felt, or what I learned. Mostly I learned that 96 per cent of what leaves my brain and travels out my mouth is totally unnecessary bullshit commentary. And, more surprisingly, a large percentage of that is useless criticism about the world.

My truth machine gun, rammed shut with the hippie flower of vocal surgery. Perfect. Some things are just facts. Truth. Information.

I want a sandwich. I'll meet you at eight. I found it fascinating that I'd want to make some snarky (or kind) comment about something, but typing it into my Blackberry and flashing the screen at whoever was close by was just not really worth the effort. So I sat back and was allowed to take a sabbatical (that I didn't even know I needed) from the job of shaping my opinions with whoever was in my company.

The biggest thing I noticed was that it was impossible for people to dislike me at parties. If I'd been divisive before, I was now instantly likeable. I was a *mute rock star*. I was a mystery to everybody, and the actual *polar* opposite of how I'd been, always foisting my personality loudly on everyone in the room to make sure they all knew I was fucking worth liking and if they didn't like me then fuck them, I didn't need them anyway. I became the opposite magnet. The thing people had to come to.

How'd I wind up like that, anyway? We know the answer to that – and I shouldn't start dragging my mother into this. You're a shrink. You're versed in the fine art of not talking and measuring what the relative truth is, incoming and outgoing. You've been practising for twenty years.

Have I ever told you that when I get in a certain mood, I stop talking and want to communicate by writing? The first time I remember doing it was with Jonah. I was twenty-three and I'd just come back from the party at the Cloud Club and been told that there might be a chance I could live there. I was so beside myself with excitement when I got to his apartment that night, I didn't speak. I think I didn't want to ruin the magic. Instead I sat on the couch with him and a pad of paper, describing what happened: I wanted to keep it perfect in my head, as if it was going to get ruined if it came out of my mouth, which was filthy, ruined by being a passage for millions of exclamations and exaggerations in the course of my lifetime.

Last year on Neil's birthday, we'd been joking for a while about how we communicated best by text and Twitter. We had an epic dinner in Seattle planned for his birthday at a little dark restaurant with magical food. I asked him for a pen and paper and we spent the three-hour meal writing back and forth instead of talking. The restaurant thought we were a little weird but they were kind enough to provide a flashlight since the tables were so dimly lit. The best part was not having the running commentary about how incredible the food was, as it arrived, course by course. We just *ate* it.

No wonder monks take vows of silence. Nobody can possibly fuck with them. Nobody can argue with silence – it's always the truth.

Anthony, I love you so much. I'm going to miss you so, so much when you go. You – you who did what no one else has ever done so well.

Thank you for shutting me up. Like Depeche Mode says:

Enjoy the silence.

Love,
Amanda

A letter to my other half

BENJAMIN LAW & MEGAN WASHINGTON

BENJAMIN

Dear Meg,

For years now, there has been a mystery in my life I've needed to solve. And I'm bringing this up today because it involves you. Here's the thing. Whenever I leave you alone with my boyfriend, he returns to me significantly *gayer*, almost in exact proportion to how much time he's spent with you. It's noticeable. Leave him with you for a few hours and Scott comes back having bought what he says is 'only *technically* a woman's blouse'. Leave him with you for a day and he comes back with an embroidered jacket that appears to have been auctioned off from Bea Arthur's estate. So when he went to New York for three months after winning that music fellowship and we realised you would be in New York the entire time too, I had to brace myself. The next time I would see him, it was possible there would be nothing left of him except a giant pink triangle with a bleached arsehole.

What do you *do* to him when I'm not around, Megan?

In all seriousness though, you recently told me that Scott and I were the first gay couple you ever befriended in your life. And I'll admit it: hearing this from you was a point of pride. And surprising, considering: (1) you have many friends; and (2) you work in an industry saturated with faggotry.

We all met well over half a decade ago. It was the mid 2000s and Scott and I had just moved into our first apartment together. We'd met at someone's gig – yours? Scott's? Your then boyfriend's? It's hard to remember – and to cement our friendship, you'd brought over, as a housewarming gift, a fishbowl with two fish: a species apparently so robust, they even survive in Chinese rice paddies.

(And even though I'm Chinese, they are dead now.)

It feels like we've known each other for longer, though. We've had picnics in the park littered with used condoms, drunken late-night conversations in the corner of parties. You've educated Scott and me about the best methods of pubic hair removal, while we introduced the concepts of Grindr and fisting into your life. (The concepts, not the practices.) Your mother has accused me of cheating at Scrabble, and she has also asked us to stage an intervention for your chain smoking. You fell asleep on our sofa watching that gay zombie wound-fucking film that was banned at the Melbourne International Film Festival. You would have normally found it shocking, but you'd been recording and were just too tired. Scott was with you when you bought the prescription Ray-Bans that would become your trademark. We've seen the blonde hair, brown hair, black hair, purple hair, long hair, killer dyke undercuts.

Still, it's the music I remember. For you, it used to be small jazz shows or the gross late-night ones at Ric's. Now it's standing ovations in the main hall of the Sydney Opera House. It started off with regional prizes, now it's ARIAs. For most of the songs you've written, Scott and I still remember the demos or early mixes. When I was in India, homesick and miserable (and I'm still not sure if you know this), I'd walk down the streets of New Delhi, blocking out every other sound – the engines, the cows bellowing, the kids crying – listening to an early version of 'Sentimental Education' nonstop. It felt like the only thing that kept me sane over that month.

Scott's recording in LA right now. They've finished BVs and now they're onto strings. It's very possible he wouldn't be doing any of this if it weren't for you. Years ago, you told him, 'Hey, I've been listening to your demos and we'll have to do a gig together some time,' then added that because of schedules, it probably wouldn't happen until the following year. Then you phoned him and asked him to do a gig the very next night at Ric's. This is typical Megan Washington: love expressed via chaos. 'If it wasn't for Megan,' Scott told me recently, 'I would have found my feet in some way. But she was the first person who gave a shit about me and what I did. That meant a lot.' And those nights – when the two of you have sat at his piano to harmonise on a new song he's written, or the time you came over to play *How to Tame Lions* on Scott's Boston upright the day you wrote it – they mean a lot to me.

I mention Scott a lot. We both know why. The other night, after the Bon Iver concert, we talked about what we were going to write to each other for today. And without any prompting, we both immediately said the same thing: you and I are friends, but we are actually friends *through* Scott. Other friends, I think, would be offended, but I think we're both confident enough in our friendship to also understand how it works.

Because I've been developing this theory for a while. We're all someone's other half, but not in the way books and films would have us think. We are all someone's other half, but they are someone else's, who is someone else's in turn. For instance, you will eventually marry this man – a kind, handsome son-of-a-bitch Scott and I consider to be perfect for you – and he will be your other half. Scott is also your other half, and I'm his other half, and my other half is my friend Anna, who will marry her other half, and on and on and on it goes.

We're all halves of each other, like overlapping Venn diagrams. This is how love works.

On the morning Scott's father died, it was impossible to call people one by one. As Scott spent time with his mother, I sent out the SMS to our friends to tell them what had happened. Out of courtesy, most people didn't call back; they simply messaged, which is good. Only two people called me back that day, the only people whose voices I really wanted to hear. Anna called back, my other half. And you called back, Scott's other half. We didn't talk much through the crying, but it helped.

Nowadays, Scott wears a single ring, roughly the width of a human hair. I didn't give it to him; you did. It was one of your rings in New York and you told him to try it on then decided it looked better on him. He never takes it off. And when he returns in a month, he and I will fall asleep together, holding hands, and I will feel grateful that the ring is there. It represents a pact, a guarantee, not just between the two of you, but also that if anything should happen to me, you'll still have his back. I hold this hand most nights of my life as I sleep – his hand, which also holds yours.

Thank you for being my friend, and for being Scott's other half.

All my love,
Ben

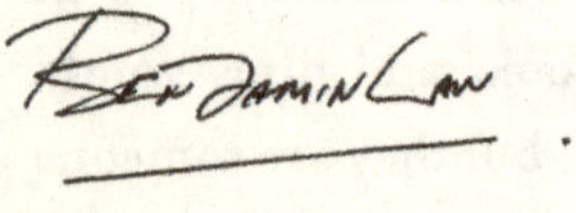

MEGAN

This letter is at once so easy and so difficult to write. Easy because I love you. Hard because I don't think I know you. Which is weird, you know, because I've known you for such a long time, and when I thought about writing this I thought it would be a piece of cake. But then when I started to write about you, I realised: shit, I barely know you. Because every time we're together, we have a translator. My best friend is your boyfriend. You're actually not my other half. Scott is. And you're his other half, which kind of makes you my *quarter*. But 'my other quarter' doesn't really have the same ring to it.

So then I thought about how fucking weird it is to love somebody you hardly know.

I was thinking about the law of the universe, which is that 'like attracts like', in relation to the three of us. But here it's kind of 'love attracts love', I suppose. I don't need to know you because the one I love loves you, so I love you, and that's as complex as my algorithm needs to be.

It's funny, because I bet you know me. I bet you do, because you see me more readily than I see other people. My first instinct is not to ask who one is, or even how one is – my habit is to tell you who *I* am. You've attended so many of my life's milestones – been attentive and proud when I've taken a risk and succeeded, been honest and supportive when I've failed. Maybe that's a thing: that real friends are people who have seen you fail. More than once. More than twice.

So maybe I don't feel that I know you because I've never seen you fail. Because you haven't, to my knowledge. In the seven or so years that I've known you, not once have you made a mistake. Not that I've seen. Every time I see your work in print or in the press or on TV. You're always clear, and concise, and thoughtful, and funny, and *you*. Every time you do something, it works. Because you've designed it to be that way. You've made it so.

It's weird; with most people, their relationship is the thing that outsiders know the least about. But in this case, I know you best through Scott. And through his eyes, almost. How strange; I don't really know how you create, or how you write, or how you cook, or how you shop, or cry, but I know how you love.

There's one thing you've always done with me that I wanted to thank you for. When you met me I was nineteen and, if my memory serves me correctly, fairly *enthusiastic* about my opinions and ideas of the world. I'm sure that you saw me very clearly then, but you never treated me like a kid. Which helped me grow into a grown-up.

Maybe I don't give you the claps and praise and applause that you give me, because you don't ask for them. Maybe you don't want them; I'm not sure, but I wish I'd paid more attention when they were due.

This letter doesn't really have a point, or an angle; it's a kind of meditation on you, and us, and why we're here.

But if I ever get to write this letter again, I want it to read differently. I hope that we can make that shift from quarter into half. I really do love you, but I want to know you, for myself now, including Scott, but not requiring him. I don't know what else to say. That's all.

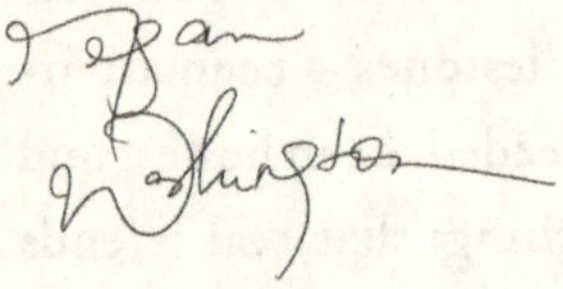

BEN BALL & GEORGE MEGALOGENIS

BEN

Dear George,

Congratulations on the book. It's out, and now the writing begins. There are speeches for launches, talks for festivals, columns about a few of your favourite things for the weekend mags. The writing about the writing. And the talking about the writing, let's not forget that. All those meta-words.

I wonder whether you feel any closer to the ex-prime ministers you interviewed, now that you've put your author's hat back on, now that you've set the agenda, and are answering questions rather than asking them.

One often hears politicians described as being children, squabbling and vainglorious. Oddly enough, in my line of work one sometimes hears about people in other publishing houses having described authors as being like children too.

And it's not intended to mean that they are replete with the innocent joy of creation. It is intended to mean that they don't always play well with others. That they're demanding and competitive. That they like to draw their own pictures on the front of your books.

This is just fine by me. This is, in fact, just what I like. I'm with Martin Amis, who said, 'I think all writers, if they mean business, if they're ambitious, have got to think they're the best.' Who wants to publish – or read – a writer who doesn't mean business? So – demand away. Compete away. Mean business.

EM Forster had something to say about children. He wrote that a 'wonderful physical bond binds the parents to the children; and – by some strange, sad irony – it does not bind us children to our parents. For if it did, if we could answer their love not with gratitude but with equal love, life would lose much of its pathos and much of its squalor, and we might be wonderfully happy.' Well, it's not Forster himself saying that, it's a character in *Where Angels Fear to Tread*, but let's not get into that distinction, George.

Forster himself didn't have children. As a parent, I don't agree with his suggestion that love ought to be equal, for maximum happiness. How could my children go out in the world, if they felt as attached to me as I do to them? What lecture or match or party would be worth going to, when the alternative is hanging out at home with Dad? What would be left to look for?

I'd like to think that for my children, I was a baseline, not the high point. I hope that my love for them will be the X-axis from which point their loves and their lives shoot outwards and upwards. Perhaps it's writing to you, George, that makes me think of graphs and lines. Please don't point out that graphs don't always go upwards and outwards.

You work with, or around, or in spite of – or possibly on – politicians. So you know about children. You have children, so you know about politics. And you're a reader so you know about unequal love. You know that the book you love can't love you back, and although its writer might love you in an abstracted, sometimes monetised, sense, it's not with the specific devotion of the reader for the work, or the parent for the child.

And – again – by me, that's just fine. That's what we want, us readers. We don't want – at least, the sort of reader I'm talking about doesn't want – to choose our own adventures. We don't want to alter the plot, or to participate in the story, or have embedded video or links to the post-punk kabuki performance. We don't want the book to listen to us.

We want to hear the writer's story. We want to learn something, or to hear in it something of ourselves that we didn't know to listen out for.

As you know better than most, George, editors are readers who *do* ask questions. They ask things like: 'But *why* was floating the dollar a good idea?' 'Remind me what a banana republic is, again.' 'What were we *thinking* in the seventies?'

'Just pretend I don't know anything about economics,' I said. Kindly, you didn't say, 'Who's pretending?'

I like to think ignorance is a professional strength. In classrooms and training days all over the world, learners are encouraged to put up their hands, because if they have a question, they can be sure that others will too. Editors are the kids who've always got a question.

The teacher takes a deep breath. The parent at the wheel tries to concentrate on the road.

This participation sometimes leads editors and publishers to think of themselves as the better half, the essential component, the half that makes it work. But editors don't make the book, and marketing people don't make the book, and sales people don't make the book. Even production people, who do make the books, don't make the book. What the editor tries to do is to help the writer take the reader where the writer wants to go.

But, George, don't writers know about unequal love too? How else to think about someone who spends years making something that will bring an uncertain number of others a week or so of pleasure or information? The writer worries a lot more about the reader than the reader worries about the writer. Some authors happily stride about that world basking in the reciprocal adoration of their readers, wonderfully happy with a life without pathos and squalor.

But mostly, the author's the one at home, chewing their nails and worrying when the reader's going to turn up, watching the dinner go cold, finally switching off the lights and going to bed alone. Or – to use an image that might have more resonance in your own life – the writer's the one with the filing cabinet of clippings, still campaigning years after the election was decided – whether it was lost or won. Readers, voters, fans – they move on. They're the ones who leave.

So what are we to make of all this, George, this business of unequal love in the business of writing? We're all coming out losers. It's that sort of attitude that sent Clive Palmer into politics.

All I've got to offer on the subject is this – that the better half of all of us poor saps who are interested in this sort of thing is the book. As readers, writers, editors, that's the thing that completes us. Forster's also famous for encouraging us to connect – but not through the book, not to connect the reader to the writer and the writer to the reader. People making that mistake meant that JD Salinger didn't answer the door for fifty years.

If it's any good, if it means business, we'll connect with the work, as some sort of tool for helping think about the world around us, with a little more compassion, a little more insight, a little more complexity.

Of course the love is unequal. But it's entering the relationship that counts. Isn't it the sense that there's something greater than ourselves that makes life less pathetic and squalid? Who but a child wouldn't be satisfied to be the lesser half?

I appreciate that this is going to be a hard sell to Malcolm and Bob and Paul and John and Kevin. Good luck.

Yours, with all best wishes,
Your reader

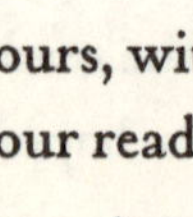

GEORGE

Dear Ben,

We've had a year of talking followed by a year of writing. This year, our third together, is the year of delivery.

Governments do these things the other way around. They deliver policies, then they write new ones, then they try to talk their way to another three-year contract with the public.

What binds author and politician is the campaign. Unfortunately, it is also what separates author from publisher, child from parent. I assume you think this is as it should be.

You write, 'How could my children go out into the world, if they felt as attached to me as I do to them? What party could appear worth going to, when the alternative is hanging around at home with Dad?'

You are right, if what you are saying is a book needs to be pushed out of the door. But have you thought about the consequences of sending an author on tour, on their own?

You dispatched me to Sydney, then Brisbane, then Perth in the first week of publication. Canberra the following week, Canberra again in the third week, and then on to Adelaide.

The publicist you assigned to our campaign told me she is the best in the business. She lasted just one night in Brisbane before begging off the tour. Something about having to hold the hand of Alain de Botton back in Sydney, I think it was.

Without passing judgement, I note that in the first three weeks of our book's life on the shelf, it has sat at number two on the independent charts, behind de Botton. Ben, is he the son you wished you had?

Relax, I'm messing with you.

What I really wanted to say is that your letter arrived too late for a thoughtful reply. You see, my other parent, Patricia Karvelas, the chief of staff in *The Australian*'s Melbourne bureau, had just barked an order for me to join Twitter.

Patricia had been nagging me for some time. But I said, 'No, I am writing a book for Ben and I don't want to give away a good line to the Twittersphere.' 'Don't be a wimp,' she replied.

Which reminds me, at the one event you did turn up to – our book's official launch in Canberra – the prime minister asked how the tour was going. I told her I now had a better understanding of the pressure the media places on politicians, because the radio and TV appearances, the public speaking and especially the commuting from taxi to airport to taxi to hotel were exhausting me.

'Oh, you get used to it,' she replied. It was her way of saying I was a wimp.

Then again, she has staff to write her speeches, bully her interrogators and ensure her credit card bill is paid on time so she gets to keep the points.

I'm not saying I want someone to hold my hand. I'm not even saying we should slow the tempo of appearances. To be honest, I have never had more fun.

But I do believe you should have given me some advice before I left home.

Let me put it this way: if this were a postcard, it would say:

'Hi Dad, thrown off one flight, trashed two hotel rooms and thumped three shock jocks, in no particular order. Just thought you should know, before their lawyers write to tell you what they claim I've been up to.'

Yours,
George

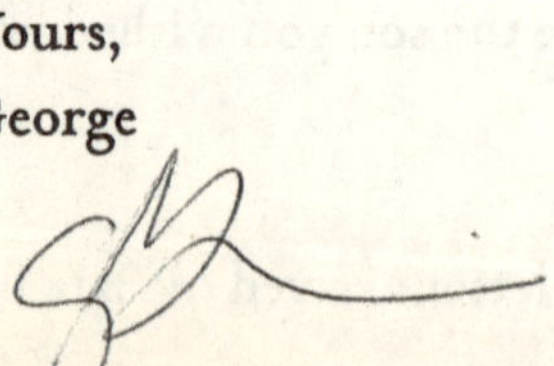

SOFIJA STEFANOVIC & THOMAS HENNING

SOFIJA

Hi Thomas,

I know you've been back in Melbourne for a while and I haven't heard from you. So, I guess, we broke up.

The night before I left Ethiopia was so crazy and every time I think about you, I feel sad and strange. I find it hard to forgive you for being mean to the people who were looking out for me. Also, you lost my phone, abandoned me in a brothel, attacked my friends and made a scene in the cultural centre.

But after all that, when you eventually came back to our hotel room with the fancy wine, it was nice. I don't even remember what we talked about, but we didn't fight. We went to bed like every other night, except that it was our last one.

I'm writing to you because I got a weird email from Yonathan. He says that those guys we were with on the last night are in gaol. Do you know anything about this?

—

Thomas,

I can't believe I was surprised you didn't respond to my email. I can only assume you were too preoccupied with yourself to take any responsibility for anything, as usual.

Yonathan sent another email. He says *you* called the cops and told them that the Eritrean guys we were hanging out with were terrorists. He wants me to send money to get them out. This sounds crazy to me, so I thought I'd ask you about it, assuming you will have the decency to stop drinking and writing poetry, or whatever it is you do, and answer me.

I really consider Yonathan a friend, even if he's opportunistic. Like when he took us to that brothel-pretending-to-be-a-nightclub – I know he only took us there because we are westerners; it was the only way he and his friends would get let in. And then he got into a fight with one of the girls sitting on some fat white guy's lap. I felt bad for him. What if she was his neighbour and he's in love with her and she won't even look at him because she's spending all her time with sweaty white guys with money? I developed a soft spot for him then. You, of course, didn't see this because you'd disappeared with some Israeli jerk who offered you a joint. By the way, I later saw that guy making out with what seemed to be an underage boy.

And, of course, you were off your face when you finally did find us in that cultural club hours later. You left me, in the middle of the night, to be raped, killed or robbed in Addis Ababa, in favour of doing God-knows-what in a brothel with a paedophilic junky. Lucky for me, Yonathan and those guys looked out for me. I think I will send him the money after all.

Sofija

THOMAS

Hi Sofija,

I'm incredibly sorry it's taken me so long to reply. I don't have the internet where I am now and I've had to do a bit of running around, so I haven't made it to an internet cafe for at least a week. Anyway, it's great to hear from you again. Your bile has been sorely missed.

I'm sorry for everything, truly I am.

Don't send Yonathon any money. He's full of shit, and whatever he said about me is a lie.

I'm not sure how he knows it was me who called the cops on them, unless he still had a friend on the hotel staff, but I doubt it. *I* didn't even know it was me until the next morning. Apparently I was ranting about an attack on the hotel or something when they wouldn't sell me cigarettes and wine.

I would assume they just got a smack on the wrist for all of that palaver and are out now. Personally, I think, Fuck him. He's to blame, I think, for everything that happened. He took us to the brothel, he's the one who foisted that hyper-tense Israeli guy on me in the first place, and he's the one who took you out dancing with King-of-Bed and all those other weasels who pretended to be your friends.

I'm sorry; it all still irks me. And though I do accept that I am to blame for a lot, it is somewhat unfair to paint me as a snivelling junky. Honestly, the joint smoked with the Israeli was the only drug I even brushed against the whole time in Ethiopia. It was a total fuck up, but it was an accident, and I do hope you can forgive that.

Also, just to clear things up: I didn't intentionally abandon you in the brothel. I got thrown out. The bouncer found me when I was throwing up in the urinal. Your phone is probably somewhere on the men's room floor there. Well, probably not any more, but still.

They threw me out the back way, and I tried to tell them my girlfriend was in there, but they thought I was just trying to get at the whores and ignored me. I tried to walk back around to the front so you could see me when you left, but the streets were fucked and I got lost in the middle of some Addis slum. But I didn't want to leave you in a brothel so I kept walking. When I finally found the place again, the bouncers wouldn't let me in. So I waited, and eventually Yonathon came out and I waved him over, but he said you'd already gone.

Honestly, I didn't abandon you, and I spent the whole night trying to find out where you were. You should have left me a note at the Taitu. I found out from that one-legged kid, Hop-a-Long, that you were in the cultural club. I had to pay him thirty birr to take me to the bloody place as well.

Anyway, I'm glad to hear from you. I'm sorry about everything, and I do hope one day we can converse as friends. Don't believe that weasel Yonathon: he's a fucking liar.

Very sorry about it all, but perhaps one day you'll look back and laugh, even if in a nervous and hysterical manner.

SOFIJA

Why would I look back and laugh? Why did you call the cops? Do you realise that all those men have been in an Ethiopian gaol for a month because of you?

You know all those guys were students. And poor King-of-Bed, he actually told me that his mother (who was also called Sofia, by the way) was dead.

So comparing his life to ours is unfair, and since he's trying to get back to study, mooching off inner-city Australians isn't such an offence. And he *has* to have a distinctive nickname. How else are people going to remember him? I thought he was quite brave, actually.

And before you showed up with Hop-a-Long, I was talking to another guy, Michael, about how he's interested in sociology and wants to write about arranged marriages. He wanted to start an internet forum with me and other Australians who are interested in cross-cultural communications. I imagine I haven't heard from him as he is probably being raped in gaol, courtesy of you.

I don't think they 'pretended' to be my friends, Thomas. The amount they wanted was only about fifty bucks. And their behaviour that night was far, far more decent than yours.

I have sent Yonathan $800 through Western Union. I'm not sure if that will be enough.

THOMAS

Cancel the money transfer! Cancel it! It's a bad idea to encourage him, a very, very bad idea. Look, they're all taking you for a ride, just like they were in that cultural club. They were clearly, clearly involved in the scam that was going on, which is why they were so insistent on you doing 'the right thing'. That bill should definitely not have been 900 birr – that's more than four times what it should have been. I already gave them a massive amount for that instrument I broke when I fell on that musician. That club had made a heap off us already; to keep the scam going was excessive.

Your friends were a bunch of charlatans and they would've told you any old thing to get what they wanted. They may have been charming, but you were willing to throw money at them, and King-of-Bed's nickname speaks clearly about other motives they may have held. Do you really think they all call him 'King-of-Bed' in daily life? Nonsense. They're all only after one thing. Well, in your case, two things, but either way, they want to take what they can.

I understand you were pissed at me, and why. Sure, from your point of view I'd run off with a whore. But I hadn't! I spent the whole bloody night trying to find you, in an absolute mess of a state. And then, after that fucking scene in the cultural club, to be surrounded by a pack of hustlers baying for money – it was all too much. I felt utterly betrayed.

The only reason I was in that place was because I was looking for you. I didn't want to dance with that woman, and I clearly didn't want to fall on the musician, and I didn't want to have to give them all my money. All I wanted was to go back to the hotel and sleep. And then you encouraged that herd of morons to come back with us so you could give them a heap more money to settle a debt that shouldn't have even existed? It didn't make an inch of sense. They were laughing at me. Openly laughing at me. That whole walk home was humiliating, particularly since I'd just made an absolute mess of that bar.

At least you decided to let me take the money out to them and have a shower. I'm sorry I lied about having paid them, but it seemed at the time to be the only way to make the situation disappear without creating any more problems than we already had.

And just to let you know, I didn't call the cops. The doorman did. I didn't ask for them to be arrested. I just wanted to make them go away. I was trying to buy cigarettes or wine but the bar was closed, so I started explaining what a shit the night had become, and said there were a bunch of guys outside planning to attack the hotel. So the doorman went and got the cops from over the road. I honestly didn't know that's what happened until the morning.

It is highly, highly unlikely that they've been charged with terrorism. They probably all got out a few days later and were told to stay away from the Taitu.

Cancel the money, really. All you're doing is encouraging a bunch of leeches to keep feeding.

I hope you're well.

SOFIJA

Dear Thomas,

At this point, I am *not* well. I'm very concerned. Attached is an article citing a UN report that says four Eritrean men were arrested for planning an attack on Addis Ababa. Quote: 'The Ethiopian government is claiming to have thwarted a large bomb plot by its tiny neighbour and foe, Eritrea. It is the latest in a series of accusations and counter-accusations by the two governments.'

So there you are. Leeches or not, they're in gaol.

And *how come* you never called me when you got back, anyway? How come we never properly broke up?

Did you ever really like me?

THOMAS

Hi Sofija,

Okay, clearly something went horribly wrong there. I've called the embassy and explained what happened. They want written explanations from both of us. I need to meet with some representative of ASIS this Tuesday, so if you could email me your statement regarding all this, that'd be great. If not, I've pasted the embassy's email address below. You'll likely get a call from ASIS soon. They've been reasonably understanding thus far.

I'm immensely sorry, and if you can send me Yonathon's details, I'd like to forward him some money as well, if possible. I'm not sure why they've been mistaken for Eritreans. King-of-Bed was from Harrar. He told me. And I'm pretty convinced those young, bald guys claiming to be Rastas were from Shashamane, which was why they kept saying they'd take you there to meet their families.

As to whether I liked you or not, I did. You were great. In the end, though, it all became a bit too much. The whole event made a mess of me. Until now I just assumed you were either crazy or dangerously naive. I'm glad to learn now that I was wrong.

And I was in love with my ex. I'm sorry to be telling you that now, and I know I should have at the time. I tried to blot her out, but she kept haunting me. If it's any consolation, I've made her life horrible ever since.

I hope you're okay.

SOFIJA

Dear Thomas,

That's what I was after. I wanted to hear you admit it. Of course I knew something was going on. I came overseas to meet you and the minute I saw you I knew something had happened. Then all the new things paled into the background, and all I could think of was how you didn't really want me.

And then I found out it was because of your ex. I saw an email you sent her, because you left it open at the internet cafe when you went to buy cigarettes. I guess I just wanted you to admit to it.

I'm not stupid. You're not that good an actor, and you certainly never fooled me.

THOMAS

Hi Sofija,

I'm immensely sorry to have caused you such pain and difficulty. Honestly, I didn't intend to. I am undeniably a horrible shit of a person. If ever you stab me in the back of the head as I walk down the street, I will consider it justice and within your rights.

If you have the time and are willing, although I do understand if you are not, would you email me your statement of events? I'm meeting with this person from ASIS tomorrow and I'd like to have as much prepared for them as possible.

Once again, I'm really, really sorry I did this to you. I hope one day you can forgive me, but if not, that's fine.

SOFIJA

Okay, so I've got to come clean about something that happened at the brothel. King-of-Bed told me you were vomiting in the men's bathroom and I got security to throw you out.

And then, when you were looking for me, I told Yonathan to tell you I'd already left. Actually, I was inside eating injera with the prostitutes.

And the reason there were no taxis outside the brothel when you came out was because I got King-of-Bed to send them all away, so you'd be stuck.

I wanted to punish you for everything. I wanted you to realise how much you'd miss me if I was gone, and I wanted you to want me back. I wanted you to realise that your ex was a loser and that you needed *me* in your life instead. Like in *Reality Bites* when Winona Ryder discovers that she doesn't love Ben Stiller but Ethan Hawke, who was staring her in the face the whole time, even if he was behaving dickishly!

That's why I got so upset when you showed up drunk – I hoped you'd be desperate, scared I'd been killed or something, but instead, you just started dancing and broke that traditional instrument and then became a tight-arse to the guys who had helped me out the whole night. So I'm asking you not to be angry about it, because my motivation – winning your love – was pure.

Also, about the letters from Yonathan. He *did* write me one, telling me that you'd got those guys kicked out of the Taitu Hotel. But I lied about them being arrested.

I spent a lot of time thinking about how cruel it was that you never even called me after you got back to Melbourne. So I just found that article about the Eritreans getting arrested for terrorism and thought I could pretend it was our friends and engage you in conversation again. I wanted you to pay attention to me, like when we first met.

Anyway, sorry about all that. I wasn't actually anticipating that you'd get the embassy involved. I guess you should probably get in touch with them. Also, I hope you didn't tell them you took drugs. I think drugs are really illegal over there.

THOMAS

I see . . .

This is all rather disconcerting and I'm not quite sure what to make of it. On one hand, I'm incredibly sorry I upset you so much and drove you to such lengths. On the other hand, you're a loony.

I'm not quite sure how to put any of this delicately, so I've decided to just go for the tactless route.

Sofija, you abandoned me in an Ethiopian ghetto. I spent an entire night hunting for you through a city I don't know. I bribed a handicapped child to find you, and forced him to walk for forty minutes to show me where you were. He had only one leg and that's a long way to travel on one leg. I am now currently in discussions with ASIS and the Australian embassy in Addis regarding all of this and likely they're going through my entire personal history. I understand you were upset, and I'm very sorry about that, but this is kind of insane and worrying. I'm sure you have your reasons, but you're out of your mind.

I was recently talking to an Afghani cab driver about the merits of arranged marriage, about how happy he and his wife were and had been for thirty-odd years. And I was looking at the messages in my phone from my ex, saying that I'm a terrible lover and she's going off on a BDSM tour of Germany with an Icelandic composer, and thinking about this email – which I'm sorry I've taken so long to write, but after your last email I was drunk for several days and lost control of my eyes. Anyway, I was thinking that perhaps if my parents had married me off to someone they liked, I'd maybe be a lot more calm and happy.

I sincerely hope you're okay, really, I do. I hope you have some good friends around you and things like that.

Feel free not to write back.

Okay.
Goodbye.
Thomas

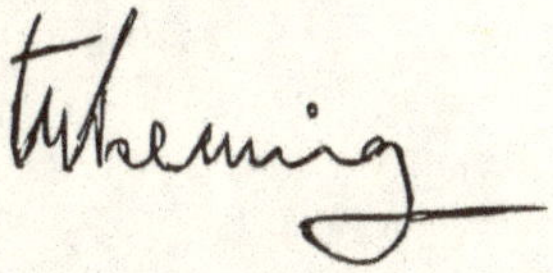

SOFIJA

Dear Thomas,

I'm sorry about Hop-a-Long, really. I didn't want him to suffer; I just wanted you to. I felt that it was the correct amount of revenge for what you'd done, and I guess Hop-a-Long was collateral damage.

I hope everything went well with the embassy – which, obviously, wasn't part of my revenge fantasy. Sorry.

Best wishes,
Sofija

Thomas,

I was hoping for an embassy update. I think it's quite immature that you aren't answering.

Anyway, just wanted to say that it's unfortunate your ex left you to go on a sex tour of Germany because she thought you were bad in bed. In case you're wondering, I didn't think you were bad, I just found you un-resilient and a bit faulty.

From,
Sofija

Hi Thomas,

I hope the embassy worked out well.

I hope you don't still feel bad about your ex. Everyone knows that anyone who is into S and M is really boring in normal life. Seriously. You are *much* better off without her. She sounded quite nuts.

So, guess we're both single . . . I'm not saying we should definitely go out again, I'm just saying that I think we ended on the wrong foot, so, I, for one, would be willing to explore the option of getting back together, if you were.

Or we could just have a coffee. Whatever. No pressure.

xx Sofija

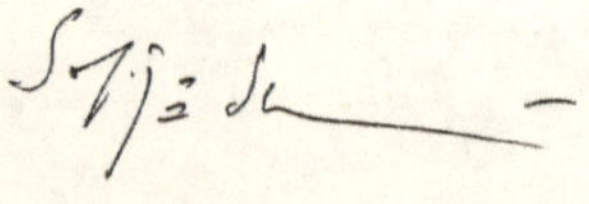

HAMISH BLAKE & ZOË FOSTER BLAKE

HAMISH

My girl, I know we need to come up with a clever, funny idea for that letter thing on Sunday but, you know, I got to thinking and . . . I just wanted to say I love you, I cant wait to marry you, I'm in awe of you, I adore you and you make everything better (a bit like salt), but you also add kick to my life (a bit like pepper).

You gettin' me?

Mebot xxxxxxx

ZOË

I love you too, but that does *nay* help with our subject matter for People of Letters.

So, I was thinking. What if we were to take a really well-known fictional or animated duo and write as them? Like, Bert and Ernie for instance. So, I'd be all like, 'Bert, if I trip on another one of your goddamn rubber duckies on the bathroom floor, I am going to put that little fucker in the blender!' Oh, hang on, I think it's actually *Ernie* that's into rubber duckies . . . But you get what I mean. We could make them really twisted and depraved.

Or! We could do Tarzan and Jane! Buzz and Woody! Or what about Batman and Robin, and we reveal that actually *Robin* is the superhero and Batman has really just been his puppet this whole time, and maybe Robin even created Batman in a lab, ('Frankenbat'), to protect his name and fortune . . .

Whatever we do, it has to be funny and it has to be clever. Let's put our thinking beanies on.

Love,
Frankenbatbot xxxx

HAMISH

Hey honey, yeah, that could work. We did go as Catwoman and Batman to that party – maybe I could wear my Catwoman suit on stage? Although it *is* on this Sunday and the only anti-chafing powder I find is effective has to be ordered from America so it might not get here in time.

But you know, there might not be anything wrong with just writing to each other about love and how you do beautiful things for me, like write love notes from the cat and take photos of him next to them so it looks like he did it. Unless that actually is him writing the notes, in which case please thank him.

I'm at the shops; let me know if you want anything. I already got popcorn.

xxxxx Popbot

ZOË

Hi Puss!

While irrefutably striking, your PVC Catwoman outfit a) smells a bit like rotting brie, and b) is perhaps is a bit too . . . showy? For a

Sunday afternoon.

Also, I've been thinking about the Bert and Ernie, Batman and Robin thing. They have the potential to become a bit laboured. We don't really have that much to work with, sans homosexual undertones and a basic understanding of their living spaces and favourite clothes.

Re: your idea of love notes, I'm sorry, darling, but I just don't think anyone wants to hear a couple of love-drugged fiancés read out their syrupy scribbles to each other. How spectacularly nauseating! No. We must not expose a theatre full of intelligent, literary-loving types to our mush. I won't have it.

Oh! Would we dare to do Katniss and Gale? Or even Katniss and Peeta, perhaps? *The Hunger Games* is top of everyone's mind at the moment – it would be *very* clever to tap into that, wouldn't you agree? Think of all that thrilling geese talk. Speaking of geese, please bring home some almond milk.

Goosebot xxxx

HAMISH

Hi honey,

Good idea to cash in on *Hunger Games*. I could dress as the girl and shoot an apple out of your mouth! Remember how in New Zealand I hit the second most difficult target after a few tries at the archery place? Let me know if you want me to start organising a bow.

So yeah, that's a good idea, buuuuuut . . . Speaking of couples and good ideas – seriously, why don't we write as us?

We could share a bit of personal stuff. Not pet names necessarily. I probably wouldn't be comfortable with everyone knowing my nickname is 'Puss'. Don't get me wrong, I *love* the nickname when it's just between us, but I think some people might think it's because I'm a pussy. And not just a pussy sometimes, a pussy so often it is actually the word most synonymous with me. As opposed to the real origin of the nickname, which is that I have the reflexes of a cat, and sometimes cough up fur and chase small balls of tinfoil around.

I could write about how tolerant and beautiful you are, like during that night when I tried to fancy it up in New York and took us to a swanky hotel and snored so much you had to move into the bathroom with spare blankets and pillows and build a little nest to sleep in. Then when I got up in the middle of the night and found you, I had to kick you out of your nest to take a whiz and you wouldn't let me swap places with you because you said I needed my sleep more than you because I had to work the next day and hadn't been sleeping well. This was after I'd essentially kicked you out of your bedroom to piss in it! And you were just totally thinking with my interests in mind and I found it incredibly selfless. I did actually need to poo as well, but I didn't want to push it. Not that I'm trying to be a hero here, you were awesome, just thought I'd share with you that little DVD extra from one of our more memorable nights. But you really did humble me with your kindness that night. What a teammate. So that could be the kind of gear I do in my letter to you, then obviously you would pick a story about me being great. I have a few in mind if you want to workshop it.

Sorry, I didn't get almond milk. You know I think it's a scam. Almonds don't have teats. And also, they're, like, the driest things in the world. If this so-called milk is actually their juice, it would take about 25000 nuts to produce a carton and it'd cost $500. I can pour some amaretto in regular milk when I get home if you like.

xxxxxxxx Hamebot

ZOË

But Puss, you love being called Puss! We do that cute kissy come-here-kitty noise to each other! And anyway, everyone heard me call you that at the Australia Day barbecue and gave you heaps of shit about it, so you've seen the worst of it. Plus, it's just easier with you and Meowbert both running around the house, a one-name-fits-all kind of thing. I will nickname our firstborn Puss also.

How kind of you not to defecate in the bathroom as I slept on its cold floor. Also you forgot the part about your putrid wet gym socks being in there too, and being so nasally offensive that even when I shifted my whole nest to open the doors to put them outside the bathroom door they were *still* molesting my poor, sweet lady nostrils, and so I ended up putting them in a plastic bag and then the bin, such was my fury at that time of the night and my sleeping and the noise situation in general. It was hard to love you as much as I usually do the next morning, but then you took me for pancakes and a peanut-butter thickshake and my hands were jittery with sugar and my heart beamed with forgiveness for your late-night lorry honking.

But look, I don't think we need to do that personal stuff, Puss. I really don't. Let's be creative fiction rascals instead.

Maaaaaybe we could do something that plays with the form and template we've been given – like, maybe 'my other half' literally, so, I don't know, conjoined twins, maybe! Or Jekyll and Hyde? Or even a known duo, like salt and pepper (the condiments, not the popular '90s RnB outfit)? Or we could do a fictional relationship between Coke and Pepsi, because, you know, they're kind of a couple, I guess . . .

I'm starting to get a bit anxious now. We only have two days left and I don't want to do some shitty half-cooked idea, which is about all my brain stove is serving right now. Okay, that was pretty good actually.

Anxiousbot xxxxx

HAMISH

Hi honey,

Coke and Pepsi is funny. I always think Coke would on one hand be constantly smug that they're dominant, but also annoyed that Pepsi is still hanging around. Coke could tease Pepsi about the fact that none of the guys who know the Coke recipe are allowed to fly together in case the plane crashes, while you never hear that fact repeated about Pepsi because evidently no one cares as much about the Pepsi formula. Same goes for all drinks, now I think about it. I bet the heads of Solo are allowed to fly together because there are more people at the company that know the secret formula of water and sugar and three drops of lemon juice.

I wonder what we would be if we were drinks? I'd probably be Pepsi Max: likes to be associated with extreme sports but when you think about it the association makes no sense. You'd be Diet Vanilla Coke, for no other reason than it's my favourite and it's not available any more, like you! You're only available to me! Remember how I bought you that diamond and proposed and it was super romantic? I don't like to go on about it but since we're on the topic now – that was great, wasn't it? Real fairytale stuff that could be the kind of thing you might like to share with a room full of strangers. I'm not saying the letter should be a thank-you letter for the proposal – I mean, I'm over the moon and you saying yes was a dream come true – it could just be a lovely stroll down memory lane for both of us, don't you think? It's not that I want to be put on a pedestal here at all, honey, and in my letters I'll downplay it so people don't know this was my idea, but don't you think it could be fun for you to write down all the details in your letter of all the things that really blew you away that day, really just so you've got it as a historical document? I could help you remember some of the finer details of the subtler things I did that you might have missed in the excitement, if you want.

Then I can list some of the five billo reasons I want to marry you, not least of which would be the hilarious love notes you write on our bathroom mirror, how generous you are with everyone, or the fact you spent six weeks in the bottom of New Zealand being my best friend while I shot a movie, even though the town we were in only had about sixteen people living there and you had to spend all day alone next door to a guy who'd turned his house into a creepy place called 'Dolly Land' and we later learned he'd done gaol time for attempted murder. Sorry again about that, but also thank you again.

Let me know if we've got the green light here. I'm seeing Ry tonight but can knock it off when I get home, or at the very least tomorrow morning, since the thing doesn't start 'til 5.

BIG love.
xxxxxxx Hamebot

ZOË

Honeybee,

I will always support my man, no matter where his work may take him. Hopefully wherever it takes us next, I'll leave with a better highlight than not being slashed to death in the middle of the night.

Yes, People of Letters starts at 5, if by 5 you mean 1. So we will *definitely* need to write this in the morning. Like, strong coffees, no distractions, wi-fi definitely off and phones on silent. Ooh, maybe

I will make *pancakes!* That can't be considered a distraction because it is food-based and brain need food to do good job.

I'm home tonight and will maybe even jot down some ideas on the Coke–Pepsi thing, just because we need to get this dingin' thing underway.

I love you to pieces and back together,

Cokebot xxxxx

Honey, it's fine, I've done it for both of us.

I'm pretty unthrilled you scheduled in a table-tennis match for this morning, knowing we had People of Letters on this afternoon and we are incapable of ever doing anything until the last second, but I got up early and knuckled down on behalf of both of us.

I ended up going with the queen and the king from chess, and the power struggle they encounter in their marriage, what with her being the most powerful on the board, but him the most important, and the battles and insecurities surrounding that. It's fun, I think, but there are also some really important messages in there about being supportive and non-threatened when your partner just gets in there and takes care of business like the awesome queen she is.

I hope you like it. I had to race off to meet Jess for brunch, and couldn't work out that fucking printer as usual, so would you please print out two copies and bring them with you?

I love you, honey. This is gonna be fun.

Queenbot xxxxxx

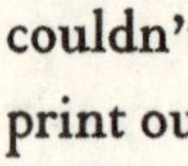

HAMISH

Hey lady baby,

I'm so sorry about pong this morning. I totally forgot and it was with Aaron and it's a trophy game. I would have cancelled in a second were it not a trophy game, but you know how he gets about that trophy.

THANK YOU, though, for doing the letters. I'm sure they're great; you're great so it makes sense they will be. My phone is doing that weird thing where it's only letting me read the first few lines of each email, so I couldn't read the rest of what you wrote but to answer the question I'm pretty sure was in there: yes, I won table tennis. Thanks again for covering for me, can't wait to read the letter, you're awesome, I'll see you there!

xxxxxxxx Slackbot

PS To make it up to you I have bought three cartons of almond milk.

To my petty crimes

KATE McLENNAN

I've never really had a taste for crime. I mean, sure, my skincare regime largely subsists on the use of swiped sample products from my local Aesop store and naturally I've scanned through the odd vine-ripened tomato as a bog-standard gourmet at Coles, but hey, haven't we all? It's not like I'm a graduate of the Winona Ryder School of Shoplifting. I hardly think these minor misdemeanours a criminal make. I prefer to think of my felonies as piddling rather than petty. But then again, maybe I would, after all – it hasn't always been this way . . .

I'm from a good family – a country girl raised by a loving panelbeater father and schoolteacher mother. We didn't have a lot of money when I was a child, and in the winter months I stayed warm by wearing a coat of many colours, which my mother had made by hand. No, wait, hang on, that wasn't me, that was Dolly Parton. My mistake. I had homemade *undies,* not a coat. I guess what I'm trying to say is that we weren't exactly rolling in it, but we didn't want for anything either.

As a kid I was content with my lot in life: riding my banana-seat bike, selling dried flowers by the side of the road and cooking tadpoles with matches. You know, just doing my best to recreate the plotlines of Enid Blyton adventure stories. I possessed no great desire for anything more than I had.

But all that changed on 8 October 1985. It was Saskia French's birthday and when she brought every single one of her presents to school for show-and-tell, I decided, rather matter-of-factly, that I wanted them. Actually, not all of them, just one – a cold, crisp, shiny box of . . .

Wait. First, let me take you back. I was in grade prep and Saskia French was my best friend in the whole world. Saskia had skin like honey and beautiful white-blonde hair that looked like the icing on top of a Boston bun, which she'd always tie back loosely with a green and navy tartan ribbon. Her hair always flopped just so – you know, in that way some girls can wear their hair so that it looks like they've just casually dismounted a pony?

Saskia's family were wealthy graziers who lived in an architecturally designed house that featured lots of natural light, parquetry floors and shelves that were stacked from floor to ceiling with books that weren't written by Max Walker. Their indoor pot plants were *alive*. Artefacts from overseas trips sat atop musical instruments, which in turn sat atop Persian rugs that were most definitely not bought on sale from a warehouse located next to a racecourse. Saskia's mother wore Jenny Kee jumpers and her dad was an artist. One of his paintings had made the front cover of the white pages. There's not much more you can say about that: he was as close to a celebrity as our town got.

I loved going to play at Saskia's house – it was always filled with music – music that wasn't Neil Diamond or the Delltones. There was no television and they called their evening meal 'dinner' not 'tea', and her parents drank wine from *bottles* and in *glasses*. They ate meals like 'chilli' and duck crepes with a selection of chutneys on the side. Their mustard was kept in jars. Not like at our house. We didn't have mustard in jars; we had mustard *powder* and it came in a tin and we put it on sausages to make casseroles. Based on their condiment selection alone I deduced that our house was *disgusting* and Saskia's house was a *wonderland*.

Whenever I went to Saskia's house I didn't want to leave.

I wanted to ride her horse and have picnics by the river and learn to play the piano and eat duck crepes and swan about the house with my floppy ponytail all day long. I wanted Saskia's life. I wanted her to be me and me to be her.

On 8 October 1985, when Saskia French displayed all of her birthday presents for show-and-tell, she produced picture books and puzzles and wooden dolls inside other wooden dolls and Twister the board game and a galaxy of stars to stick on her wall. These presents were all *okay*, but the present that really caught my eye, the pick of the bunch, the gift that encapsulated all of what was brilliant about Saskia's life, was a shiny, crisp, perfect tin of Derwent pencils.

We didn't have Derwent pencils in our house. We didn't have polished floorboards or a piano or shelves stacked with books. We had modestly sized windows, and my hair ties were made from knickers elastic; in summer we stayed in a caravan, not a holiday house; we'd never heard of mangoes or avocados; we rode bikes, not horses; we played netball, not ballet; we drove Fords, not Volvos. We ate chips, not nuts; we drank Loy's soft drink, not barley water; we ate white bread, not brown; we had Strasburg, not salami. We weren't poor; we were 'no fuss'. We didn't like to show off. We lived within our means and living within our means meant that in our house we didn't have Derwent pencils.

But on 8 October 1985 I decided that was all going to change. I was going to put Saskia French's Derwent pencils in my bag and make them mine. I knew that I could. I knew that Saskia wouldn't notice. Aside from developing an appreciation of fine mustards on our play dates, I'd also discovered that Saskia French was a little vague – in that way that a lot of rich people are. I knew it would be an easy get.

And so on 8 October at 2.45 p.m., in the hustle and bustle of a cut'n'paste session, I quickly unzipped Saskia French's schoolbag, grabbed her Derwents, and tucked them safely away in my red Target backpack. Done. I had stolen them. Saskia's pencils were mine.

On the way home my thighs burned on the hot vinyl seat of Dad's ute, but I was cooled at the thought of the pencils sitting at my feet. When we arrived home I raced up to my bedroom and crawled inside the wardrobe to hide my freshly stolen goods. I may have been a thief but I wasn't stupid – these pencils weren't for open displays of drawing on butcher's paper at the kitchen table. Oh no, these pencils were for private under-the-doona-after-*A-Country-Practice* drawing.

I clicked open the tin for a quick look at my acquisition. Inside lay all the colours of the rainbow; Magenta and Aqua and Kingfisher Blue; Zinc Yellow, Deep Vermilion and Cobalt Green. Browns to draw tree bark, greys for stormy clouds, yellows to make bright suns, greens for flower stems and deep reds for ladies' lips. I ran my nose along the line of little coloured soldiers, giddy at the bright wooden smell. I tipped the pencils on the carpet and began reordering them in the tin, mixing them up into a haphazard colour chart of contrast: blues with the pinks and white next to green, red next to yellow – shaking it up, shuffling the spectrum like a crazy god of colour.

'What are you doing?' Dad barked.

'Nothing!'

'What have you got there? They're not yours, mate!'

'They're Saskia's! She said I could borrow them for the night.'

'On her birthday?'

'Yes!' I cried weakly.

'Mate, what will her parents think when they find out you've got half of Saskia's bloody presents? They'll probably call the police, mate. They're probably calling them right now. You could go to gaol, mate!'

This was not the first time I'd been threatened with incarceration. It was a regular occurrence in our household for Dad to call our local copper, Keith Bellows, if my sister or I had been displaying some particularly robust behaviour. Dad would dial the number and say, 'Look out, Kate, if Keith answers this phone he's gonna lock you up and throw away the key.' Luckily Keith never answered. Fortune was always on my side. Not this time, though. Saskia French's parents were surely sending me to gaol.

In a final bid for my freedom, Dad suggested that I call Saskia's parents to apologise and beg for them not to put me behind bars. Bravely, I took on Dad's advice and straight after tea I made the call. The conversation was brief; as I had predicted, neither Saskia nor her parents had even realised that her pencils were missing. I cried for a bit and promised Saskia that I'd bring her pencils to school the next day. No criminal charges were laid. The matter was never raised again.

That night as I lay in bed I was riddled with guilt and hot with shame. Yet still the Derwents beckoned me from the wardrobe. Surely Saskia wouldn't mind if I used them just a bit? Deciding that she definitely wouldn't mind, I crept out from under the covers and retrieved the pencils and some paper. Once back in bed and under the doona, I opened the tin and began to draw – a picture of a sky full of clouds and birds and a shining sun. I drew Mum and Dad and my sister and me, all of us holding hands and happy, all of us standing tall and bright in the sunshine and with me not in gaol.

Two months later, on 25 December 1985, my aunty Heather arrived at Christmas with two meticulously wrapped rectangular presents – one for my sister and one for me. I carefully removed the paper and inside was a gleaming, cold tin of perfect Derwents. Tears sprung from deep inside my cheeks. 'Oh, aren't you girls both very lucky!' Mum said gently, before adding in her best teacher voice, 'Now, they are for home. Not to take to school.'

No, they weren't for school. They were precious. Precious pencils for home – where they were safe. Besides, I didn't want to show off – not everyone at my school could afford Derwent pencils and, well, it would be rude to make a fuss.

MISSY HIGGINS

Dear cow,

What part of you *was* it that landed on my plate that cold Melbourne afternoon? Was it your thigh? Your neck? A sliver of your bum, perhaps? And did you ever imagine that when you died, you'd be sliced into 500-gram pieces and dispersed all over the country? That your body would be eaten by hundreds of different people whom you'd never met? What a strange thought. You must have passed through the intestinal tracts of such a diverse range of people: a young child whose mother cut you up into little pieces to make you easier to chew; an elderly woman who drenched you in gravy, served you with mashed potato and ate you in front of the telly; a group of patriotic thirty-somethings celebrating their country by throwing you on the grill and washing you down with VB.

I never planned to eat you. I'd called myself vegetarian (sometimes even vegan) for many years, in fact. It sounds cruel but I used to kind of love the awkwardness of talking about the ethics of meat with someone while they were eating it. Watching men in suits at a business dinner looking awkwardly down at their meat-laden plates as I told them where their food came from, their forks visibly quivering as their conscience wrestled with itself. I told myself, It's not nearly as cruel as the way that animal they're eating was no doubt treated. And I certainly had a point. But there comes a time in one's life when one must finally accept that one is a hypocritical wanker.

I did something worthy of a righteous scoff from everybody at whom I had once looked down on from the saddle of my high, high horse. I ate a steak. I ate you, dear cow. And I loved it. If I could take it back, I would. I'd regurgitate you, stick you back together, take you back to the grassy field or the feedlot from whence you came, utter a hearty 'moo' of encouragement and send you back to the herd. But I can't. I did it. I was iron-deficient, premenstrual, grumpy and feeling selective in what I wanted to feel ethical about that day, i.e., nothing. I ordered you from a nice-looking young lady at the pub, hoping against hope that she wouldn't recognise me as 'Missy Higgins the vegetarian singer', and waited for you to arrive on my table. I sunk down deep in the chair, pulled my beanie low for disguise. Thirty seconds later, the waitress came back: 'Excuse me, you're Missy Higgins, right? Oh my god, I'm a fan! Can I get your autograph?'

Shit, I was sprung.

'Um, yeah, sure,' I replied quickly, fumbling with the pen she put in front of me.

'You wanted that steak medium-rare, yeah?' she seemed to announce to the *entire* pub.

'Ah, yes, yes, thank you,' I mumbled into my chest, sinking down so low I almost fell off the chair.

Oh god, would she tell her friends? Would she write a blog about it? Would she sell the story to *Meat-Eater's Digest*, become the poster girl for the All-Vegetarians-Are-Hypocrites movement, print my face in the middle of a target with a cow leg coming out of my mouth? This was disastrous. I felt like everything I had done in support of animal rights was about to be rendered useless. I stood up, went to walk out and then – *bam!* It hit me. The smell. The sizzling, meaty aroma of your cooking flesh floating towards me on the arm of the waitress. The world seemed to stop. Suddenly there was only you. And me. And the prospect of you being in me. She placed you delicately in front of me and for a while I just sat there and breathed you in. Childhood nostalgia enveloped me with swirling colour: birthday parties, balloons, family barbecues, running under sprinklers, hot dogs in white bread, chops, sticky tomato-sauce fingers. This was the smell I'd grown up with. The smell that I associated with family, love, security, tradition and, well, *home.* It'd been so long since I'd smelled anything but steamed broccoli and tofu. The thought of where you came from, dear cow, was at that moment so far from my mind that I drove my knife and fork into you like you were my last meal on death row. Or, more accurately, my last meal before my morals grabbed me by the ear and dragged me out of there.

On the walk home I put a hand to my stomach. How could I have done this? Not only do I think eating meat is unnecessary and wrong, I actively preach against it. I appear in ads holding baby pigs and cuddling dogs, saying, 'You wouldn't eat your pet – why is a cow any different?' But the truth, dear cow (and this is hard for me to admit, especially to you), is that I don't actually have an inherent problem with the idea of eating animals. Nothing about the basic act of eating another being's flesh feels wrong or makes me queasy. I could have been a surgeon if I'd had the brains, since nothing disgusts me – except when people talk with a mouth full of toothpaste spit but I don't think surgeons have to deal with that.

Anyway, the point is that it's not eating the flesh of a cute furry animal that I feel is wrong. It's the idea that that animal didn't get the same right to life as we all do. It's the idea that something can live its whole life in a dark, dirty cage not big enough for it to spread its wings or turn around, that it may never know joy or even contentment, *that's* what disgusts me. Or that we pump these animals so full of hormones that they can grow to their full body size in three months, so much so that their limbs and organs collapse on themselves and if they don't die they're in constant pain their entire lives. And all this without ever seeing sunlight! Even you, Miss Moo, if I may call you that, were no doubt painfully branded and castrated, had your sensitive horn tissue scraped out of your skull with no pain relief, and spent a good chunk of your life in a feedlot, munching on pellets that your digestive system wasn't built for. All so that your fat was nicely marbled for my pleasure. *That's* what disgusts me. That we as humans have put ourselves so far above these other creatures that we think it's okay to make their short lives absolute hell. Fuck childhood nostalgia. I could also get nostalgic about those massive, *hugely* wasteful water fights we used to have with all the neighbourhood kids during summer – they're some of the best memories I have but I wouldn't dream of doing that now. Times change. We grow up. We learn stuff. We learn that neither we nor the planet are indestructible. And that perhaps things weren't simply placed around us for our enjoyment. Perhaps we are not the kings.

So why did I eat you, Miss Moo, on that fateful afternoon, instead of ordering the eggplant parmigiana? Or perhaps slipping an iron tablet into my mouth and having a shot of vodka to get over my silly, premenstrual self? Because I'm not bloody perfect. No one is. And it's stupid for us to pretend we are. As shown by the fact that diets don't work in the long term, it's counter-productive for us to have an all-or-nothing mentality. One mistake and we're a failure! 'Ah well, I ate a Smartie, may as well eat a cheesecake and a few packets of Tim Tams.' It's the same with meat. You don't have to stop eating it if that scares you, but don't do nothing. Eating it a couple of days *less* a week is *much* better than doing nothing. If you haven't earned yourself the 'grand honour' of being able to call yourself a vegetarian, who gives a flying duck? It was stupid of me to be so hard on myself that day. Maybe I'm the kind of person who needs the reins a little looser in order to stay on course. I never wanted to stick to any sort of rules just because I had labelled myself as something once. Labels are pointless when the very thing they're labelling is mercurial, aren't they?

Look, Miss Moo, I've rambled on here, I know, but I just wanted to tell you that I know we can't keep going the way we are. I know that meat demand is rising, and as it does the quality of animal care is going down rapidly. If you and your friends once had a little bit of room to graze when you were alive, sure as the sun will rise and the population will grow, we'll soon be raising all of you in cramped indoor spaces, because we simply won't have a choice. Factory farms will buy up the family-run farms like Coles bought out Con the Fruiterer. There'll be no cute Cadbury cows on the hillside; you'll all be stuck indoors somewhere, farting a hole in the ozone layer and awaiting your miserable fate. But, Miss Moo, I really think if we humans try to do what we can instead of doing nothing at all, maybe we can change that. Maybe we can make your life actually worth living. It's the least we can do.

Anyway, sorry again.

I hope they've got some good grass up there for you in cow heaven.

Yours sincerely and (mostly) herbivorously,
Missy Higgins

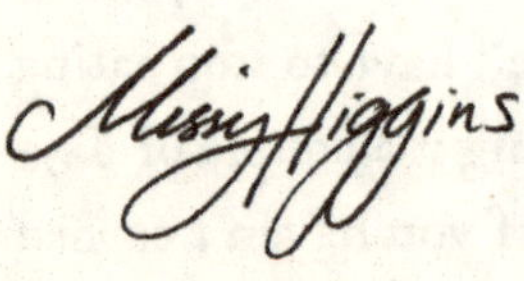

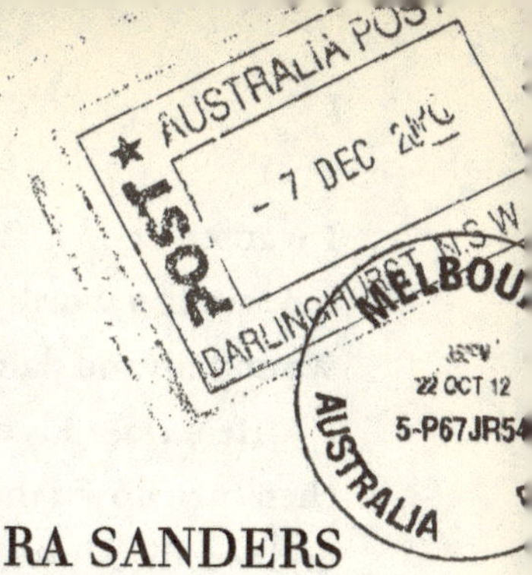

ZORA SANDERS

Dear employees of the Mooloolaba Island Family Hotel and Resort gift shop,

You may not remember me. But then again, considering what transpired between us in the summer of 1992, you may. I know that more than twenty years have passed between then and now, but I would like, at long last, to apologise for the crime I committed in your shop, and more importantly, more painfully, I would like to apologise for my subsequent cowardice.

You see, although I was only five at the time, I must admit to you here and now that I was already in the grip of an addiction. A vice in whose power I was a tiny, helpless pawn, driven to acts of degradation and, yes, even criminality. My four-year-old self was consumed, compelled and seduced by the feverish pursuit of that beguiling mistress, la dolce blanca, the white witch, the snowy temptress. Yes, employees of the Mooloolaba Island Family Hotel and Resort gift shop, I was a sugar addict.

Even at that tender age my entire life was dedicated to the pursuit of lollies, sweets, bonbons, candy . . . They had many street names, and I knew 'em all.

The elderly Greek man who owned the milk bar at our local shops was my dealer, but, like so many junkies, I convinced myself he was, you know, more like a friend. Sure, there was a mercenary aspect to our relationship, but beneath that, we really *got* each other.

I wanted candy, and he wanted to sell candy. Well, 'want' might be too strong a word, but a suburban Canberra milk bar was where he'd wound up and damned if he could do anything about it now.

He'd raise his eyebrows in my direction when I entered the shop, then turn down the dial of the small TV on a shelf behind the counter and wordlessly pull a white paper bag from a string by the five-cent pick-and-mix selection. He was the only person who really knew and accepted my particular . . . predilections. Milk bottles and gummy worms were my opiates, caramel mates my cocaine, Redskins my heroin. He would pluck my selection from the various plastic trays, drop them into that little white paper bag, lick his fingers clean of residual sugar and seal it with a practised flip and twist.

I'd hand over my money and get a second eyebrow lift in exchange. There was no need for idle chatter between two people who understood each other so well.

By this time I'd also figured out a very reliable scam to get enough money to finance my habit. In the first weeks of kindergarten we were all encouraged to open savings accounts and bring some money to put in every week. It was basically a racket run by one of the Big Four banks to establish brand loyalty in children as early as possible. But little did they know, the scammers were soon to become the scammees.

Every Monday morning my mother would give me three dollars to hand over to the smiling, perfumed woman who came to our classroom to collect and, presumably, deposit our funds into our accounts on our behalves. However, very early on I discovered that the minimum you could deposit was actually just fifty cents. This put a full $2.50 into play for me every single week. And $2.50 to a five year old in 1991 was nothing to sneeze at.

My mother never seemed to notice the discrepancy between what she was giving me and what the occasional bank statements showed. By the end of the seven years of primary school, some of the kids could have put a down payment on a reasonable house in an up-and-coming neighbourhood. I had saved just under $75.

The point of all this is to make you understand the state of mind I was in when I committed my crime. My older sister, my mother and I had been on the road for two days. I hadn't been out of my mother's sight for more than a minute in all that time, and my usual source of funds had been cut off by the accursed summer holidays. It had been more than forty-eight hours since my last hit, and the icy fingers of sugar withdrawal were playing my spine like a goddamn xylophone.

When we finally arrived in the hotel lobby, my mother went to check us in, sending my sister and I to wait in that fateful gift shop. My sister abandoned me in favour of a rack of magazines, while I, of course, was drawn at once to the glittering display of lollies on a shelf right at my eye level. We were the only people in the shop, and I have to say that neither of you, the women behind the counter, were paying us any attention, being deep in conversation with one another (for which, understand, I do not blame you whatsoever). The conditions were right. It was the perfect storm of opportunity and desperation.

Without a second thought, without even a first thought, I reached out, my hand steady as a rock, and casually lifted a packet of five-flavour Life Savers from the display stand. Maintaining a casual nonchalance, I dropped them soundlessly into the case of my beloved comfort pillow, Pilly, making it an unwilling accomplice to the whole sordid episode. I had the grace and confidence of a young Artful Dodger and then some.

But I want you to know that while, yes, this was a criminal act, it was also an act of desperation.

Up in the hotel room, locked in the bathroom, that first hit of glistening glucose tasted better to me than the ambrosia of the gods themselves. It was pure bliss.

Unfortunately, although I was capable of carrying out the crime with consummate ease, when it came to covering my tracks afterwards, I was less cunning cat burglar, and more hapless lolcat.

This had always been the case. Back at home, when left alone in the house after school, I would invariably gravitate to my sister's forbidden bedroom to riffle, quite harmlessly, through her many fascinating possessions. If I remained focused, I could return the room to its original state and she'd be none the wiser. But more often than not I would simply get distracted mid-riffle and wander merrily back into the lounge room to watch TV or go looking for the next-door neighbour to play with. My sister would come home some time later and find that her immaculately tidy room now appeared to be the site of a momentous troll-doll massacre. Not even sad-clown troll or her prized Buckingham Palace-guard troll would have survived the slaughter that swept them and their many (*many*) comrades from their custom-built display stand into a higgledy-piggledy pile of carnage on the floor.

My sister would angrily confront me, but I would stoutly deny all accusations, although even I had to admit that a burglar who left all valuables untouched while he played with her troll dolls, tried on her makeup and wore her shoes around was an unlikely (though potentially terrifying) explanation.

And so it was in the aftermath of my great crime in the Mooloolaba Island Family Hotel and Resort gift shop.

For a full twenty-four hours I hid the slowly diminishing roll of Life Savers in my pillowcase. My family was used to me carrying Pilly around with me wherever I went, so that didn't raise any suspicion. And although I was definitely sneaking off on my own and claiming to have been in the toilet more often than usual, I was a small child, and everyone knows they are basically mobile urine factories.

It reached a point when I felt certain that my crime would never be discovered, that I was free to savour my Life Savers without punishment or retribution. And that, of course, is when I let my guard down.

The next afternoon as we were getting ready to go to the beach, the one place I wouldn't take Pilly, I used the distraction of gathering towels and sunscreen and inflatable li-los to slip a Life Saver out of its paper and into my mouth. I tried not to make any obvious sucking motions or sounds, but as we stood in the lift going down to the lobby, my mother suddenly stiffened and sniffed the air.

'What's that smell?' she asked, turning to me. 'Are you eating lollies?'

'No,' I replied.

'Open your mouth.'

'No.'

'Open your mouth!'

'No!'

'You are eating lollies!'

'I am not!' I shouted indignantly.

But even getting those words out had given my mother and sister a glimpse of my scarlet, sugar-coated tongue.

At this point the lift doors opened and we stepped out. My sister, the betrayer, pointed at me, eyes alight with a hellish glee and shrieked:

'She's got Life Savers!'

My mother, who is well-known among her friends and family, as well as the local council, constabulary and law courts, as a terrifyingly, morbidly honest and upstanding citizen, leaned down to my level and, in a voice made of ice and fury, whispered, 'And where, exactly, did you get those from?'

The recriminations went on for hours. All my mother's powers of guilt inducement were brought to bear upon me, and I was left a tearful wreck. Didn't I know that *stealing* (there was no room in my mother's vocabulary for something as euphemistic as 'shoplifting') was the worst crime a person could commit? Who knew what the follow-on effects of my actions might be? What if one of the women in the shop was held responsible? What if she was blamed for *my* crime? What if she lost her job *because of me*? How could I have been so selfish! My mother didn't even know who I was any more.

We never made it to the beach that day. Eventually I was beaten down so much that my denials could go on no longer. Sobbing, I upended Pilly, letting the remaining quarter of the roll fall out in a shower of torn paper and tinfoil onto the hotel bedspread.

Then came the true ordeal.

As punishment, my mother and I would go downstairs and I would be sent into the shop to confess my crime, pay for the Life Savers I had stolen, apologise and promise to never, ever steal again. The real kicker was that I would have to go on my own. She would stand outside to make sure I went in, but I'd have to do all the talking by myself.

As soon as I heard what she was proposing, I became petrified with fear. Confessing to my mother had been bad enough, but the thought of admitting what I'd done to the people I'd done it to (assuming, of course, they hadn't been fired already and were living in an alleyway, cursing the unknown Life Savers thief who'd brung them low) was terrifying.

On the way down in the lift I begged my mother to change her mind. I'd accept any other punishment she could think of! I howled, I sobbed, I begged her to reconsider, but she remained resolute.

We walked across the lobby and stopped in sight of the gift shop.

'Off you go, then.'

'Please, Mum, *please!*' I begged. But she was silent, refusing to look me in the eye.

I began the walk across the lobby. I tried to calm the heaving sobs that were rippling through me. I crossed the threshold of the gift shop. As before, there were no customers inside, but you, the two employees, were again behind the counter, chatting to each other, unaware that a notorious criminal had entered your midst.

I walked up to the counter. One of you saw me and paused in conversation.

'Hello!' you said, so kindly I felt the tears begin to well again. 'What do you want, sweetie?'

To me you both seemed like adults, forbidding in your authority, but you were probably only in your late teens at most. You looked down at my tear-stained face with concern.

'Are you lost?' asked the other one. 'Shall we go and find Mum?'

Still I couldn't speak.

I reached out and opened my palm, showing the gold dollar coin I'd been given to pay for my stolen goods.

'Do you want to buy something? We've got lollies over on those shelves,' said the first, pointing to the exact scene of my crime.

At this point the sobs returned with full force. I knew there was no way I could explain to these angelic women, who fussed so sweetly over me, that I was not, in fact, an innocent child, but a hardened criminal, and that they themselves were my victims.

I dropped the remains of the Life Savers on the counter, damp and sticky from my sweaty palms, and placed the dollar coin beside them.

Then I turned and fled, ignoring your cries of concern. I ran past my mother who reached automatically to stop me, then let her arms drop to her sides. I rounded a corner and climbed the nearest flight of stairs. I hid on the first landing, from where, peering cautiously over the railing, I could see the entrance of the gift shop and the expanse of the lobby below.

You were in conversation with my mother, who looked resigned and tired. You listened for a while, and then, inexplicably, you both began to laugh. My mother's expression didn't change. I couldn't understand how you could laugh at the discovery of how close you'd come to losing your jobs, to being destitute and homeless, begging for charity from uncaring strangers on the street.

My mother spoke a little longer, then you both turned and went back into the shop. I could tell from the movement of your shoulders that you were still giggling together as you passed out of my sight.

I crouched down and buried my face in my knees. Crying with shame and humiliation.

Some time later, I heard my mother's voice above me.

'I've talked to them. They were very, very upset.'

'I'm sorry,' I whispered.

'It isn't going to happen again, is it?'

'No. I promise.'

And to this day, I have kept that promise. I may not have broken my addiction to all things sweet, sticky and delicious, but I have at least refrained from thievery to obtain them. My aversion to stealing is so strong that I can't even see someone 'sampling' grapes in the supermarket without breaking out in a cold sweat. While my friends gleefully enter all their produce as 'brown onions' at the self checkout, I feel faint if I accidentally enter a poppy seed Kaiser roll as a sesame seed one.

But despite my pristine behaviour, in this respect at least, ever since that summer afternoon in 1992, it is my failure to own up to my crime that still haunts me. I know I should have had the fortitude to confess to you, and apologise. Perhaps it would have been the beginning of a life of dignity and restraint. Not terribly likely, I admit, but maybe.

And so, dear employees of the Mooloolaba Island Family Hotel and Resort gift shop, let me say, from the bottom of my heart and the core of my soul, for once and for all: sorry.

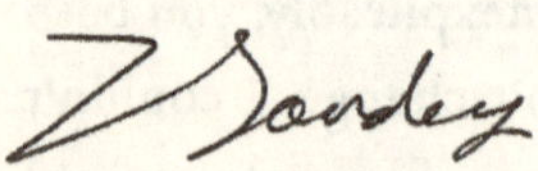

JANE CLIFTON

'Bless me father, for I have sinned. It's been forty-five years since my last confession, so, hang on to your rosary beads, we're in for a bumpy ride.'

That's how I would begin if I was to ever again creak open the carved wooden door of God's own TARDIS, the confessional box, and throw myself upon the faded purple satin knee cushion and His mercy, to whisper into the ear of His representative averting his old face and trying to stay awake on the other side of the curtained grill.

Being brought up Roman Catholic introduces you early on to the notion of wrongdoing and its consequences. Words like 'mortal' and 'venial' trip off the tongues of seven-year-old Micks in training for their First Communion. The catechism had already taught us words like 'penance' and 'purgatory' and 'absolution', 'benediction', 'consecration' and 'transubstantiation'.

We learned early about sin. And even though sin didn't always equate with criminal behaviour – no matter how sinful your mother told you it was to leave any food on your plate, you knew they wouldn't send you to gaol for it – we got the picture.

But I won't be visiting any confessional box any time soon because, sadly, they no longer have any power over me.

I live in the absurd universe Camus and Sartre alerted me to when I was just eighteen, where I have to sort out my transgressions all by myself.

So, I'm writing to you, my petty crimes – my PCs – in order to set the record straight. Who or what are you? Can I live with you? Am I a bad, morally corrupt person? If there really was a heaven and hell – an 'up there' or 'down there' to those flat-earthers among us – which way would I be pointed on the day of reckoning?

I'm going to start with the big ones just for a sense of perspective.

The Big Ten. The Tablets. Moses' Rules, fresh from the mount. Downloaded to the original stone iPad – hashtag #iamtheword.

I'm going out of order and starting at five, because I want to be perfectly clear: I have not killed anyone.

I have been heard to utter the words 'I'm gonna kill you' and 'If you don't stop drumming on the table, I will stab you through the heart with a spoon'. But these are just phrases. Petty phrases, if you will. And even though they do say that the pen is mightier than the sword, in this instance they're wrong.

I don't even kill spiders. I'm a glass-jar-and-cardboard-release-into-the-wild-to-kill-other-species kind of gal.

'Thou shalt not kill'? I haven't.

Now, back to the first commandment.

'I am the Lord thy God. Thou shalt have no other Gods before me.'

He-with-a-capital-H goes on:

'For I, the lord thy God, am a jealous God.'

And you can pretty much deduce from that 'He the Lord thy God' is also a pretty uptight, egocentric God. Almost an insecure kind of God.

I mean, really, if you have to tell people not to consider any of the competition – and, let's face it, there are a lot of contenders for top dog up there in the clouds – you're pretty much working from a loser position.

A secure God would not need to issue that first commandment.

A commandment I have to confess that I have disobeyed many, many times. I have, indeed, placed many other gods before Him.

It began with Cliff Richard – so, not so bad – then Billy Thorpe and Johnny O'Keefe. Followed, of course, by the Beatles, the Rolling Stones and the whole Baby Boomers' major arcana of dead-at-27s. There's been Paul Newman, Steve McQueen, Terence Stamp, Alan Bates, Hugh Grant, Colin Firth and Dominic West. But now it's simply James Hird. [*makes sign of the cross*]

The first commandment also rules out the worship of graven images 'or any likeness of anything that is in heaven above, or that is in earth beneath, or that is in the water under the earth'. (Water under the earth? Who knew? And how to make a graven image of that? The Jenolan Caves done in rose quartz, perhaps?)

I have worshipped the sun – sometimes topless (don't spend too long on that picture) – until my skin peeled. Or roasted it in Coppertone to a scarlet shade of brown – except for the bits where I wrote the name of my boyfriend in lipstick and it showed through as a pink tattoo. I have already received my punishment for this heathen sun-worshipping, in the form of a plague of age spots that now cover my ancient epidermis.

I have worshipped – and continue to worship – the moon. All women's bodies pay homage to the moon whether they like it or not. It tugs at our hormonal tides.

I wish upon the new moon, bowing three times and turning over any coins I have in my pocket for good luck. I drive with the sun visor down on some nights because it's bad luck to see the new moon through glass.

And I'm a subscriber to Mystic Medusa's fabulous astrology website, and when I was in Ireland last year I had my tea leaves read by a Mrs Johnson.

My desk is littered with false idols: statues of Our Lady, the BVM, in varying sizes and types; Infants of Prague; laminated holy cards; rosary beads of every shade and weight; a stone Winged Victory from Athens; mother-of-pearl crucifixes; a miniature Stonehenge (straight out of Spinal Tap); and a tin of decorative Jesus bandaids.

I worship these icons while rejecting their inspiration. Like visiting the Louvre and heading straight to the souvenir shop. I'm cravin' those graven images.

OMG – I think it may be time to review Commandment Two: 'Thou shalt not take the name of the Lord thy God in vain.'

Christ Almighty and for God's sake, you've been reduced to a text icon! Time to build a bridge.

Commandment Three: 'You mustn't work on Sundays.' Well, these days I'm a marriage celebrant and Sundays are my busiest days – especially for gay commitment ceremonies. God.

And if I'm not supervising unholy unions in parks, gardens and wineries all over Victoria, I am kicking back at the mall, with a little retail therapy, being served by sinners in shops that never close.

'Thou shalt not do any work, thou, nor thy son, nor thy daughter.' Well, my son and daughter get paid double-time at Grill'd on Sundays, and those kids have phone plans to maintain.

And while we're on the kids, a little of the Fourth Commandment wouldn't go astray. There was a lot more 'honouring of thy father and mother' when I was a young sinner. Ably assisted by a clip across the ear that, these days, would have put my mother behind bars.

We've covered Five, and so to Six. Here, in all its uncovered, alluring, buffed and oiled loveliness, struts adultery. Now, technically, I have never been married (never been asked, thanks for asking), but I've been living in sin with the one bloke for thirty years, so I'm not sure which is the bigger misdemeanour.

In the thirty-three years prior to meeting him I did put it about a bit. But now I'm just bragging – that clearly wasn't adultery, that was fornication.

I have, in fact, been a very chaste de facto over the past three decades – jazzed up from time to time with my fair share of harmless crushes. But Catholics are taught that if you even think about someone in a lustful, sexy-rexy kind of way it's the same as actually doing it – like they'd know . . . Here in the secular world we have rules.

I'm going to skip forward to the ninth and tenth commandments, which concern coveting.

Dear PCs, it is safe to say that I am coveting dot com.

I have coveted my neighbour's house and my neighbour's lap pool and jacuzzi. I have coveted my neighbour's manservant, and their maidservant. I have not coveted his wife, nor his ox, but definitely his ass, and so much more that is my neighbour's.

Obviously not my immediate neighbours – I live in the western suburbs – but other-people-in-general's good fortune and stuff: yes! I have coveted.

I covet the book sales of Wendy Harmer, the corporate appearance fees of Kate Ceberano, the acting CV of Lisa McCune, and Delta Goodrem's hair.

I covet the small breasts of every woman in the world, and take out Tatts tickets each week hoping to win enough money to get mine reduced.

I covet everyone's radio job and envy every blonde with a weekly magazine column featuring a full-length, zany photo that takes up half the page.

I want shoes by Louboutin, a holiday house at Dromana and a lover in his early forties. I want a VW Tiguan and a pearly pink Vespa. I covet, I covet, I covet!

My mother used to say, 'I want, never gets,' and she was right!

And that is why I am guilty of Commandments Nine and Ten.

I plead *not* guilty to Commandment Eight – because I cannot tell a lie – but guilty as charged to Seven – 'Thou shalt not steal' – because I was a teenage shoplifter. I know I'm not alone. Testify, ladies and gentlemen: who else among you was, or continues to be, a teenage shoplifter?

My first petty crime – yes, here we come to the nub of it – was committed in Cardiff, Wales in 1960, when I stole a pair of café au lait fifteen-denier seamed stockings from a downtown department store named Littlewoods.

I didn't even own a suspender belt! But I wanted those stockings and I took them. And then, the worst thing that could have happened to an eleven year old happened to me – I got away with it.

So there were other occasions. You know who you are, PCs. Step forward, the chocolate bars and the LPs, the lime-green hot pants and the pixie boots.

This gives me a whopping 60 per cent failure rate on the Big Ten, and don't get me started on the Deadlies, where I would score a perfect seven for lust, envy, avarice, pride, sloth, wrath and gluttony.

There are no religious terms for the most blatant among you, my petty crimes:

- shooting my mouth off
- being a know-it-all
- being an oxygen thief
- telling people what I *really* think when a little white lie would be so much kinder – especially when pissed . . .
- speaking of pissed – driving home drunk from gigs singing along at the top of my voice to Sharon Jones or Ike and Tina Turner.

This letter has involved such rigorous self-examination I now know how the nuns felt when we giggling teenage scourges would ask them what *they* confessed to each week – impure thoughts, perhaps?

I do miss those weekly trips to God's own TARDIS and the act of confession. I miss that light, guilt-free feeling of wiping the slate clean and starting each week afresh, after saying a few decades of the rosary and reciting the Act of Contrition. A feeling you hoped would last all the way from Saturday afternoon confession to Sunday morning Holy Communion without getting pissed on brandy crusters and letting a boy from Aquinas College crack five on you ('inside, upstairs' on the Ladder of Love).

Here, in the cold, hard, absurd universe, one must forge one's own moral code. On the plus side of growing up Catholic, you do develop a powerful sense of the notion of forgiveness.

Dear petty crimes, I know you for what you are and I forgive myself, and I try to live life to the best of my moral abilities.

But, look, you know what's going to happen if I'm wrong and there is actually a set of pearly gates up there beyond the ozone layer:

Saint Peter will see me coming and yell out, 'Holy hell, it's Margo Gaffney from *Prisoner*!' and down I will go.

Jane Clifton

ELMO KEEP

Dear Modestly Complex Analogue Music Piracy Ring of the Mid-to-Late 1990s,

It was a heady and yet, in hindsight, quaint time, the mid-to-late 1990s. I'm going to lay the blame for my dalliance with petty crime squarely at the feet of grunge music, where it belongs. Grunge was already to blame for the premature death of hair metal and terrible 'slacker' film *Singles*, and would be, eventually, for the existence of the band Nickelback. That I facilitated the theft of possibly dozens of copies of grunge records had nothing to do with my own moral turpitude and everything to do with the fact that this kind of thing was sewn into the very fabric of the Alternative Nation itself – the neatly packaged corporate rebellion, which we, the nubile, flannel-wearing, corruptible youth of the day, were being sold in the form of endless Nirvana-lite records. It was essentially about all the many and varied ways a young person might be able to stick it to the man. So of course stealing these records was absolutely logically, if not ethically sound. But then it *was* ethically sound, because, as all those rock stars told us, record companies were greedy, money-hungry corporate whores, and *fuck them!*

So it was fine.

'Not being able to afford something is not a reason to steal it,' my mother would say. 'It's a reason to not buy it.' To which I would say, 'Don't tell me what to do, you're not my real mum. Except that you are.'

As a teenager, after watching *Empire Records* probably one too many times, I determinedly set myself the not-too-lofty goal of getting a job in a record store. The reason for this was two-fold: one, I desperately wanted to leave my horribly paying job at the local Woolworths; and two, who wouldn't want to work in a record store? Believe it or not, young people, but there once was a time when the record store functioned as the internet does today: you could get into nasty, largely pointless arguments about miniscule matters of taste with real live human beings – but face to face!

In the end, I did not get hired by a charmingly eclectic indie store populated by an unlikely cast of counter-culturally archetypal young people coming of age. No, I was hired by a filthy big chain outlet, such as the one the cast of counter-culturally archetypal young people coming of age fought off so valiantly in *Empire Records*. To get hired I did not have to dazzle the intimidating, cool boss with an encyclopedic knowledge of the history of pop music; I just had to fill out a form. And, looking back, I can see that it wasn't the charming, self-administered, asymmetrical, bright-orange haircut I was proudly sporting at the time that made me so attractive. It was my youth. My youth meant that I could be paid much, much less than other people working there, most of whom were well into their twenties and thirties. If memory serves me correctly, it was fourteen dollars an hour, which was to me an absolute fortune. Especially compared to the paltry eight dollars an hour I was getting at the supermarket, and with the added bonus of never having to handle poultry at the deli counter ever again.

I won't lie: working at the record store made me pretty cool at school, even if we did all have to wear the same horribly daggy black polyester collared shirt with the store name emblazoned on the breast pocket. Even if I did have to be at work first thing Saturday *and* Sunday mornings to fill those costly shifts that paid loading rates on weekends. I had managed to clamber above the milieu of after-school jobs at bakeries and supermarkets and newsagents that the rest of my friends were still mired in. So, of course, it was time to share the spoils of war with my comrades.

Now cast your mind back, if you can, to the cost of a compact disc in the mid-to-late 1990s. If you can't, or weren't born at that point, I'll remind you: an album cost up to $32.95. I know, it's crazy to think that the record industry survived as long as it did. $32.95 was a cost equal to two hours work, closer to three after tax. But blank tapes were really, really cheap, at only $1 each. So I would buy a bunch of tapes and I would sneak home the CDs I wanted to copy onto said tapes.

You'll note here that I didn't just keep the CDs, which would have been so easy. I wasn't some kind of common thief – I had morals! I would take three or four albums home on the Saturday afternoon, copy them to tape that night, and then return them to the store on the Sunday morning. No one at work ever knew. I made tapes of the tapes and gave them to my friends for free, which produced a fidelity similar to a crappy mp3. As I never actually profited from this piracy, I felt like it was a victimless crime. I was a socialist. It was a very Robin Hood thing of me to do, I thought, liberating this music and distributing it to the poor.

Pretty soon people started requesting specific albums they wanted me to tape for them. When this was confined to a couple of my closest friends, it was totally fine. But when it got into the wider school community, I didn't want to be spending my Saturday nights staying up into the small hours making copies of Alanis Morissette albums. If I did it for everyone, it would eat up my entire life. As my scheme worked similarly to a franchise, it was easy to roll it out to other people. It was, like I said, only moderately complex. I let it be known at morning rollcall that a meeting for 'music club' would be held at lunch.

'I work Thursday nights and weekends,' I said to those assembled at the designated tuckshop meeting spot. 'When you come up to the counter, you don't know me, all right? Don't all come on the same day, either. Otherwise we don't have a deal.' What was this, *Fight Club* several years before *Fight Club* was even a thing? Whatever it was, you could not talk to me about it at work, that was for sure.

My rule was that people had to buy an album outright – I wasn't facilitating straight theft from my store. Many worked out they could split the cost of an album among a few friends, buy the blank tapes and make all the copies they wanted. When they wanted another album to copy, they would just bring the original one to me at the store and exchange it for a different one. I felt good about this, since the store was at least getting this initial $32.95 plus small change for blank tapes. I heard rumours that some kids were charging five dollars for their tape copies, which displeased me. But I was no mob boss, I had no *consigliere*, no enforcer to make people stick to my rules. I just had to trust that a swift kick of karmic justice would be delivered to their shins in good time.

Things went on in this merry way for many months. The fortune I had imagined accumulating from my new wages never materialised as I had no impulse control and the store offered great employee discounts, so no sooner would my shift end than I would buy as many records and music magazines as my bank balance would allow. I loved the people I worked with, even if I was too young to see that they did not love working at the store like I did. It wasn't an after-school job to them; it was what they did five days a week. Listening to the pounding volume at which new releases were played on repeat for days on end would have sent anyone insane. But I was in ignorant bliss of any of these adult realities. To me, it just felt like I had won the job lottery, and if I grew up to work there every single day? That would be totally awesome.

One Thursday night my boss called me into his office. 'I have to talk with you about something at the end of your shift.' Which was, at that point, two hours away. 'Come back in here when you're done.'

My blood ran cold. Did he know, somehow, about the piracy ring? He must! Why else would he want to talk to me? My mind span while I stacked and restacked the classical jazz section. *Did I slip up? Get lazy? Did someone see something? Was there a mole? Why didn't I have a* consigliere *at a time like this?* I was totally going to be fired. My life was over.

Two sweaty hours later I was in the office behind the store, down labyrinthine messy corridors stacked with CDs, kind of like the hidden tunnels at Disneyland where the employees take the heads off their Daffy Duck costumes away from the eyes of children.

'So,' he said as I sat down. 'There are going to be some changes here with how we allocate hours to everyone.'

'Great!' I blurted, thinking at least I probably wasn't fired.

'Well, okay. You need to take this home, read it, and come back and sign it if you agree. If you don't agree, you can't be rostered on. You have until Monday to decide what you want to do.'

'No problem!' I tore out of there with my heart singing, flooded with relief but still thinking that probably I should cool it on the CD returns for a while, just to be safe.

'This is a collective bargaining agreement,' my father said to me that night, looking over the document I'd been given. 'It means they want you all to agree to earning a lower wage with no penalties in return for getting a certain amount of guaranteed hours a week.'

'What should I do?'

'You shouldn't sign it, that's what you should do!' he said. 'You all need to be in agreement that you won't sign it. Don't let them bully you into signing it – you'd be getting a terrible deal. They want to halve your wages.'

'Oh, that sucks!'

'Yes, it does. You guys are the workers,' my father said, imparting to me a valuable life lesson. 'You have the power. They can't do anything without you.'

So began my brief career as a socialist agitator. It lasted for exactly the length of one weekend. I lobbied and cajoled my co-workers. I pumped them for information. I appealed to their sense of civic responsibility. I reminded them that we were basically a family and that we had to support each other. By the end of the weekend I was convinced that no one was signing this outrageous flaunting of our civil rights. Everyone agreed it was monstrously unfair, unethical. Bullshit, basically. The workers were going to win this round, dealing a crushing blow to our corporate overlords.

I went into work after school that Monday and straight to my boss's office.

'So, have you signed it?' he asked.

'No, I'm not signing it,' I said, delivering the deathblow. 'No one is.'

'You're sure you don't want to sign it? Last chance.'

'I'm totally sure.'

'I'm sorry to do this,' he said. 'But you're fired. You're the only hold-out.'

My disillusionment was crushing. I was speechless. I couldn't believe it. Again, I was blind to the adult realities of making a living. No one wanted to lose their job for the sake of a principle, so they just put up with losing their benefits and earning less money in exchange for job security. They didn't have a choice. They were, like me, brought down by the man.

'And I need you to return your shirt,' he said as I got up to leave.

I said that would be no problem, I would bring it in the following afternoon. But I never did. My cheeks burning, I walked out through the crowded store unable to look my now ex-colleagues in the eye. I never set foot in there again.

So I want to thank you, Modestly Complex Analogue Music Piracy Ring of the Mid-to-Late 1990s, for teaching me these harsh lessons in the most poetic way possible, while also letting me grow fat on the fruits of my labours, both legitimate and otherwise. All things told, in the end, with the money I lost when my job ended and the money the store lost on all those pirated records, I'd say we were just about even.

To my biggest fright

TONI JORDAN

Dear Fright,

Holy fuck, you are scary. You are the scariest thing that has ever happened to me. You're still the thing that keeps me up nights, the thing that terrifies me beyond all reason.

I stand before you as Brucette Banner, mild-mannered novelist. You, Fright, are the six months wherein I revealed myself as a green-skinned, clothes-splitting, raging semi-human hulk. You, Fright, are the knowledge that deep inside me is a psycho, stalking nutjob.

It started on a normal night. A party. I was twenty-seven, with a great job as a laboratory manager. I had a red Nissan, a degree in molecular biology and I shared a flat in Hamilton in Brisbane with a girlfriend. I had no boyfriend. It was the nineties, and it was Brisbane, so it wasn't quite *Sex and the City*. It was more like 'XXXX and the Endless Suburbs'. But I was a normal woman. Rational.

At that party, the party that will live in infamy in my memory forever, the host was introducing me to his friends. I shook the hand of a man I hadn't met before. Spunky. Tallish. Dark hair. That very second, the instant I took his hand, I could feel the transformation begin. My skin took on a greenish tinge. I felt my clothes tighten, the seams begin to split under my arms and across my back. It was irreversible. Just like the real Bruce Banner, I had been accidently exposed to gamma radiation, in the form of that man, whom, to save us all from embarrassment, I shall call Mr X.

Then and there, I made my plans. The first step was to get him home. I stopped drinking – soft drink only for me, for the rest of the night. I flirted and fluttered around him, lifted and separated him from his friends. I got him horribly drunk and, as the party was winding down, offered him a ride back to his place. Heh heh heh. He was somewhat bemused, but I was a foot shorter than him and, I'm sure, looked innocent. Trustworthy. Heh heh heh. In the manner of unsuspecting victims the world over, he was compliant. I poured him into the front seat of the Nissan and strapped him in.

It was only while shagging on his couch an hour later that I realised I hadn't bothered with irrelevant details like his job, marital status or last name.

He and I had a mutual friend, the host of the party, who was highly amused by this turn of events and proved a great source of all the little details of Mr X's life, details which proved incredibly useful, and which I would have already known had this been a more normal 'courtship'.

Over the next few months, things deteriorated. Social conventions and taboos in the early nineties were just this side of Jane Austen. What women could do, what women could say. A minefield of political correctness constricting female behaviour in the most chauvinistic and ridiculous manner. There is, apparently, a limit to how many times a day you can call a man you've only just met and shagged just the once. Repression, pure and simple. It's breathtaking. Through a process of scientific investigation, that acceptable number of phone calls might have been around, say, seven. I might have exceeded seven calls a day on, perhaps, a daily basis, for say, a number of weeks, since that first night.

You might be shocked to hear that sometimes he didn't answer. This was before texting, and to leave a message for someone – who, for some unknown reason, refused to take your call – meant speaking with an actual person in a message-taking call centre. When the anonymous message taker recognises your voice and anticipates that your message will be PICK UP NOW, it could be a warning sign. So I began varying the messages I'd leave. I stopped saying PICK UP NOW. Sounds a little bossy, I thought, so sometimes I'd say, PICK UP PICK UP PICK UP. Then I got smart. My message evolved to PICK UP OR I'M COMING OVER. Success!

And that business of befriending his sister: that was just a misunderstanding. She worked in retail. When you work in retail, anyone can just go into the shop and start talking to you. Der. That's the whole point of working in a shop: talking to customers. And she was a lovely person. She worked in fashion. I bought a whole new wardrobe.

Showing up at someone's workplace in the middle of the day unannounced, even with a homemade lunch, is frowned upon. Apparently. As if nutrition and convenience count for absolutely nothing. Talk about skewed priorities.

Also unappreciated is dropping around to a man's house unannounced, even when carrying a still-warm eggplant parmigiana and the offer of a long night of shagging. More often than not, however, he'd open the door a smidge, then let me in. I was twenty-seven, did yoga three times a week, and made one hell of an eggplant parmigiana.

Don't think I spent every night for the next few months obsessively stalking a man I'd only just met with the desperate fervour of a virgin camping outside the Apple store. That would be sick. I also spent long nights sitting in my car, parked across the road from his house. Just watching. Oh, look. That flicker through the front door? He must be watching telly. And now: that light's just gone on, the one on the side. Possibly he's peeing. The back left tyre on his Corolla looks a little flat. Possibly I should ring and tell him. Though possibly not.

Meanwhile at work, things weren't going so well. I was spending less time at my desk and more time in the ladies, crying, pacing between the cubicles. I'd phone my friends at all hours, sobbing, 'Why doesn't he like me? *Why?*' (In a noteworthy aside, nearly twenty years later I retain only one friend from that mad six months. None of the others have kept in touch.) And anyway, it's a valid question. Why *didn't* he like me? I was, after all, fabulous. Aside from my superior parmigiana-making and shagging skills, I was smart, interesting and kind. What on earth was wrong with him?

Now, of course, from the perspective of almost twenty years, I can see that perhaps during that six-month blur of focus, I was a teeny bit overenthusiastic. You, my Fright, my first and only psychotic episode, showed me what I was capable of. You showed me the monster within myself, you showed me my power, you showed me my ability to scare the shit out of someone a foot taller and 20 kilos heavier than me. For that, I'll always be grateful.

Best,
Toni

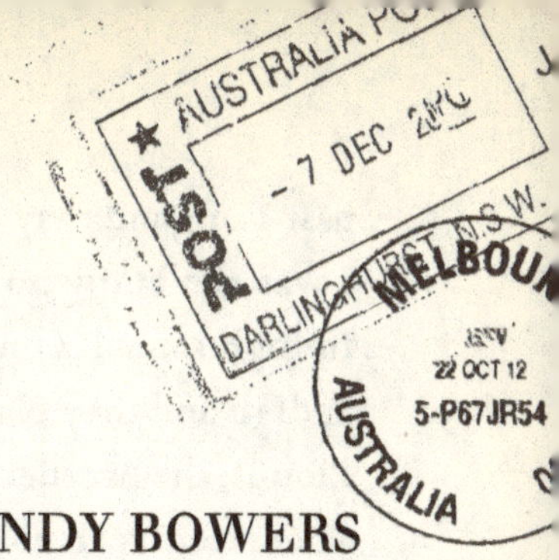

CANDY BOWERS

Dear David Bowie,

I was eight years old when you gave me the fright of my life.

Let me set the scene: it was the '80s and we were experiencing a boom in fantasy and science-fiction movies. My favourite childhood films included *E.T.*, *The Dark Crystal*, *The NeverEnding Story* and *Flight of the Navigator*. The *Ewoks* TV series (small furry creatures played by little people in *Star Wars*) and cartoon spin-offs were my staples on a Saturday morning in the lounge room at 24 Burchall Grove.

It is a little-known fact that there have been people of colour from the African Diaspora living down under since the dismantling of the White Australia Policy in the late '60s. My parents fled Apartheid South Africa in 1973 and with my oldest sister a babe in arms, they came to settle in Dandenong North, Victoria.

I am the youngest of three girls, David, and my sisters are a crucial part of this story. Kim and Tania are five and four years older than me respectively, and growing up we often found they had to come down to my level or I had to go up to theirs. For example, I probably read *Catcher in the Rye* and watched *Twin Peaks* a little too young, and I probably kept them playing with Barbie Dolls well beyond a suitable age. I remember Tania watching me styling my Barbie's extra-long blonde hair on the front steps of our house and saying, 'I'm going to play with you right now, but if anyone comes past I'm gonna say Mum made me do it, okay?' When we got older I was the one who desperately wanted to be a part of their scene. In high school Kim and Tania were in an indie grunge band called Spdfgh and they played with the likes of Ratcat, the Falling Joys, the Clouds, the Breeders, Elastica, Ben Lee and the Lemonheads. Having a fourteen year old in apricot culottes and peace-sign earrings tag along seemed to cramp their style a little. Let's just say I spent a lot of time looking after the equipment in the van.

My sisters introduced me to the concept of 'cool', and also 'uncool', very early on. 'Cool' was music, 'cool' was difference, 'cool' was art, 'cool' was queer, 'cool' could be quite harsh and moody and often ended with the sentence, 'And if you cry to Mum about this, Candice, we will never take you out ever again.' 'Cool' was cutting your own path whether the 'status quo' understood you or not. In fact, being misunderstood was proof of your ultimate 'coolness'. When Spdfgh performed the song 'Yo Mutha-fucker, Mutha-fucker Mutha Yo Yo!' at the Annandale Hotel in Sydney, in front of our ultra-conservative South African mother, I remember thinking, This is freaking cool.

David, it was in 1986 at the movies in Dandenong, sitting with my sisters (three little brown girls with homemade popcorn and no-name lollies), when you rocketed into my world, planted a few crucial seeds and quite literally scared my afro straight.

When you appeared on screen juggling a crystal orb, wearing a velvet cape and extraordinarily high-waisted pants, and sporting a blonde spiked mullet, I was bolted to my chair. It's possible that no breath escaped my lungs whenever you were on screen.

Jareth, the Goblin King sparked an otherworldly and thrilling fear in me.

I was enthralled, in love and totally afraid of you. I remember this deep desire to see you kiss Sarah and to see her kick you very hard in the shins. You were so scary and so queer, so male and female all at once. You were something else and I became obsessed to the point where I left my window open at night hoping you would visit – which was pretty daring for a seven year old with a morbid fear of possums. One night, Tania put a mop on her head and crawled through my window; my blood-curdling scream woke up the neighbours and she had a healthy red slipper mark on her bottom for about a week afterwards.

It was around that time that I also became taken with Boy George. It was as if you both opened my soul to the world in between: to a third space. When I look back at my taste in music I see a particular leaning towards outsiders and outliers – those who could not and would not fit in, those who became the trendsetters and created movements in music and art; those confident enough, strong enough or lucky enough to pursue their work, even when the rest of the world could not understand it.

My most recent fright came in the form of a tweet, by an Aussie hip-hop icon. He made a comment on my position as an artist, in response to a challenge my sister Kim (aka Busty Beatz) and I sent out to the Australian hip-hop scene. We wanted to riff on the dominance of the white male perspective in Australian hip-hop. We wanted to discuss the current culture in comparison to where it came from. Back in the day, hip-hop was freedom and a voice for marginalised people, for poor folks and for black folks. So what is Aussie hip-hop now and more importantly does it (by its very nature, i.e. sound and aesthetic) currently exclude people of colour? The provocation was: 'What is the relevance of a white male perspective in Oz Hip-hop, when the dominant culture is white?'

Ozi Batla tweeted: 'While we were building a scene in early 2000s one comedy act were PARODYING hip-hop culture. Now they're cut cos they're outsiders.'

That was his response to our provocation – to cut down the messengers rather than engage in the debate, which seemed weak to me. He was referring to my cult hip-hop comedy act Sista She. We had a song on triple j about being harassed at a train station called 'What Are Youse Girls Doin'?' Our success somewhat riled the 'purists' in the Aussie hip-hop scene and I've gotta say that fact still makes me giggle to this day.

I replied to Ozi: 'Outsiders fella, we're blak women and we're queer – y'all were never about to open that door.' And, 'An act that spoke directly to young Australian women. It was fun makin' fun of y'all but we were in it for the feminism.'

No doubt the Aussie hip-hop scene could not acknowledge the breakthrough nature of our act. Our outright silliness slammed up against serious activism, and annoyed, angered and possibly frightened many who were building their kingdom, fully equipped with drawbridge and army to keep out folks who didn't sound Aussie enough or battle rap like bogans. I am still surprised by the covert racism and fear of difference that exists in even the most 'political' corners of the Australian hip-hop community. What a freaking bummer.

I guess when you speak out against the norm and interrupt oppression, life gets dangerous, especially when your perspective threatens to highlight hypocrisy. In the case of Aussie hip-hop, no doubt our magnifying glass frightened the DC logo off their flat caps . . . Like they say about log jams and dynamite, the only way forward is to blow shit up!

It takes courage and huge self-belief.

David, if there's one thing *Labyrinth* taught me, it was to be bold and courageous even in the face of those most dominant of all. The revelation that the whole movie had actually been a personal battle to teach Sarah how to stand up for herself is brilliant and something all little girls and grown women and Warrior Princesses need to remember on a daily basis.

The words that break the spell (oppression/perceived power) are simple: 'You have no power over me.'

You have no power over me.

Dope.

Thanks for frightening me, David, and thanks for the music.

All the best,
Love,
Candy B

MOJO JUJU

To my biggest fright,

It's taken me a long time to write this letter. Twenty years, in fact – it might seem a little out of the blue. But I dare say at least some of the adrenaline and maybe even a little of the fear you once gifted me might be present here today as I read this letter aloud. So it's fitting in a way.

I was nine years old when we met. I guess I've got a lot to fill you in on that's happened since then. Like that you made an impact on me, in more ways than one. You left a mark, to say the least.

Anyone who knows me could probably vouch for the fact that I've never had much trouble finding things to say. At the same time, I've grown up writing songs and playing in bands, and, you see, most songs now don't go over five minutes – under four if you want them on radio. Not to mention I've always been more of a postcard kind of kid than a letter writer. Really, I don't know why I haven't written 'til now, but I figure it's gonna take me a little longer than a postcard to say what I gotta say, and the way I see it, you owe me as long as it takes to get this off my chest.

Now, it might hurt you to hear this, and, truthfully, it wouldn't make me terribly sad if it did. A long time went by when you didn't much come to mind for me. Occasionally you'd come up in conversation, and I learned to laugh about it. But there's still a part of me that ain't all that sure it's funny.

See, sometimes I get these headaches and sinus pain. And I know it's because of you – or, rather, how we came to know each other.

Maybe six or seven years ago, I started having pain in my hips. And more recently that pain started moving up my back. I never really put two and two together until eventually it got so bad I had to start seeing doctors and sports therapists. I had X-rays and everything. For a while I had to use a walking stick and every month or two I had to get my shoes re-soled because I'd wear out the right heel.

Everyone I saw who tried to fix it asked me the same question:

'What kind of accident did you have?'

That's when it occurred to me that you were responsible for this. And I do hold you responsible.

Finally an osteopath friend had a look and gave me some tips and sorted me out. It's been two years now, though, and the pain has started coming back. Some days I think it's worse than ever.

But it's nothing. Nothing compared to the pain I felt that day.

Do you remember that day? I feel like I ought to be able to say I'll never forget it.

But honestly, I don't remember all that much about the day itself.

I do remember being excited about saddling up and putting my boots on.

See, I wasn't much liked by the other kids. Mostly because the town was too small and my name was too long. Or something like that.

Anyway, I was excited. I was going out riding with some other kids.

Most of the time I would ride by myself, down along the Baradine Creek, out in the Pilliga Scrub. Which is something I'd probably enjoy now, but, being nine years old, at the time I kinda just wanted some company my own age.

Well, you really fucked that up with your big, grand entrance.

I know what you're thinking. I played my part in it too, right? Trying to impress those other kids. Yeah, you're right. It's true, I was likely riding too fast. In fact, I know I was.

I never blamed Charlie for anything. He was a good horse. But I got the feeling he blamed himself. I still feel bad about that.

I rode him once more afterwards, because I wanted him to know it was okay. But I gave up riding altogether after that.

I don't exactly know if it was the moment when I felt Charlie trip over that rock and lose his footing, or if it was when I was in midair when I first made your acquaintance. But I do know for sure it was your arms wrapped around me when I woke up on the ground, covered from head to toe in my own blood. I was staring you right in the face.

Well, that's when I first learned the power of my own voice. I thank you for that. I've been standing on stage wailing at people for a long time since.

As surprised as I was at the time, in hindsight it's no surprise at all that you were there at that moment. What truly intrigues me, though, was the way you hung around waiting to see what would happen next.

You waited for my mum and dad to arrive and introduced yourself to them. I don't think they were all that impressed or pleased to meet you, really. I guess they felt as though they didn't have time to sit around and get to know you.

I've never really known why you chose me.

Maybe you just saw an opportunity. Maybe you thought of it as a bit of harmless fun that just went too far. Maybe it was the fact that my dad was an ambulance officer and we lived at the station, and I was almost home when you revealed yourself. I made you think it wasn't that big of a deal, but seriously, you scared the shit out of me.

Blackout. Shower.

Blackout. Hospital.

They didn't have an X-ray or a CAT scan there, so Dad had to drive the ambulance all the way to Coonabarabran. Dad in the front, you and Mum in the back, trying to keep me awake.

A broken nose and a fractured lip. And of course an impressively sized mark of an upside-down horseshoe right there on my face. That led most folk I saw for weeks to come to inquire as to the condition of Charlie's foot. His foot was fine.

My face went black and blue and swelled up so I could only open one eye.

I don't even remember how badly I landed on my back. I figure it was lost in the throbbing of my head.

I tried to forget about you mostly. But I know I dreamed of you for a good while after that.

I've met some of your relatives since. You seem to be the biggest member of the family. Or perhaps you just seem bigger in my memory.

I don't know if this letter will ever find you. You seem to be long gone. Maybe you're still out there hiding in the scrub, playing tricks on kids. But I wanted to let you know I haven't forgotten.

It's more than just a deviated septum or a twisted pelvis, more than backaches or headaches. There's something else you left me with. Some kind of callus. Something numb.

It's not that I don't feel pain – obviously I do. And I still get scared. But I don't flinch or turn away.

Maybe that's not so bad. Maybe I even ought to thank you for that as well.

But really, there's still a part of me that's a little bit pissed at you. I don't really hold grudges. And normally I'd just invite you for a drink, and put it all behind us. But I find it hard to imagine you've changed. I think it's best if you just stay hidden.

Sorry to bring this all up again. Especially seeing as I can't see a way to resolve it.

I wanted to be sure you knew exactly what you'd done. I needed to know that you know.

Thanks for hearing me out. And if we ever do meet again – just know I'm coming prepared.

'Til then,
Mojo

YUMI STYNES

My family all love a good fright. We like to hide in dark corridors and jump out and 'boo' each other. The other day my fella came through the front door with my mum. He feels very protective towards my mum as she's tiny and Japanese. Waiting for them in the dark was my little daughter Anouk, hiding, waiting to 'boo' them.

For a brief second, Martin thought the kid was an assailant and had his fist clenched and ready, prepared to defend his mother-in-law. Pow! Imagine if he'd punched my kid, in front of my mum!

But now to a more serious fright . . .

I have a fear of crowds. It started when I used to bar-tend at the Palace in St Kilda and drunks would shout their orders to me over the heaving music and they would lean right in towards me and accidentally spray saliva at my face, sometimes into my eyes, sometimes into my mouth!

That was gross, but the thing that frightened me was the way the crowd would lose its sense as the nights wore on. Weekend after weekend, you'd see them start to brawl, start to slur, spit on the floor, sometimes vomit, pee in the darker corners, pash a gross guy because of his passing resemblance to David Lee Roth, dance crazily to 'I Alone' by Live, and, above all, behave like arseholes.

Something about being in a crowd sets you free, allows you to lose your humanity . . .

Years later I was pregnant with my first daughter and working for a music TV channel called Channel [V]. We used to do these tours of the country in the 'Channel [V] Music Bus', broadcasting live shows from places like Townsville and Launceston. I think the idea was to take the live music experience to kids in regional areas and blow their minds with bands like Magic Dirt and Shihad. It actually worked and there were a lot of kids who'd never seen a rock band before. For the first time in their lives they felt the buzzing through their feet from really loud bass guitar and the fat drumming through car-sized amps, and these kids were allowed to scream really loud and jump up and down and shake their heads and be moved by music. It was awesome. Thousands of people would turn up to these things.

One day we were in a town on the Gold Coast and, fairly obviously pregnant, I was sent to do the very first opener of that day's show from out in the crowd. It meant talking to the camera, talking to the crowd, and at the same time trying to convey to the people watching at home through the telly some of the adrenaline and vibe in the air that day.

The audience was massive but cute and young and excited, and when the camera guys and the producer and I took our positions among them, the kids all squirmed with excitement about getting on TV and being seen by their friends.

I chatted with a few of them until the count started that WE WERE GOING TO GO LIVE!

10 . . . 9 . . . 8 . . . 7 . . .

But something happened when the camera lights came on and all these sober, good-hearted and excited kids realised that maybe if they shoved closer, squashed in a little nearer or did something outrageous like snatch the microphone out of my hand or grab my hair, they could maybe be on telly.

The crowd became an animal. And the animal was pouncing. *On me.* The way these kids each lost their individuality and became part of the aggressive wave was scary and I actually feared for my life. And I feared for my unborn baby.

We got through the link and as soon as I got free of the crowd, I ducked out of sight, burst into tears and hugged my tummy.

Recently I experienced a whole new level of crowd fury when a comment I made about a soldier and war hero made front-page news in what turned out to be a very slow news week. Slow fortnight! There was *nothing* in the news! Whitney Houston had already died, there was no leadership spill yet . . . Nothing.

I'm hesitant to bring it up because it was the ugliest thing I've ever been through – *ever* – and I did end up delivering that baby naturally and without drugs . . .

I don't wish to revive any of the ugliness by talking about it in front of people. But some of you have never seen any of the work I do on the telly, nor read anything I've written, nor heard any of the radio I broadcast. You may only know me vaguely from this one stupid incident, which, I'm happy to say, doesn't represent my career at all. I work bloody hard to support my two daughters and in this constant output of words, words, words, I said something that so inspired the ire – the *fury* – of complete strangers that I was sent death threats and hate mail and was menaced online by a mob without a face. Channel Ten clocked more than 30000 complaint phone calls; Twitter became an outlet for every racist in the country to slag off Asians; the Facebook site that my work set up two years ago was strangled by teams of vigilantes who would schedule sentinels to stay online and bully anyone who tried to defend me.

I've since realised there is a cycle in the media of finding someone and hounding them, and then forgetting about it. I've seen it happen to Christine Nixon, the Blue Wiggle, Lara Bingle, Marieke Hardy, and many more. It was my turn!

I've tried to find some of the worst tweets sent to me but most of them have since been deleted. People said horrible things – things like, I should be shot in the face or killed, my children should be hurt, I should be made to shut up by having a dick shoved in my mouth, I should be raped, World War II was my fault, I was a dirty Asian whore . . . But one of the things I found actually hurtful was women who told me I should get the sack. Didn't they know I was a single mother? I've got children to support! Why would you wish that on a person?

My posture changed. Walking down the street, I was hunched and defensive, waiting for missiles to be lobbed from moving cars.

During the worst of it I rang my boss in Sydney and asked him to either fire me or publicly defend me. He said, 'Yeah. I heard about the package.'

'What package?'

'The one that arrived today,' he said.

'I don't know anything about it,' I said.

'Oh. Uh,' he said, and changed the subject!

What package?

I rang my boss in Melbourne and got to the bottom of it.

Apparently, some guy had gone to the trouble of going out, collecting dog shit, wrapping it up and putting it in an envelope, and posting it to me, care of Channel Ten.

But, how's this? He hadn't put enough stamps on it and it was *returned to him* because he'd written his return address on the back! So he then paid the extra money and the package eventually made its way to Channel Ten! Well done, buddy!

During the absolute height of harassment and fear and threats, I took my daughters, now aged seven and ten, out to see a live stage show of *How to Train Your Dragon*. It was opening night, and crowded. I felt vulnerable and exposed. People stared at me. I'd been on *A Current Affair* the night before. I was page three of the *Herald Sun* that actual day. There was a picture of me *this* big.

But I was proud to be with my beautiful girls, taking them out and doing normal things.

Was there danger in that crowd?

Nuh.

I looked around and saw people like me – tired parents who fuck up sometimes but try their hardest to seek entertainment for their kids and for themselves. Sometimes an entertaining media lynching might help pass the time. Other times, a dragon show. Or a movie.

While I felt a strong sense of protectiveness over my kids, I didn't feel afraid. I didn't let – I'm not letting – the crowd win.

From,
Yumi

To the stranger who hopefully doesn't know who I am

SEJA VOGEL

Dear Danny Goffey,

When I was a teenager first discovering music, there were a few bands that really changed my life. Yours was one of them. You made me want to play music, you showed me that pop songs can be powerful while being light-hearted, and you just made it all look terribly fun. Some people referred to you as 'the weird-looking one', but I always thought you were attractive. I loved that you were a skinny man who had good rhythm – a rarity, in my book. You impressed me and I loved the way your mouth looked like Paul McCartney's when you made an 'O' with it.

When I listened to your music on the way to school, I felt cooler than everyone else on the train. In reality I was most likely the only one sitting on my own with my walkman on, while everyone else giggled with their friends, actually being cool. Regardless, your intoxicating music, like a mini Britpop party in my ears, made me feel popular and slightly superior in a way. At home I had a picture of you next to my bed and I looked at it every night before I went to sleep. In the photo you were wearing a t-shirt that had a French phrase on it: '*C'est magnifique, mais ce n'est pas la guerre*'. I stared at it, wondering what it meant, wondering if you had come up with it, if you knew French, and whether it meant something sexy.

One day my curiosity got the better of me and I looked up each word separately in a French dictionary at the school library.

It means: 'It is magnificent but it is no war'. Hmm. Definitely not sexy . . . Unless one is really into war. Which, even though I'm German, I am not.

You might be relieved to know that you weren't my only obsession as a child. I had enough creepy infatuation to share around. I slept with a Beatles book next to my bed from when I was seven to when I was nine, open on a photo of John Lennon leaning up against a tree. I told my parents I would marry him when I grew up. I listened to all my dad's Beatles records a million times and watched the *Help* movie he had taped off television until the worn-out VHS went wonky. Eventually my obsessive behaviour must have become a little worrying for my parents and my dad sat me down to explain to me that my dream of marrying John was probably not going to come to fruition as he had died before I was born. I couldn't believe it. I cried for two weeks straight.

When I got a little older I went to a Pavement concert with a love-heart sticker on my forehead and stood at the front of the audience, right in the eye line of singer Stephen Malkmus, hoping to send a subliminal message to him of my undying devotion. I thought the heart sticker would make me stand out from all the other girls in the front row. In fact, I already stood out on account of my massiveness. I also stood out because I looked like a total dickhead with a sticker on my forehead. But in my fantasies he would pick me out of all the girls, invite me backstage and be my first proper kiss. He didn't, of course. I was a child; he was a grown man. It would have been illegal, not to mention immoral. But that was the way my mind worked back then.

The point I am trying to make is: John Lennon and Stephen Malkmus! At least you were in good company.

Fast forward another few years and I was still a child, but a child who had started kissing boys and smoking pot. I went to my first ever Big Day Out. You played. I stood in the front row, got kicked nearly unconscious in the mosh pit, had my shirt ripped and my hair caught between people, and actually thought I might die several times. But I loved every minute because you were right there. I saw you walking out in the 'real world' that day. I followed you around the grounds, too shy to talk to you, but trying to find the right moment to tell you how much I liked you and to make you my friend. Not surprisingly, the moment never came, seeing as I was following you around like a police officer on a stake-out, trying to be inconspicuous, ducking behind tents and strangers whenever you turned around. Before I knew it you had walked backstage, out of reach. I pressed my face up against the fence until security told me to leave. I'm not sure if you saw me – I was the one wearing the Supergrass t-shirt.

I think I grew up a little after that. I graduated high school, I started a band that sounded a bit like your band, and I stopped living vicariously through my famous crushes for a while. Playing in a band was the best, just like I knew it would be from following your career. We got signed to a cool label, put out some EPs and went on lots of tours. I went to uni and studied French. I often thought about your t-shirt, since '*C'est magnifique, mais ce n'est pas la guerre*' was the first full sentence I had learned in the language. To be honest, I thought about you less and less now that there were actual real boys right in front of me. Sure, they weren't British or quite as Paul McCartney-mouthed, but they were there nonetheless.

And just when I thought I was over the youthful, obsessive, psychoneurotic phase of my life, the head of our record label/tour promoter asked us if we were interested in supporting this band from the UK called Supergrass on their upcoming tour of Australia. I almost shit my pants. I struggled with the idea of meeting you. I wanted to be your friend, I wanted you to think I was cool, and I wanted to not shit my pants in front of you. I squirmed for weeks before the tour, agonising over what to say and how to be.

Our first show together was at the Forum in Melbourne. It was the biggest venue I had ever played and I was terrified. I walked down the stairs to the band room before the show and literally ran straight into you with a thump. You looked up and said, 'Oh, sorry!' Your mouth made an O and it was great. The next thing I noticed was that you were wearing the t-shirt with the oh-so-familiar French sentence on it, and before I could even think about why it seemed so familiar to me, I blurted out, 'Hey, that's the first thing I ever learned how to say in French!' As I heard the words come out of my mouth, I had flashbacks to staring at your photo as a teenager, looking up each word at the library, and, to my absolute horror, my face turned the reddest shade of red it had ever redded. *Please* don't let this be a homemade t-shirt! Please don't out me as the creepy punisher I have suppressed for all these years. I waited in dread for you to react for what felt like minutes, although it was probably only two seconds. You finally said, 'Oh, yeah, it's a quote from blah blah blah.' I had stopped listening – too busy trying not to spew. I mumbled a 'yeah, I must've read it,' and then excused myself to go tune my keyboard or something equally nonsensical. Tune my keyboard?! Idiot!

Needless to say, we didn't become the best of friends or lovers as I had hoped. It's never a good idea to meet your childhood crushes, but I have to say, you were very nice to me. You all were. I still have the photo of you and me that I took of us in the bathroom at the Metro in Sydney, but I keep it in a drawer now. The photo was taken because I told you my mum wanted a photo of you. I lied. It was me who wanted it. You suggested it would be funny to take one of us together in the tiny bathroom so it would have a toilet in the background. I willingly obliged.

I guess you never really lose that stalker gene if you are born with it. But what I am trying to say, now I have the level-headed hindsight to deal with it, is that I am sorry for being a creep back then. I know it can't be nice all the time to be famous, getting chumps like me memorising things on your t-shirt and following you around festivals. But surely there have been worse than me, right?

I would like to tell you that even though I haven't had nearly as much success and exposure as you have, it hasn't always been pleasant for me either. People yelling at me on the street or getting me in headlocks after shows; people sending me strange presents or emails; a doctor telling me she was a huge Regurgitator fan whilst inserting the speculum during my last pap smear. These things are uncomfortable to say the least.

But I'd like to think we can make qualitative judgements when it comes to particular stalkers. I'd consider myself to be a 'quality stalker', not your average nasty breed. I'm nice. I have things going for me. I just happen to have a small problem with drawing the line between romance and fiction occasionally.

So, Danny, next time you come to Australia, please take that into consideration, and if you walk backstage in Brisbane and there is a tiny felt drum kit waiting for you, just know that it came from a nice place.

Je suis désolée.

Best,
Seja

KRISTY CHAMBERS

Dear sir,

You don't know me, and we will probably never be anything but strangers to each other. Still, I felt compelled to write this letter to you.

I may not remember what I ate for lunch yesterday, or the surname of that weird guy I dated for six months in 2007, but I remember the day our lives converged so vividly that it's difficult to believe it was almost a decade ago. Subtle details of the moment have faded over the years. I can't recall the exact colour of your shirt, for instance, or the day of the week or the music that was quietly playing in the background at the time, but it's impossible for me to forget you. You struck like lightning. There was nothing, and then, suddenly, there was you.

Life can be very surprising sometimes, like your co-workers bringing in a cake for your birthday when you didn't think anyone even knew the day, or finding yourself in the midst of an unplanned pregnancy.

Some surprises are awesomely welcome, like reaching into the pocket of your winter coat on the first bitterly cold day of the year to discover a long lost fifty-dollar note, or finally meeting a guy who isn't emotionally fucked up *and* who is also free of sexually transmitted diseases and substance-abuse issues. They do exist.

And then there are those surprises which can best be categorised as alarming, like stealth diarrhoea hitting in public, or an indelicate boyfriend committing unintentional anal penetration on your person.

I'm not entirely sure, sir, where on the spectrum of surprises you belong, but it's somewhere after winning a raffle and well before accidental butt sex.

I learned of your existence as we both stood in line at the Commonwealth Bank on Adelaide Street. Looking back, it was a chaotic time in my life. I was a full-time student, midway through a three-year Bachelor of Nursing degree, and I was also working full-time in a bar in order to stave off homelessness and scurvy. Between work and study, I was always tired. I had climbed the ranks of my hospitality job by default – everybody else had gradually quit because our boss was a mercurial, irrational dickhead – but I was far too fatigued to even look for another position. I somehow became the 'Assistant Bar Manager', a change in job title that failed to affect my wages in any way, but which saw my responsibilities increase to include tasks like doing the banking. Which is how I came to be standing in the same line at the same bank as you, at the same time in the same tiny corner of the world, with a bag full of cash in my hands.

I stood behind you in the line. Not immediately behind you, but about three bodies across as the queue snaked through the room in a zigzag formation. My mind was elsewhere. It was on the assignment I had not yet started which was due for submission the following morning, and it was on the precious night of sleep I would have to forgo in order to complete it. I already knew that my assignment was going to be a piece of shit, but I also knew that I could hand in a piece of shit and still pass, because I'd been doing exactly that for eighteen months. I felt a physical ache for my bed at the thought of yet another all-nighter, and yawned so widely that my eyes watered. The situation was annoyingly familiar, and the only answer, as ever, was going to be a lot of strong coffee. And that's when you caught my eye, fidgeting on the spot, restlessly shifting your weight from one leg to the other.

Now *that's* a guy who's had some decent coffee, I thought. I was mildly envious.

You stood out from the rest of the customers because you were the most animated person in an otherwise static line, the only one perceptibly moving at all. I watched as you waited impatiently, glad of the distraction as my brain shifted away from my own deeply unsatisfying thoughts.

I stared at the back of your head, at the dark curly hair that was thinning slightly on top and cascading untidily over your shirt collar. Your face was obscured from my view, but I guessed that you were an older man, possibly in your late forties or early fifties. I looked more closely at the crumpled fabric of your shirt and noticed a light brown stain, like old dried blood that had never properly washed out, and a yellowing ring of grime circling the collar. As a matter of fact, you were kind of unkempt. You began to twitch slightly, appearing to grow more agitated as the cashiers continued to hold long discussions with the customers already at the counter. I understood your frustration. Waiting in line is boring, but waiting in line at a bank is tedious. There's nothing to look at, nothing of interest there at all. I would hate to work in a place like this, I thought, it's so dull. And then it happened.

With a shocking, furious burst of energy, you leapt upwards and shouted:

'BIG BLACK COCK! BIG BLACK SALTY COCK!'

My mouth fell open. I was stunned. And so was everybody else in the bank, apparently, because nobody moved, nobody snickered or even acknowledged that they were hearing your outburst. You had thrown a couple of large black salty cocks into a calm, still pond of monetary transactions, and yet there was not a ripple to be seen. The cashiers carried on cashiering. The waiters carried on waiting.

You were the first person I ever met with the severe sweary kind of Tourette's that people generally associate with the disorder. Until that moment I had always thought that Tourette's was a childishly amusing idea, as far as neuropsychiatric disorders went. As someone with a great affection for swearing, it seemed like my kind of illness, a disease perhaps even tailor-made for my dirty mouth, but you, sir, took me to school. You taught me that Tourette's wasn't funny. You taught me that in the right context and location, Tourette's could be *fucking hilarious.* Arse wank dickhole vagina nutsack!

Love,
Kristy

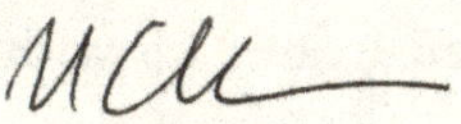

AMY INGRAM

Okay, hi!

So. I was totally excited when I got asked to do this, and then I was totally freaked out, and then excited again. Then I came up with about 800 ideas of what I could do/write about but most of those were complete balls. I have to admit, as I was thinking about all this, my mind started to drift off into all sorts of crazy scenarios like you see in the movies – you know, like up here I make some sort of huge confession that will change my life forever, like that I'm dying, or pregnant, or I have the evidence hidden that will prove who killed my best friend last summer and that person is in this room (so he can't kill me later out in the alley as I have just made this statement in front of all you witnesses). Then of course my mind went to the obvious place where I profess my love for someone in the audience and tell him how I have always loved him but have just been too stupid to see it until now. He'd stand up and look at me very seriously, so I'd think, It's too late, he doesn't love me, but then he would smile and I would smile, and I'd run into the audience and he would run to me and we'd pash and everyone would cheer. Then the bar would put on free drinks for everyone and we'd all get shit-faced and other people would be so elated from it all they'd start pashing, until the whole room was a huge love-in pash-fest.

Alas, I cannot make claim to any of those things, and must come back to reality. So I return to my first question. What am I going to write about? I have no big secrets to confess, no dead best friend, no love of my life in the audience, and I have not really done anything crazy to someone where I am glad they don't know it was me.

But then I started to think. I may not have had some huge crush who I have stalked for years, or stolen someone's life savings in a very clever worm program through the net, but I have done things here and there along the way. And when I thought about it even more, I realised that, while not earth-shattering, they could be viewed by some people as being pretty dodgy. So this is to all the people along the way to whom I have done something slightly dodgy.

So here goes.

This is a new one – I did this just outside, actually. In my car I pulled up to the lights only to see Mr Benjamin Law outside talking to friends. So I decided to beep obnoxiously and pull the finger. Naturally he decided to make 'growl out' actions with his hands/mouth which I reciprocated while ever so slightly inclining my foot on the accelerator, resulting in me smashing into the back of a dude in a huge ute. Lucky for me his car was a beast and I did no damage. So to that dude just outside who I scared the shit out of because I was too busy being an arsehole – sorry.

To my primary school principal who I saw pashing the vice principal in the sports room: it was me who told people what I had seen that afternoon, which started a huge country scandal that may or may not have resulted in divorce. And to the vice principal who I later realised was not actually in the room – it was some other teacher he was pashing – I'm sorry I told people it was you macking on with Mr Chadwick. I have at least told three people that I think I made a mistake, if that is any consolation, and in a small country town three people is the equivalent of hundreds.

To the owners of the local store in my home town, I am sorry for all the chocolate my friend stole over a period of two years or so. I didn't steal it as I was too chickenshit but I was the lookout as my friend would shove as much candy down her overalls (which we named her 'ganking pants') as humanly possible. And I did partake in the eating of said candy afterwards, even though I felt really bad about it.

Also, I should apologise to the people of Target, where I later graduated from lookout to actual thief. I still have some of the eye shadows I stealthily hid in my'90's purple faux-fur bag.

To all the op shops I swapped price tags in: seriously, I am sorry I did such a lame thing, especially when you consider that the fine ladies of OARS were donating the money to convicts on parole to start a new life. I'm sorry I was such a cheap little shit.

To Mr Dorman, my science teacher – I made out with your son.

To the people who lived in Gorman Street, Toowoomba, while I was at uni: I am sorry for the 'shopping spree' I went on one night to find my friend a birthday present. I obtained some tiki torches, a few good-looking ferns, a gnome or two and an entire outdoor setting. You will be happy to know that I was the hit of the party having given the best presents, something which I feel is key in forging any new friendship.

To the staff of Toowoomba Pizza Hut: yes, we did bring in containers and alfoil to steal as much all-you-can-eat pizza as possible to live on for the next week.

To all the boys who I entered in my equivalent of a little black book as 'Nigel' because I couldn't remember your names the mornings after during what I have named my 'summer rampage' – which worked well until there was a boy really called Nigel and it got confusing. I'm sorry; you all were very special to me.

To my mum, who I asked for money to go to the doctor for the flu but really it was for the morning-after pill. Sorry your daughter is a tramp.

To the flight attendants from Qantas who I told it was my first time flying when they found me sitting in my seat covered in my own vomit from a not-so-handy vomit bag breakage. I'm sorry, it was not my first time flying – I'd got incredibly drunk the night before and then made the mistake of eating Hungry Jack's during the stopover in Sydney. I'd also like to thank them especially for giving me the Qantas blanket I wore as a skirt to walk into the terminal to meet my mother, who then proceeded to ask why I always have to wear hideous op shop clothes. She was delighted when I handed her a bag with my vomit skirt in it and told her what I was really wearing.

To the people shopping in the furnishings department of Spotlight who asked for my help with DIY curtain making. There are people all over north Brisbane with fucked curtains because I had no idea what I was talking about.

And sorry to Spotlight for that time I just stopped coming to work. Forever.

To the people of Newcastle and This is Not Art 2009: I understand that the ginger beer that year was not a favourite – this was my fault as I was incredibly in love with the ginger beer boy and decided getting him a job was clearly the best way to get a date. This did not work. Nor did buying copious amounts of boutique wine I could not afford from the place he worked. He did give me a discount every time, though, which I thought was a clear sign of love. I had ridiculous fantasies wherein he would teach me more about wine and we would go on extravagant tasting expeditions across the world and be incredibly happy. That this did not happen is just another fail in the many chapters of Amy's fantasy life.

To all the people that I was a fucking moll of a waitress to when I worked in hospitality: I had graphic flashes of wanting to beat the shit out of you all with baseball-bat pepper grinders. Sorry, but you really should stop being jerks to waitresses. Just order what's on the menu. Seriously, how hard can it be? And to all the men who I thought were hot until they ordered a chai latte or a skinny soy half-strength decaf: I am sorry for judging you.

To an ex-boyfriend from high school: I hate your band, and have told everyone I can behind your back.

To Campbell Newman: you are a cunt.

To all the DJs across Australia whose music I have repeatedly said is shithouse: me dancing like a maniac to the song afterwards does not mean I really like it; it means I am mocking you through interpretive dance.

To everyone I have ever lied to just because it was easier.

To everyone I have ever decided was a fucking idiot only three seconds after meeting you – I am sorry. Look, we all do it and we shouldn't, I know, but sometimes I just can't help myself.

And I really need to apologise to some of my clients at my current day job – I am really happy that you can't see my face or read my mind while I am massaging you. I am sure I would be a) fired or b) put in gaol for some of my thoughts. Here are just a few things you should all know so you get an idea of what I am talking about:

1. I don't care about your wedding.
2. I don't want to know about the funny thing your kid did on the weekend involving their own excrement.
3. Don't joke about how I'll have to use extra oil on you because you are so hairy. If you could see my face you would know that this is no laughing matter. In fact, you should be concerned because in order to get through the hour I have to go to my special place where sometimes I imagine a rope knitted from your back hair which I then strangle you with. I have rage issues, I know.
4. If I go to get you a heat pack during a massage, it is not for your benefit but mine, as chances are I need to go to the bathroom – more often than not to do a poo.
5. I now know what you sound like while having sex. I can picture it vividly in my mind. I know if you are a screamer, a swearer, a groaner, a moaner, a biter, a clutcher, a sigher, a giggler or just

> a bite-down-and-take-it kinda gal. And to a few select clients out there upon whom I have formed somewhat of a crush, I have also imagined you having sex with me – sometimes there on the massage table sometimes in one of my elaborate fantasy tales where we meet in public and you say, Wow, Amy, you look different outside of work, and I'll make a funny quip about how you do too with all your clothes on, and then we obviously fall in love immediately.

I can form an entire fantasy relationship with a person in just an hour. In fact, even after just one conversation, I can imagine the place where we could go on holiday and that funny Christmas where you meet my family and it is oh so crazy but we all come together at the end. I don't know if this is just me; I suspect most girls have this skill.

So, I am sorry. This is not everything I have done, just a taster, but to everyone else out there whom I may have forgotten, I am very sorry for being such a fail of a human sometimes and I will try to do better. I will become a real grown-up who owns things and talks about decor and buying antique furniture on the weekend. I will be nicer and stop fantasising about strange boys I meet. I will become sensible. I will have a great career, I will speak to family more, I will make more time for my friends, I will stop eating chocolate and drinking through the week. I will look to the future and it will be bright. I will marry Ryan Gosling, have an affair with James McAvoy and get child support from Zac Efron. These things I promise you all here now.

LARISSA WATERS

Dear stranger who hopefully doesn't know who I am,

I have a confession to make: sometimes I hate my job. Take this morning. A beautiful rainy morning, perfect for croissants on the back deck with my three-year-old daughter, noisy small dog and long-suffering partner. So why did I feel guilty about not watching the Sunday political TV shows? And why did I flip past the only page with actual news on it in the *Sunday Mail*, straight to the Donna Hay recipes and the Sudoku and quiz page?

I confess, I don't want my Sunday morning interrupted with politics. I just want to have a nice morning.

I worry this means I am actually crap at my job. Because I groan when at family events I get asked about politics. Frankly, I just want to switch off on the rare occasions when I'm not actually at work.

I was at a schmoozy media event recently, and do you know the bit I enjoyed the most? Not talking to a senior political reporter about the history of Queensland politics – I might have even fooled him that I knew a bit about that – but talking to a female journo I'd just met who worked at a big Sydney paper, and asking about her love life. She'd just booted out her flattie and The Boy had moved in and it was going really well, and she seemed really lovely, and I was thrilled for her. I love romance. It's one of those rare things that unites us, no matter what creed or culture or country we're from. I love that no matter where you are in the world, and whether you don't know where your next meal is coming from or which pair of shoes to wear that day, we all get a little thrill from seeking love. Is it wrong that I'd rather gossip about love lives than talk about the latest political scandal?

If this politics gig doesn't work out so well, maybe I should run off and write for Mills & Boon!

But I do think about running off. I think about living on a farm somewhere, growing my own vegies, cooking lovely, fresh, healthy food; the clean air, the idyllic lifestyle. Maybe writing a book – maybe even a Mills & Boon! – or finally taking up meditation, or yoga, and burning incense. And I know it's only a dream, and that I'd probably kill the vegies if the truth be known, and actually incense pisses me off, and I'd miss the hustle and bustle of the city soon enough, and probably get bored and isolated. But I have to cling to that dream, that dream of escaping to a simpler world, a world where I can just ignore all the problems that in my job I'm somehow meant to be helping to fix.

Because sometimes it's all too much. I feel helpless to make a difference, frustrated at the lack of progress I'm making, or, sometimes, just over it! Sometimes the greed destroying our planet and our need to keep killing each other over made-up deities are too big for me, and I just want to bludge on the couch for a bit. Or go for a nice bushwalk. Or a swim in a crystal-blue sea, on a perfect sunny day, without a care in the world. I just want to enjoy the beauty of this world and hope everything will be okay without having to fight for it.

But then I think of my beautiful little girl. And I tell myself that I'm doing it for her, and for the other kids in this world who deserve the brightest future. Still, it doesn't make it any easier to not see her much and to miss some of those precious moments. She gives the best hugs, but you've got to earn them. I earned one this morning and felt like the luckiest mum in the world. So, my darling girl, please forgive me for missing any of your daily fifty-four renditions of 'Galumph, goes the little green frog'. I'm trying to do my best to make sure that the world is still going to be as rich, beautiful, diverse, clean and fair as you deserve it to be. Sorry if I let you down while I try to do that. And sorry if I fail at that, as well as at being a good mum. It's a pretty tough gig, this, and I'm just little old me.

So, stranger, sorry if sometimes I can't sustain it, and I just need to switch off and live in a bubble for a bit. Which can sometimes involve crappy reality TV instead of *Lateline*, or cooking up a storm to Fleetwood Mac instead of Radio National. Or gossiping with my staff about love. Or daydreaming about escaping to an island in the Great Barrier Reef and watching turtles hatch and soaking up the sun and eating fresh pineapple and tinned spaghetti. Not together. But you can't deny that tinned spaghetti rocks.

Anyway, stranger, you are the Queenslander who I speak for in federal parliament. I hope you don't know who I really am. Or at least I hope you can forgive me for being only human. I am trying to do my best, but sometimes I'll fail, and sometimes I'll disappoint you, and sometimes I'll disappoint myself. And my daughter.

But I reckon it is all gonna be okay. For all my self-doubt, I do think humanity is going to make it, and overcome our selfishness, our greed, our obsession with consumption. I think we'll find a way to live on this planet that doesn't destroy it, or each other. I think that, despite the fact we're right on the edge of a global environmental crisis, we'll pull together and we'll somehow make a better future for ourselves and this earth. I don't have all the answers, and sometimes you'll find me on the couch, but you can rely on my unshakeable optimism and hope for our future.

So, stranger, I wish you all the best. In love, at work, in yourself. And I wish you hope. For it's not just love that conquers all, it's hope.

But sorry about all the other lot in parliament. They tend to act like pork chops most of the time. It bugs me, too.

Love,
Your Greens Senator x

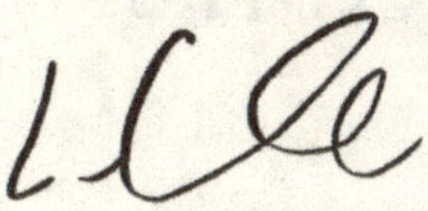

ROWENA GRANT-FROST

Dear Rowena,

When I think of myself in the future, I like to think of someone who sits comfortably on the chair that represents her place in the world. My arms are hanging loose, my legs are stretched out, and I'm smiling as I lean into its soft, squashy back.

'Aaah,' I say, 'this is it, right here: my place in the world. I have found it and it is comfortable.'

And then I might put on a hat, light a cigarette and solve a crime, because when I imagine myself in the future, I also like to imagine that I am Humphrey Bogart.

When I think of myself in the future, I like to think of someone who stands straight and speaks confidently. I like to imagine someone who walks across frozen ground, climbs to the tops of mountains and watches the sun rise and fall, as it turns the sky types of colours usually found in cocktail glasses.

I think of someone who wrestles a bear with her bare hands and wins, because that is how I imagine myself, Rowena of the future.

When I think of myself in the future, I do not think of someone who lies on her bed, staring at the ceiling, repeating the proverb: 'This too shall pass.' I do not think of someone who cries easily, worries about the future and struggles under the weight of uncertainty and insecurity. When I think of myself in the future, I think of someone who looks to the past and laughs.

Tell me, Rowena, does it turn out this way? Will I find my chair, my place, and laugh? I wish that you could tell me, and whisper the answers across the years and decades that separate us.

'It will be all right,' you will say. 'Stop worrying and dry your eyes. Everything will be fine. Just wait. You won't believe it.'

If you could time travel, would you recognise me? I think about this quite a lot. Would I know you if I saw you and would you know me, or would we be strangers, both in appearance and experience, and fail to recognise and acknowledge each other? I hope we aren't so different—I hope we still look the same and sound the same and I haven't been made bitter and angry by the world. I hope I don't own 1 million cats, I hope I still shower, and I hope I still have Elliott, because he is just the best.

Whatever happens, I hope some things stay the same. Maybe nothing will change, or everything will at once. There is comfort in knowing, but frustration that I can't – at least, not before it's time. Until then, I will be standing here awkwardly, uncomfortably, shifting my weight from foot to foot, waiting for my moment to sit down.

With lots of love across space and time,
Your friend,
Rowena

Rowena / xx

To the woman who changed my life

ADAM LIAW

To my grandmother,

Ahpor. I have called you that all my life and now, at the age of thirty-four, I can finally tell you that I have no earthly idea what it means. My suspicion, of course, is that it means 'grandmother', but if it does I'm not even sure what language it is.

You grew up in a place and time so different from mine that it is hard to imagine us having anything in common at all. And let's be honest, other than a shared appreciation of the acrobatic slapstick of a young Jackie Chan, we really don't.

When you were fifteen, you were married and pregnant with your first child. When I was fifteen, I was studying for my final exams at school. I should note here that school was a thing that I did too much of and that you hardly did at all, and yet you read and write seven languages while I can confidently speak only one and know slang terms for genitals in just a handful of others.

When you were nineteen, your sister was shot and killed by a policeman on suspicion of being a communist sympathiser. When I was nineteen, communist sympathisers sold me copies of *Green Left Weekly* on the university lawns.

By the time you were twenty-one, you'd had three children and lost a husband.

For the past sixty years, you've asked your own children to call you 'Aunty' rather than 'Mother' because you believed a fool of a fortune teller who once told you your life was cursed, and that having your children never acknowledge you as their mother would save them from your fate.

I remember watching you cry when you lost your son, my uncle. You were seventy-five and he was sixty, and your sadness grew from a belief that your curse had followed you for five decades across the seas of the world to strike down your first-born.

What kind of curse is it that causes a single mother – an impoverished and uneducated washerwoman – to fight to send every one of her children to university, so that they may become doctors, scientists and successful businessmen? Does the same curse see that woman's grandchildren become surgeons, lawyers and engineers, and, in at least one case, achieve moderate success through an ill-conceived stint on a reality-TV cooking competition? What wretched curse would force that woman to be surrounded by a dynasty of children, grandchildren and great-grandchildren, who will all love her and care for her until her last breath?

Ahpor, Grandma (possibly), our relationship itself is an anachronism; a generation or two earlier and we'd likely never have even met. But we are bonded by blood: a connection that is as much primal instinct as it is love and respect. That's what makes us a family, and one that has been created by the sheer force of your will.

To my mother,

What can I say to the woman who created me from nothing? Who stood between me and death until I was strong enough to stand for myself? Who taught me to speak, to read, to write and to count? To tie my shoes, the correct table manners for drinking soup, how to draw a person's face, and how to ask my boss for a raise?

How on earth you have amassed the wisdom you have in just one lifetime is beyond me. You are my own private oracle. But not like the irritatingly folksy one from *The Matrix*, nor the one with the laser eyes from *The NeverEnding Story*.

All I can say, dearest Mother, is, 'Thanks a bunch!'

I know you're proud of me, as all mothers are of their sons, but I'm not sure if I've ever told you how proud I am of you.

Nearly twenty years ago, when the task of raising your own children was all but done, you decided to devote your remaining energies to helping orphaned and disabled babies in rural China. You'd say God called you, but regardless of whose idea it was, the fact remains that you've built orphanages, hospital units and care facilities that have improved the lives of people who, without you, would have had no chance at all.

I've been lucky enough to grow up with an amazing mother, and I'm proud that children who are not as lucky can experience a mother's love from the best in the business.

There are thousands out in the world right now who, like me, have you to thank for the very fact that they are walking, smiling and breathing today. What a magnificent stroke of luck for all of us that you are the person you are!

To my wife,

I remember the first time I ever saw you. You walked through the room, a vision of beauty, elegance and grace, and I turned to my friend and I said: 'I'd hit that.'

You call it love at first sight, but my recollection of the emotion was slightly less romantic. And, if I'm to be honest, that's the way it should be. Only the creepiest of stalkers fall in love with people they don't even know.

My love for you comes not from a moment's smile or a glance at a shapely bosom, but from our years together, our shared experiences and the way we learn from each other. And as we continue to live and share and learn, that love continues to grow stronger.

What I'm trying to say is: the more I know you, the more I like you.

You've guided me through some of the most dramatic changes in my life, and had to leave your friends, family, career and country in doing so. Sometimes you've supported me, sometimes you've pushed me, and sometimes you've dragged me kicking and screaming into being a better man.

I hope that what we have is forever, but who knows? Statistically at least, cross-cultural marriages like ours are fighting a losing battle. Perhaps one day you'll fall out of love with me and break my heart. Perhaps in time I will take leave of my senses and be struck by that twisted arrow that blind Cupid shoots at old men with deep pockets when they're around young women with fake breasts. Or perhaps we'll grow old together, see the world together, and die in each other's arms at 120. No matter how it turns out, my wife, I'm glad to have met you.

To my daughter,

First of all, you don't actually exist yet so please forgive me if this letter comes across as slightly impersonal.

I don't know what kind of music you'll like, what clothes you'll wear or what brand of mobile phone you'll want to use to call your good-for-nothing boyfriend who you shouldn't even be seeing in the first place.

In fact, I know about as much about growing up as a young woman in the twenty-first century as my grandmother did about being a teenage boy in an age when Rick Astley was allowed to achieve success non-ironically.

What I do know is that you come from a long line of impressive and powerful women; women who can and have changed the future, and improved the lives of thousands.

These women who have come before you have affected my life in ways that you'll come to understand over the years. And when you come into this world my life will change again.

As you learn about these women in your family, you may decide that they are extraordinary. But I prefer to think of them as exactly ordinary – testament and example to the incredible power of ordinary women.

For my part, what I hope you take from their experiences is the right to self-determination – the belief in your ability to become the person that you want to be, rather than the person I or anyone else may want you to be. Whatever you choose as the grist to your mill, know that it is your choice, and that you have my support as a father, and the support of the generations of women that have lived, fought and loved in our family.

Forever with gratitude,
Your grandson, son, husband and father,
Adam

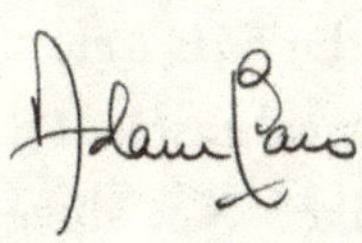

PAUL CAPSIS

Dear Janis,

My mother, who was born the same year as you, in 1943, was dating a very handsome Sicilian man by the name of Sam in 1976. I'd been a mad Skyhooks fan since the age of ten, after discovering them on *Countdown*. Then I moved on to Suzi Quatro. Hers was the first concert I ever saw, in 1975, aged eleven. That was an event I'll never forget: Suzi, in her black stretchy leather jumpsuit with a big zip from her chest to her crotch. Shaking her blonde hair and wielding her big bad-arse bass guitar at the Sydney Hordern Pavilion. Legs apart, pounding the bass between her thighs. This event marked my future.

One night, however, Sam was talking to my older brother, Manuel, about you. I was in the next room but I could still hear them. Manuel was a mad Bruce Lee fan and also in the Kiss Army. I think Sam was trying to broaden my brother's musical tastes. I'd heard of you through reading about Suzi. Things like, 'Not since Janis Joplin has a woman rocked so hard' – that sort of stuff. My ears were pricked and I stopped what I was doing and listened to Sam describe you to my brother: 'Janis Joplin, she used to stand on stage, drunk, holding a bottle of Southern Comfort, screaming and swearing, with her tits falling out of her dress, beads flying, high on drugs.' I needed to know more.

One day, some months later, I was standing at the bus stop on

Castlereagh Street in my school uniform, outside my favourite second-hand record and book shop, and I saw a book displayed in the window. A big book with a photo in red and orange of a woman with her hair flying and a microphone pressed up against her mouth and the words 'JANIS written and edited by David Dalton'. It was you, Janis, it was you.

From that moment, our long-term connection began. I went into the bookstore and asked the hippie lady with the big afro behind the counter if I could look at the book. She smiled and handed it to me the book. I flicked through it with the very grown-up writing and sheet music and came to the black-and-white photos of you. Now I was totally intrigued, by your pock-marked face, your wide smile, squinty eyes, broad nose, loose hooker clothing, stringy hair, shiny shoes, rings, bracelets and beads. You looked totally wild, but you also looked serious, screaming into the mic. Outside on the street in your massive white fur coat and hat; inside and on the rooftop of the Chelsea Hotel in New York; onstage at Monterey Pop, Newport, Woodstock, Madison Square Garden . . . In each and every photo you looked different. I handed the book back to the lady and caught the bus home so I could make my curfew.

I couldn't stop thinking about you that afternoon and into the night, and about the book and the photos. I went back to the store the very next day and bought the book. It cost me four dollars. Four dollars was a lot of money for a twelve year old back then.

When I got home, I found a floppy red 33 RPM disc inside the book. I played it on the stereo and you sounded like an old blues singer. The disc had early recordings of you singing Bessie Smith songs at Threadgill's in Texas in 1962 and some audio of you talking about life on the road on the festival express train in Canada in 1970. You sounded sad.

By the end of 1976, I'd saved more money and bought your greatest hits album on vinyl. Now I got to hear you, the rock star, and your voice startled me, scared me even – the power, the strength and ferocity. I had heard early recordings of Ike and Tina Turner and I thought you sounded like a black woman singer in a lot of pain. I was a heavily bullied little faggot wog kid at school in Surry Hills and there was something about that pain that I got hooked into. I related to it; I understood it.

I wanted to know as much as I could about you and I dedicated a lot of time to investigating you and that obsession eventually led to me becoming a performer myself. That's where my passion came from: you. Through listening to and reading about you, I learned about other styles of music and singers. You totally changed my entire life and what I ended up doing. To you I am eternally grateful.

I jigged two days of school to see you in a film – *Janis: The Way She Was* – showing as part of a rock documentary film festival in the city. You flashed on the big screen, neon feathers flying, voice like a volcano going off, in colour and black-and-white footage.

The images of you captivated me just as much as your voice. Your look was androgynous, like a man/woman, and you looked free. The stories about you – the drinking, your tattoos, drugging and fucking – all these things caught my orthodox Catholic twelve-year-old interest.

Nanna's house was full of Kiss and you playing on the stereo. My brother's and my music replaced my mother's Rod Stewart, Supremes and Richard Clapton singles. I used to turn off the lights, put on my brother's white headphones and lie down on the poo-brown shag pile rug in the pitch black with my eyes closed and listen intently to you, to your voice, your screams and wails, trying to understand your secret messages of pain, to me, to the faggot kid bullied at school. Your toughness helped, your voice soothed me, rescued me. It was like you were saying, 'It gets better, honey, just hang in there and don't take no shit from any fucker, man.' You helped me, protected me.

At the height of my obsession with you, I used to dream of seeing you live in concert at Winterland in San Francisco with Big Brother and the Holding Company, and hanging out with you and your dog George in The Panhandle, driving around in your psychedelic-painted Porsche, and, most important, I dreamed of saving you, from that last hit of heroin that took you out, took you away from the world at the age of twenty-seven, on 4 October 1970, in the Landmark Hotel in Hollywood. I dreamed that I tried to wake you, out of your overdose, and save you. I had that dream for years. But I'd always wake up at the crucial moment and then realise that I couldn't save you – you were gone.

Sam and my mother dated for a few more years and Sam eventually became a Jehovah's Witness. I started studying with them myself – my brother, my mum and I would have weekly Bible studies – but that's another story . . . After two years of studying with them, I was told that listening to you and rock and roll meant that I would die for all eternity (which, by the way, was only days away, back in 1977). I then made the decision that listening to you was more important than living in Paradise forever and I stopped my weekly Bible studies. My mother stopped too because she refused to give up her nicotine addiction, and she and Sam broke up. I went on happily listening to you, kept building my collection of you, and just continued being who I wanted to be.

Love always,
Paul XXXXX

Love
Paul xxxxx

ANTON ENUS

This is a 'coming out' letter to Foziah Davidson, a friend from high school in Cape Town, South Africa. Unusually, I have not composed this especially for Men of Letters. It is not a reconstruction of thoughts from the time or, indeed, a kind of fantasy letter to a younger self. This is a conglomerate letter, condensed from actual correspondence between Foziah and myself in the period of 1980 to 1982. I have changed just one word, correcting 'divorced' to 'separated'.

Thursday, 21 August 1980

I've also just read a novel by EM Forster which has really made an impression on me. This is mainly because it has more relevance than it appears to have initially. It's called *Maurice* – if you can get hold of it, do – if only to find out how narrow-minded we, the quasi-liberal, really are.

What do you do, Miss D, when you have a very serious problem and want to talk about it, but cannot for fear of the consequences? I've had such a problem, a skeleton in the dark reaches of my cupboard, for many years. I've never ever spoken about it, mainly because I haven't a confidant. (I have yet to come across anyone who'd understand, or the guts to spill the beans). I long to tell someone and I guess I will – someday. It's like this: it's something that everyone I know has never encountered before, so what's the use of embarrassing them and myself for nothing? Years ago I thought that if I ignored it long enough, it would go away, but no such luck. You're about the only person I know who might understand. Got time to listen? At your own risk, of course. And I'd better warn you, it will most certainly change your whole attitude towards me. Anyway, we'll discuss it at length if and when I can pluck up the courage. I assure you, you won't be prepared for this one!

Saturday, 6 September 1980

You know, I think you'd better forget what I said in my last letter about having a skeleton in the cupboard. No, it hasn't suddenly disappeared, but I think it would be exceedingly foolhardy of me to incriminate myself. Maybe in twenty years' time I'll have plucked up enough guts to actually talk about it. Believe me, it's a very real problem – something like cancer: nothing much you can do about it but pray, and I've done quite a bit of that. And people have been known to conquer cancer, so who knows? I believe – very firmly – that much can be achieved by good old willpower. Am I wasting your time? Believe me, you're better off not knowing – for my sake anyway, because whenever you look at me I'll be wondering what you're thinking.

Wednesday, 1 October 1980

Romance is in the air, albeit only in my imagination. That is just a fancy way of saying it's a nice evening. I have been sitting out on the verandah in the dark. The air is caressingly warm, with just the hint of a breeze to rustle the hair and excite the senses: the ideal conditions for the mind to stray to things desired. I've been sitting here thinking about many things. How perfect a single moment can be if we just want it to be so. In the moments I am meandering along the pathways of the land of 'if', nothing – absolutely nothing – matters. Problems are like sand in a sieve. Anything goes. Who cares about my faults, what I did wrong and what I didn't do right in my life? If you had been here, my dear Miss D, I'd have told you about my 'problem', about which so much has been said already. I so need someone to talk to, to confide in; someone who will understand when even I don't. I feel so alone even when I'm surrounded by people. There's no one who's one of 'my' kind rather than one of 'them'. I wish I had someone who I could relate to. But I'm scared to talk, to once and for all get it off my chest. I'm so afraid of the consequences, because once a skeleton is allowed out of the cupboard, it's never going back again. Why can't life be perfect at least some of the time? Why do we have to discover that we have shortcomings (major ones)?

I know how you would react if I told you about me. You wouldn't believe me first of all; then you'd think I was funny, which I am not. I cannot bear to have anyone laugh at me. It makes me feel inferior. As if I've let someone – me – down. The stars say that Virgoans are perfectionists. I'm a Virgoan. The discrepancy between one's idealistic ambitions and what we actually attain in life leads, according to sociologist Durkheim, to anomic suicide. I think I'm a prime target. I know very well that my lot in life can never be what I want it to be and yet I cannot accept that. So how am I expected to accept that I have major personal imperfections? It's not fair. I didn't ask to be made like this.

I feel so emotional right now. And there's no one to talk to! The trouble, someone once said, with loneliness is not that there's no one to listen to our problems, but that we have only *our* problems to solve. I have such great needs; so much do I want people to be in my life that it maddens and frustrates me when I get rejected and treated in an offhand manner.

Well, I haven't told you what I set out to do, largely because

I don't think you would understand. When I'm in your company I still feel we're total strangers, which is as much my fault. Have you learned anything about Anton Albert Enus tonight, my dear Miss D?

Monday, 31 May 1982

I've decided there's no point in staying in South Africa for longer than I have to. My parents have been [separated] for seven months now and I feel more and more that I have to make a clean break. I'm glad in a way that the break-up came when I'm old enough to take it. It's been one of the more unpleasant periods of my life. I found myself crying alone when I realised this was it. No going back to old times. It's not an experience I would recommend. But life isn't always what we'd like it to be. Is it ever?

Wednesday, 8 September 1982

Remember when I was [in] first year I told you about a special problem I had but couldn't talk about? Well, I'm ready to talk about it if you're prepared to listen. I'll elaborate in my next letter. That will give you a chance to confirm you're willing to take on the huge responsibility of being a confidante, and furthermore I'll be past the magical age of twenty-one by then (maybe I'll undergo a magical transformation and become an adult).

Tuesday, 28 September 1982, noon

I'm glad you're prepared to listen, Foziah. I so need someone to talk to. You know, being something of a loner tends to get incredibly lonely most of the time. You'll appreciate, of course, that this is something I haven't told any other friend and it's something which scares me immensely.

The bottom line is that I've accepted that I'm not 'normal'. I'm not into girls. Do you understand what I'm saying? The word for it is gay (a terribly misleading word because it's anything but). It sounds quite silly saying it, but it's all too true. The first thing, you'll be wondering, is, 'What about Trudy?' [My teen sweetheart.] I don't know. I really cannot explain it. I'm attracted to her in a different sort of way. It's a *romantic* rather than sexual attraction. It's strange, but when I'm with her I feel normal (what the hell does that word mean?). But I just cannot go on denying, suppressing these feelings. I tried to fight it, to convince myself it was just a passing phase, but I know now it's for real and it's here to stay. And it scares the shit out of me.

Continued on Sunday, 31 October 1982

One month later and I've finally decided to actually send this letter to you. There's been a slight change since then. I've told someone else: my friend Chris, who was marvellously understanding (in spite of being a Zimbabwean). No, to be really honest, I didn't have the guts to actually tell him, so I just showed him the half-written letter to you. I was so afraid he'd just walk out. But he didn't. Instead he went out of his way to help, arranging a meeting with a psychologist. After agreeing to see him, I chickened out. I went through an incredible two weeks. I was just totally out of it, not attending more than a handful of lectures (none at all in the last ten days of that period). All I did was sit in my room on my bed and stare at nothing. All I could think about was what a failure I was. If I had more guts I'd probably be dead now. It was that bad.

I hope I haven't embarrassed you (too much). Please don't be stiff and formal about this. I'm not any more. I've accepted that it's a very real situation and one that should be faced head-on. Chris insists something can be done about it (I have my doubts). Who knows? I'd change tomorrow if I knew how. I firmly believe the root of the problem is my incredibly negative self-image and my concomitant lack of self-confidence. I'm attracted to other guys because I see in them things I'd like to see in myself. Is that crazy?

Anyway, I'm glad I had this little talk with you. Perhaps you know me a bit better now. Whether or not you like me any better is a totally different matter.

Be good.

Love,
Anton

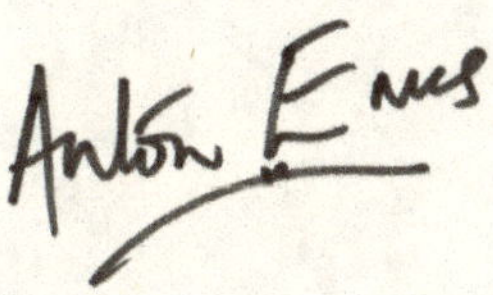

ADAM GIBSON

BLANCHEY

Ah, you were beautiful,
You were a beauty.
A pale-eyed daughter of
The Carlton Careys.
A square-shouldered rake of a thing
To lead the local lads astray,
On smoke-factory streets,
On winter trams,
On hot, north-wind days
And the smell of bushfires
And Australia fanning out,
Growing and groaning

Ah, you were beautiful, Blanchey,
You were a beauty.
Watched over by five black-haired
County Kerry brothers,
Those who got lost along the way;
Along the paling-fence afternoons,
The stolen-milk-bottle mornings,

The skinned rabbit,
'14–'18 Great War, hungry years
And the horse-drawn
416 Cardigan Street days

Ah, you walked everywhere,
Everyone did,
Across the hard-scrabble town
To the MCG and under the clocks
And back again
With dirty knees and
Trouble rising at home
With brother Freddy or
Frankie or Billy
Up to their mischief again

Ah, you were beautiful,
You were a beauty.
But oh, Jesus Christ, a wild one.
Those blue eyes of ice and
A withering glance –
I can see you right now
Holding court at a
Town Hall dance
Or at one of those Christmas parties
With the dark-haired aunties
When beer and blood hit the walls
And the young men
Turned old from the war
Still thought they were half a chance –

And maybe they were;
Their numbers were thin.

Ah, you were beautiful,
You were trouble from the start.
And if you look at your
Sister's husband like that
You're putting the
Horse before the cart.
Anything could've happened
And it actually did
For a child is born,
At Essendon hospital
And God, what a furore,
Where do we start?
God, what a scene,
This could tear the family apart
And so it did.

Oh, you were tough,
Oh jeez, you were tough,
And nobody could keep
Your Little Joanie
From you
And after five years
You'd had enough.

A train to Sydney
In the rattle-cold night,

A train to Sydney,
Bugger them, we'll be all right.

Central Station,
Country Platforms,
The great horizontal scaffold
Of this train-track nation.
Then a house at the back of the Cross
As they barricaded Bondi
And sailors fought in pubs
And the sirens screamed all night
When into the harbour
Came the Japanese midget subs
Just down the road
Just down the road
Just down the road
Just down the end of the street.

Ah, you were beautiful,
I've seen the photos.
You were a beauty,
Oh, God knows.
And you caught the eye of the
Randwick lads and the Bronte boys
With that sideways glance
And a merchant seaman
Named O'Keefe
With the same Irish eyes and
A boxer's stance.

And little Joanie grows up
And goes to the Tivoli
And the Trocadero
And you both join the
Parade of hats on
Victory in the Pacific Day
And you swear you saw
The Dancing Man
Dancing his way,
You swear you saw
The Dancing Man
Dancing his way.

Oxford Street, Moore Park Road,
Driver Avenue, the Sydney Test Match,
Your name changes to Mrs Jerry O'Keefe
And a formidable pair forms at
Roosters games, believing in Easts and
The beauty of rugby league –
They got to the moon in '69 but
You were still getting over '66 when
The Chooks did not win
A single game.

Ah, you were beautiful,
You were a beauty, Blanchey.
Moving towards fifty and sixty and seventy
That still remained.
Working in the Red Cross Shop, Edgecliff,
Before the homeware stores,

You told stories of the olden days,
Believed in soup and buttons and
Helped out with Meals on Wheels
And stood at the rally
Shouting, 'Its time, it's time, it's time.'

The cats stretched on footpaths,
Ah, those coastal town nights.
Coolangatta what's the matter
Red-brick holiday flats,
You went around the world on a
Cunard Liner
That left from Pier 2
And gave us the world as a vision
And you taught us how to catch buses
Gave us twenty dollar bills to
Buy crackers on Cracker Night
And everything, everything.

Ah, you were beautiful,
You were a beauty.
But life turns a wheel,
You can't hold back a thing,
Better just to move and change
And love and learn.

A phone call in the middle of the night,
War Memorial Hospital –
'I think you'd better come.'

Those dreadful nights that follow,
We hold your hands,
Feel them eggshell-fine,
And slowly, slowly . . .
It's not a tragedy,
It's simply the time
And something we all know
And the air skips a beat,
The room stops still,
And we feel your hand soften
And we feel you go.

Ah, you were beautiful, Blanchey,
You were a beauty.
Ah, you were beautiful, Blanchey,
You were a beauty.

JOHN WATERS

Dear Gloria,

How are things wherever German-Greek-Jewish people end up? It's a small demographic, so perhaps you all have a little private club up on a discreetly hidden cloud somewhere. For your sake, I hope it has blackjack tables.

Anyway, I am writing you a letter. I know, it's weird, but I am. I've been forced into it by an extremely demanding child. Not mine; someone else's. But at any rate, I believe there are some things I never said to you. I have talked about you ad infinitum – but not to your face, and I may just have to seize this opportunity to rectify that a little. If, of course, you should receive this letter. In wherever you are. Maybe an owl will take it or something . . . Anyway.

I would like to start by taking you back to the Metro Theatre in Orwell Street, Kings Cross, in 1969. You had come backstage briefly after seeing Reg when he was brought in to instil some professionalism in the cast of *Hair*. (I'm saying that was the aim, but of course it was misguided, because the whole idea of putting kids off the street into our production was Jim's way of making it as unprofessional as possible, and instead of Reg changing us, we managed very quickly to bring him down to our level of anarchy.) I remember you fighting your way through the clouds of marijuana smoke and walking up to me and saying, 'I'm Gloria Payten. You show promise as an actor. Here's my card.' Then you walked away. Reg told me he had never seen you do that before, to anyone, ever. I just thought you'd mistaken me for someone else. But somehow that card itself knew it was destined to become significant, because it stayed in my possession for the next two years; utterly un-loseable, like a pair of ten-dollar sunglasses. So, two years later, having just got back from six months in London, I walked into your office holding up that card, and you said without looking up from your desk, 'I'm sending you to audition for a New South Wales Arts Council tour. If you get it I'll put you on the books. Here's the address.' The next day, I had an agent. And the next week I found out what an Arts Council Tour really meant. Thanks for that. Great initiation into finding unpronounceable towns in a clapped-out panel van.

Actually, Gloria – and this is one of those things I never told you – I didn't just have an agent. I had a friend and a mentor. Somebody who spoke in weirdly short sentences that meant exactly what they said. Someone who cared enough to drip-feed me the most meagre scraps of information, so that I would feel all the more empowered when I finally achieved things for myself. My very own Mr Miyagi. Wax on, wax off.

And you know what, Gloria: to this day I keep on finding you out. About ten years after you made your exit, I worked in a play with Googie and John. The same John McCallum who, along with Lee Robinson, was the producer of *Boney*. I think you can guess what's coming next: John told me that on that day in late 1971 when he called you to say that an actor in a leading guest role had fallen ill and could you recommend someone to fly to Wilpena Pound in South Australia to start shooting the next day, you said to him: 'Got this new guy: John Waters. Newly arrived from England. He's brilliant. Television experience? Oh yes. What has he been in? Oh! What *hasn't* he been in? Let me see, er, *Z-Cars*; *No Hiding Place*; *Dixon of Dock Green . . .' Dixon of Dock Green*! Jesus, Gloria, you just dragged up the only cop shows you could remember from your brief refugee stopover in the UK years before. I was twenty-two years old – if I'd been in *Dixon of Dock Green*, I would have had to have been five or six!

You lied, Gloria! You lied through your teeth to get me a job! And it wasn't a discreet, little, entirely justifiable white lie – it was a whopping great porky pie! Gloria – *you rock!* Thank Christ there was no IMDB in 1971, though. You would have been seriously busted.

You remember that trip I made to Cannes for the festival? The one where I went broke spending thirty-five thousand dollars on an AMEX card and you advanced me the money because I had another big job coming up? Of course you do. Well, there was a movie publicist from the US there called Fred Schiff, and he told me a somewhat intriguing thing. He asked me if I had a good agent, and I said, 'Yes, I do. She's great.' To which he said:

'She? That's a good start. You see, John, I gotta kinda formula when it comes to agents: they need to score two out of three on the 'Schiff Test'. That is, they gotta be two out of three things: female, gay and Jewish. Reason being, if they're a straight shiksa, those Hollywood Jews are gonna simply try to schtupp her with no deal. If she's Jewish, there'll be a deal involved. A gay gentile man is too culturally removed from them – they don't relate. They don't got no prejudice at all, mind you. No. Prejudice can get in the way of a deal. They can't afford it. Look at the actors they gotta take care of. By the way, John, are you . . .? No. Okay. So anyway, a gay Jewish guy is cool. It was his mother's fault. They sympathise. Two outta three, John, I'm tellin' ya.'

I stopped him there.

'Fred,' I said, with my hands on his shoulders, 'I got the trifecta!'

Fred was impressed. 'Don't leave her' were his final words to me that night.

And I didn't, did I? It was you who . . . Well, no, I'm not remotely thinking that you left me. You left us all, but you had no choice in the matter. And it certainly wasn't just me. Every actor, writer and director that you took under your wing came to you whenever they needed anything. Help; guidance; investment advice. As I have said, you dispensed this wisdom in a very cryptic form. You were never a shoulder to cry on. It wasn't your style to patronise with sympathy. You didn't want to talk about problems – only solutions.

There were some at ICS who nicknamed you 'The Dragon'. I can understand why they did that. They were the ones who wanted an easy ride. I'm not saying I was entirely altruistic and dedicated – not at all: I was just lucky enough to 'get' you. For some reason, when I gazed at your face (which was, let's be honest, capable of making the Easter Island Monuments look animated), I didn't see a dragon. I saw the nineteen-year-old girl who arrived in Sydney not long after the war and wanted to be an actress. But you had an accent then, didn't you? Well, you still did years later, but it was much softer. I guess being an actress was not made easy for you. Paul Riomfalvy of JC Williamson's once said to me, 'I love that woman. I know I told her that if she gave me any more trouble about your salary I'd have her banned from all the gambling clubs in Sydney, but what I should have said was, "Go back to acting – you were good at that too, but you never broke anybody's balls!"'

So why did you become an agent? I think it was because you rose to the challenge of making it easier for others. That was your solution, and it was inspired. You belie the old joke – you remember; the one about the heart transplant recipient who was told there were two hearts that had become available: one was from a 65-year-old theatrical agent, and the other from a 23-year-old marathon runner. The recipient said, 'I'll take the agent's heart.' The doctor said, 'Are you sure?' and the guy said: 'Yes. I want one that hasn't been used.'

I think you liked that joke, but it sure wasn't about you. When I told others about how we at ICS would go into King Street and get paid half our earnings for that week out of your own bank account, well before you had received anything from our employers, they were simply gob-smacked. 'That can't be right . . .' 'Who would do that?' 'Unheard of . . .' Etc., etc. And they were right. Ours can be a self-serving and competitive world. Doing things purely because they will make struggling people's lives more manageable is not exactly a typical entertainment industry philosophy. But then neither is delaying your death by an extra twenty-four hours so that you can sign the final documents to set up a foundation in your name to help young Australians study drama. That's what you did. Philomena was there, and she saw you put down the pen and give one of your enigmatic smiles.

I miss you, Gloria. And I don't know if you're anywhere or nowhere. I haven't got the security of any doctrine to tell me what happens to us. Where we go. Or if we just cease to be. So I don't know if you know this, but there was a time a dozen or so years ago when I wasn't sure if I would be able to keep going in this business. I had to step back, and somehow rediscover everything that I was losing more and more with every day that went by. You know what I did one day? I went and stood outside 147a King Street in the city. Just stood there, looking at where ICS used to be. On the fourth floor. Rickety, clanking old lift like something out of a Parisian movie on SBS. Your office, with its big cedar desk and blown-up photos of a handful of your favourites: John Gaden, Anne Haddy, Jacki Weaver – me. I missed you a lot, right at that moment. But I did imagine you saying, 'Either do something about this, or don't. It doesn't matter. And the office is now in Crown Street, by the way.'

A lot has happened that I don't know if you know about. I have three more children, apart from Bec and Ivan. There's Archie, who's about to be ten; and there are the twins, who have just turned six. They are a girl and a boy. The boy's name is Rusty, after my dad, Russell, who you got more work for during his year living in Sydney in 1973 than he'd had in yonks. (My mother, by the way, is still going strong at ninety-four – living in her own flat and holding dinner parties for overseas visitors.) The girl twin is a feisty little number with a knack for getting what she wants. Her name is Gloria.

With love,
From John

WILLIAM McINNES

Dear Wendy,

Wendy Sykes, the first time I saw you was at the Rollerdrome in 1977, when I was thirteen. It was Christmas holidays and you weren't much older than me. You were wearing an ABBA t-shirt and jeans. You had dark hair.

And you went in the open speed skaters race. The open speed skaters were mostly men in tough-guy tight t-shirts with packets of cigarettes, usually Winfield Reds, tucked into their already strained sleeves. And there was you.

Usually when they played music for the speed skaters, it was Deep Purple's 'Black Night' or the terrifying Iron Butterfly's 'In-A-Gadda-Da-Vida'. It never seemed to stop; on and on the hairy toughs would circle the skating floor. When we lesser amoebae on rollerskates heard the first chords of those dreaded tunes, we ran to the edges and clung there, away from the maelstrom of roller testosterone. These toughs would swing their arms low and fast and howl around the 'drome.

But on that Saturday when you speed skated, whoever it was that usually played the music stuck on an ABBA song for you: 'I Do, I Do, I Do, I Do, I Do'.

And suddenly the guys with the tatts and the fags and the t-shirts and the big belt buckles didn't look so scary.

You skated so fast. And, clinging to the wire on the sides, I looked at you as you sped past smiling and I mouthed the chorus:

Oh, Wendy Sykes – I do, I do, I do, I do, I do.

Later when I was leaving the Rollerdrome, one of the toughs, who would usually instil terror as he leaned on his car in the car park and tried to spit on us lesser beings as we scurried past, was met not with averted eyes but with a shrill chorus of dweeby voices: 'I do, I do, I do, I do, I do.'

He tried to chase us but slipped. We looked down at him: his t-shirt wasn't that tight and he didn't smoke the tough man's choice of Winfield Reds but rather the bingo tragic's Ardath Menthols. And some us called out to him, 'Abba dabba do!'

You went to a different school, Wendy, but the town we lived in wasn't that big. I saw you occasionally, enough to know that the wonder of that Rollerdrome morning wasn't a passing fancy. I always thought you were lovely.

Then, two and a half years later, it happened. You spoke to me. And not long after that, you touched me. Your hands held me and stroked my hair. And you gave me something that did change my life.

You gave me a perm.

Not just any perm, but an apprentice hairdresser's first perm. It was the perm of perms.

I had wandered up and down an arcade that first morning of the school holidays because I had been sent to get my hair cut. A massive send-off by a sportsmaster on Friday afternoon was followed by a letter home to my parents threatening suspension or a school haircut if my hair length was not attended to. My mother was too busy to give me one of her furious homemade mower jobs so I was sent to a barber. You had just begun work at Maurice and Doug's Unisex Hair Salon.

In reality it was an undercover barbershop – it still had the red-and-white pole out the front. But it also, to my amazement, had you. You were the apprentice hairdresser.

The first words you ever spoke to me were, 'Hey, would you like a perm?'

I had no idea what a perm was and said so. You said, 'Well, you're here so you might as well have a go.'

My father always said that – not that I should get a perm, but that I should never be afraid of having a go.

And so I did.

I was there for hours. When it was finished and I stared at my face full of acne and hair like an electrocuted poodle, you smiled and said, 'Well, there you are!'

You never said anything else to me. You never caressed my head again – but you had changed my life.

I walked home. A maths teacher who was a friend and ally of the sportsmaster saw me as I went past the fish and chip shop in a daze. He stalked out and pointed an accusatory and freshly purchased crumbed sausage at me. 'McInnes – you clown. After a job at Bullen's with that hair? Don't bring it to school.'

Thereafter at school the maths teacher and the sportsmaster always referred to me as Bullen's.

When I got home it was worse. My mother screamed, 'Holy Christ, you stupid boy.' My father ran in from chopping down some banana trees – always a bad sign that he had nothing else to do with his weekend and wanted to work out a bit of whatever might have been frustrating him. He appeared with his huge chest heaving and in his hand, just above the top of his Stubbies work shorts, he held a machete.

'Love, are you all right?' he asked. And, Wendy, then he saw me.

He pointed his machete at me and gave me one of his usual appraisals of me, his youngest son: 'Jesus wept! When I was near your age I was jumping out of bloody planes and fighting! For what? For the likes of you, you cabbage-headed fool!'

Wendy, my sisters and brother thought it wonderful, and this led to unexpected interactions with my parents. For example, my sister talked me into wearing a hairnet over my perm while I slept. I came downstairs wearing my PJ pants and my rugby jersey and my hairnet, and my father stared balefully at me. Without blinking and breathing heavily, he held a knife in his hand ready to attack his breakfast.

'It's for my skin,' I told him.

He seethed. I thought perhaps he may have thought I was behaving like a cardigan.

Let me explain, Wendy. In our family's unreconstructed home language of the 1970s, a homosexual reverted to the commonly thrown-about diminutive 'homo', which in turn became a 'Perry Como' in rhyming slang. Later, because Perry Como, a crooner on lots of Mum's albums, wore cardigans, the insult became 'cardigan!'

One morning, my brother gave me twenty dollars to go down and tell our dad that I was a 'Perry Como'. We thought it a great joke. I went down and greeted my father tucking into his hearty breakfast. I acted out my part: 'Dad ... There is something you should know ... Daddy, I'm a Perry Como. A homosexual.'

Dad didn't explode or scream. He just stopped eating and stared at me. 'You're a fool,' he said quietly. 'You're a bloody fool.

'I had an officer who was as bent as an S-bend. But that was his business. I saw him fighting to save men with half his body blown away. He was a man. A fine man. You'd be lucky to be a tenth of the man he was. If you ever judge somebody by what they are and not what they do, then you are a bloody fool.'

Before he shovelled another forkful of fry-up into his mouth he added, 'You go tell that clown upstairs to give me the twenty dollars.'

My dad had learned tolerance through the bloodiest and harshest experience of all – war. And, Wendy, I hope we don't waste that tolerance.

You know, Wendy, there is nothing like that wonderful feeling of falling in love with another person. But sometimes it can be embarrassing if that affection isn't returned.

I remember becoming convinced that I had found my true love many years ago at a university sports competition. She was a competitor and to say she caught my attention is an understatement. The Girl from Lane Six.

Completely smitten, I brought to bear all the sophistication and debonair charm an undergraduate boofhead can muster.

I remembered those words of yours, Wendy: 'Well, you're here so you might as well have a go.' So I did. I approached her that night at a bar and uttered the words that would begin our love story: 'You have the legs of an athlete.' Smooth, William.

She looked at me with very fetching eyes and said, 'Who do you think I am? Mal fucking Meninga?'And she walked off.

And that was that. I must admit that Big Mal's legs served him very well but I never quite made the connection between hers and his. Still, there's a little wistful moment for me come State of Origin time every year when the cameras catch Mal in the coach's box. I think of the Girl from Lane Six. And perms.

Wendy, you marked my life with two women I loved unreservedly.

Near the end of her life, my mother, a very brave and courageous woman, decided to stop all treatment and medications.

She told a palliative care doctor that she'd been looked after and that everything she was given was 'okey-dokey', but it was just time to go.

After he asked her if she was very sure, she smiled and gave him a trembling thumbs up.

In her hospital room one of her children would always sit with her. Once, as I was taking my turn in the chair by her bed, I entered the room to find a sister of mercy there with my mother.

'Who is it?' asked my mother.

'Your son,' replied the sister.

'Which one? The fat one or the stupid one?'

The sister half smiled and said she couldn't tell.

My mother looked up at me and said sweetly, 'The stupid one!' And she turned to me and laughed. Really laughed.

Dying isn't particularly dignified in any way, Wendy, but to hear my mother's laugh was astonishing.

I asked her if she was all right and my mother said to the sister of mercy, 'Can you believe this stupid bugger of a boy went out for a number three and came back with a head full of spots and a perm?' And she laughed again.

'Then that was money well spent,' said the sister.

Money well spent indeed.

But as I was saying, Wendy, there's nothing quite like the feeling of falling and being in love with another person. Really falling.

I still remember the day I saw my wife for the first time.

There was knock at the door and I opened it to see her standing before me. She stood in a green dress and black boots, Ray-Ban sunglasses perched on her head, jingling in her hand the keys of her S series Valiant. We stared at each other for what seemed like a very long time, but what was probably only a few seconds, until she said with a smile, 'Hello.' I can hear her say that hello now.

And I looked at her. Into her green eyes. Those of eyes of hers that were so watchful and wise and keen.

She looked at me. Really looked.

I paused and stared back.

I drew a breath and said a phrase that you once said to me as we stared at my perm: 'Well, there you are.'

And then my wife-to-be laughed. It was the first time I heard her laugh. And it is still one of the most beautiful sounds that I will ever hear. Wendy, I kept that moment and the sound of her laugh deep in my soul.

So for all those things – thanks, Wendy Sykes.

You did change my life. You are an example of how a memory unlocks a hundred different doors and joins so many different people together.

And you know, I did try to thank you, Wendy. Earlier this year I saw you in Kmart in the town where we grew up. You were with your grandchildren, I think. I saw you – I wasn't sure but then you clicked into my memory. You were the girl in the ABBA shirt.

Wendy, I thought about just letting you go about your business in the toy section.

But then I thought better. I opened a fancy-dress packet and put on a frizzy clown's wig. I darted down an aisle and walked up to you and your daughter and your grandchildren and said, 'Wendy Sykes. Well, there you are!'

And you had no fucking idea who I was.

But thank you. Thank you for changing my life, and for making me buy a frizzy clown wig that now sits in my study.

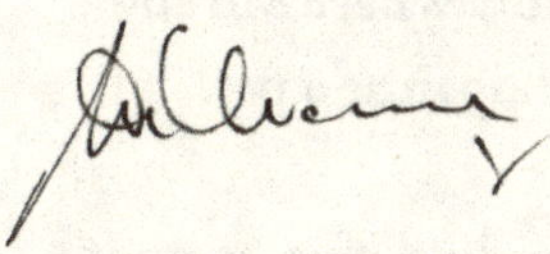

TOM BALLARD

Dear Miranda Devine,

Hello! It's me, Tom Ballard, that left-leaning homosexual ABC employee that you blocked on Twitter! Hello!

Seeing as how you don't seem to want to receive any tweets I send to you, I thought I'd get in touch by writing a letter, because you seem to like things that are outdated. While you read this you can pretend it's the 1950s – just think of me as your friendly neighbourhood confirmed bachelor.

Ah, the 1950s, when the only thing missing was AIDS . . .

I'm trying to picture you reading this. Perhaps you're spread out on your golden chaise lounge on the balcony of your Northern Beaches home with your pet taipan wrapped lovingly around your shoulders, occasionally sampling the delights of the small bowl on the coffee table beside you: your favourite delicacy, babies' eyeballs.

(That could be inaccurate, that bit. I don't know where Miranda Devine lives. But I'm almost positive she keeps a taipan as a pet.

I say 'pet'; I mean 'familiar'.)

Perhaps that's too much. Perhaps you're reading this at your stainless steel desk in your stainless steel apartment filled with stainless steel plants and stainless steel dreams. Perhaps you yourself are made of stainless steel and this letter is being digitally downloaded into your mainframe and your maker, Dr Devine, will shortly weld your face facade back to your mechanical head plate, returning you to full functionality, allowing you to continue to work towards the goal you have always been programmed to complete: TO KILL ALL HUMANS SLOWLY THROUGH A LONG-RUNNING SERIES OF QUESTIONABLE OPINION PIECES IN THE *DAILY TELEGRAPH*.

Or perhaps I'm completely wrong. Perhaps your conservative, ice queen demeanour is all a cover, and you're actually reading this in your grubby Newtown share house while sucking down a beer bong, having just returned from a passionate bisexual orgy downstairs in your fuck dungeon, all the while fantasising about forming a republic and recycling.

I hope it's that one.

However you're positioned while reading this, I hope you'll stay with it until the end, because this is important. This letter is about how, over the past two years, you've slowly changed my perspective on things and, by extension, my life.

We have a history, you and I, Miranda. Prior to my move to Sydney from my home state of Victoria in 2010, I didn't really know you existed, to be honest. I read *The Age* – mainly during Comedy Festival season, desperately flicking through the pages for a review of my own shows, or, as I like to call it, 'old-school googling yourself' – and I only ever read the *Herald Sun* when I was bored in a cafe and I wanted to read Andrew Bolt's opinion piece because I wanted something easy to hate. Fortunately, Bolt is no longer contained to just the print media; his special brand of poppycock has branched out into television, with him hosting his own Sunday morning political discussion show with all the confidence of an adolescent McDonald's employee at the helm of the *Costa Concordia*. His show's called *The Bolt Report*, which is odd; I thought they would've gone with the original title they were looking at: *Mein Kampf*.

Ah well, that's the Jew-run media for you, right, Miranda?

Anyway, I moved here and I got accustomed to the new lay of the land and figured out who I could hate here: people like Alan Jones and Kyle Sandilands and Janet Albrechtsen. And you. You're very easy to hate for a gay, Gen Y, middle-class, public school-educated son of left-leaning parents like me, Miranda.

(Sorry if that description of myself just made you projectile vomit or something – hopefully the taipan's okay!)

The only thing I liked about you was your name. If the time ever comes where I relent and try my hand at drag, there is no doubt in my mind that I shall perform under the title of MIRANDA DEVINE.

So I hated you, but so did everyone in my life, so it wasn't such a big deal. I hated you like I hate abstract concepts, like famine or disease or the Logies, but hey – *whaddyagonnado?*

Then, in August of last year, you wrote a column entitled 'The Problem of a Fatherless Society', in which you argued that Penny Wong should not be praised for deciding to have a child with her lesbian partner, Sophie Allouache, because, according to you, the ideal situation for a child to be raised in is an intact family with a father and a mother, and the 2011 London riots illustrated the catastrophic implications of a 'fatherless society'.

I read the opinion piece on my laptop while curled up in bed on a Sunday morning. I was in disbelief. I know there are some pretty shitty things on the internet, but I just couldn't believe that this monstrosity got on there. How did you do that? How did people who work at a newspaper look at the thing I presumed you created by boiling up turds and salt in a cauldron in Fred Nile's bungalow – how did they look at that and go, 'Yep! *This* deserves to go in people's heads!'?

I just couldn't work out what you were *saying*, Miranda. Your piece was riddled with twists of logic and contradictions and crazy claims; I'm worried there's something wrong with your keyboard – I think someone must have replaced one of the keys with a Bullshit Button. You need to call the *Daily Telegraph* IT Department and get them to help you, provided they're not too busy erecting paywalls for content nobody wants.

Your piece made me so angry that I felt like I had to do something, and that's quite rare for me, especially on a Sunday. I attacked my own keyboard, wrote a thing, put on a jacket, set up my laptop's camera and recorded a monologue response called 'Miranda Devine: What the Fuck Are You Talking About?'. Through a lot of swearing and jump cuts, I tried to communicate to you that, in fact, the overwhelming opinion of the scientific community is that same-sex couples are just as capable of raising happy, healthy children as opposite-sex couples are, and of *course* there's a link between Penny Wong's story and the same-sex marriage debate, and of *course* heterosexual people aren't expected to hide or be ashamed of their spouses and children for fear of 'offending' the politically correct twitterati, and *clearly* there's a difference between the social impacts of economic disadvantage and young fathers shirking their parental responsibilities and those of two women having and raising a child together in a financially stable, loving environment, and hey, also, when you post tripe like this in the public sphere it can actually have a pretty detrimental impact on the mental health of young GLTBIQ youth out there, a group of young people who are up to six times more likely to commit suicide than their heterosexual peers.

I put the video on YouTube and it now sits at over 40000 views (which means it's actually out-rated Andrew Denton's *Randling*) and I got quite a few emails from people – some amazing and uplifting and supportive and touching, some . . . not so much – and it got a bit of media coverage.

But despite my provision of my email address and my request for you to respond to me and explain what the fuck you were talking about, I never heard from you, Miranda. All you did was write a follow-up article in which you took one of my jokes out of context and claimed you were under attack from politically correct McCarthyists and you said your words had been twisted. And I assume you were referring to my response when you described the visceral reaction to your column as 'performance rage, played out online looking for more hits', which, I gotta say, I thought was pretty ballsy, seeing as how you get paid to perform your outrage on the *Daily Telegraph* website so that it gets more hits to increase its advertising premium.

You seem to have a bit of a problem with the gays, Miranda. There was that time in May of 2010 when you posted a link to an article you'd written about Catherine Deveny being fired from *The Age*. Justin Barbour, a twenty-year-old openly gay university student, tweeted at your account in response, 'You've had enough of attacking the gays for now I see. Great. Thanks.'

You tweeted back by saying, 'You've had enough of rogering gerbils for now I see. Great. Thanks.'

So as far as I can tell, when you see a twenty-year-old university student who's openly gay, you assume he must be sticking a gerbil up his jacksey, which I think is, at the very least, quite presumptuous. You have absolutely no idea what that young man has ever placed up his anus; for all you know, he could have a nest of guinea pigs up there, hibernating for the winter. You can't just *assume* what people have had up their arses, Miranda. When you assume things about my arse, you make an arse out of you and me and also *my arse*.

Also – side note: you know 'rogering a gerbil' is a *truly* bizarre idea, right? Gerbils aren't even native to Australia. That guy would have to *ship gerbils in* for a good rogering and uni students don't have that kind of money, Miranda.

You deleted that tweet and you never apologised. You didn't stand by it as a joke or anything, you just . . . carried on.

This week you were responsible for a truly odious piece of work. A front-page story and an opinion piece about how the Proud Schools pilot program currently being trialled in NSW schools was indoctrinating our children into believing that homosexuality is 'the norm' and that heterosexuality *isn't* the conventional arrangement for human relationships. You're scared of the 'thought police' beating leftie ideas into our kids' heads. You had the fucking gall to try to underplay the issue of homophobic bullying in schools, quoting research that in actual fact proves the *exact opposite*. You just blatantly misrepresented the truth and you must've known you'd be caught out; it's not a matter of shit not sticking to you, it does stick to you, but then it seems to just be absorbed into your armour of shit and only makes you stronger.

You showed zero compassion for at-risk young people out there who may be contemplating suicide, feeling cold and isolated from their peers because of this thing they have in their heads that the church and the government and history and the newspapers tell them is dirty and immoral; the kind of person I was about five years ago when I was growing up in Warrnambool in country Victoria and wrestling with my secret.

I didn't know fancy terms like 'heterosexism' and 'heteronormative', but I was sure as hell living them. Everyone was straight and that was that and if you deviated from that or questioned that you were fucked, and it was impossible, *impossible*, to imagine a world where that wouldn't be the case.

My favourite part of your piece was when you wrote: 'It's not up to academics to dictate attitudes to society via indoctrination of captive children in classrooms.'

Damn right, Miranda – only Catholic priests should be doing that! You go get 'em, girl!

Then there's the column you posted on 3 October about the march in memory of rape and murder victim Jill Meagher. You blasted, once again, the 'twitterati' for 'hijacking' the message of the march and you argued that those involved were naive and that women should still fear the night, that reclaiming it is ridiculous, and we need to live in the world as it is, not think of how we want it to be, and you used something Catherine Deveny said for some stupid reason.

You could have written anything you liked about that march, Miranda. Anything. In the aftermath of that heart-wrenching tragedy, which brought many of my friends and colleagues to their knees in grief, you could have spent your 800 words praising the truly astonishing gesture of tens of thousands of people marching in solidarity in remembrance of one innocent woman – and by extension all women who have fallen victim to sexual assault and violence. You could have spent *all 800 words celebrating that* and it wouldn't have been overdone. Because yes, as a columnist, you have a duty to speak truth to power and call bullshit on certain things when other people won't, but in this fucked-up world where fucked-up things like Jill Meagher's rape and murder can happen, the fact that incredible things like that march can happen is a fucking miracle, and if you truly are a Christian you should fall to your knees in reverence, not cynically snipe from behind your keyboard to get in a cheap shot at the 'silly idealistic feminists'. Because heaven forbid your writing could actually *elevate* the national mood in this country and unite people rather than divide us.

You know what I think we really like about American politics, Miranda? It's just so *easy*. The characters are huge, everything is set on this massive dramatic canvas: opponents don't debate – they do *battle*. It's Republican versus Democrat, red versus blue, right versus left, and never the twain shall meet. It's the place where Rush Limbaugh and Ann Coulter and Glenn Beck find audiences with their rhetoric of factual inaccuracies and fear mongering and their take-no-prisoners, God-is-on-our-side nonsense. There's no such thing as a non-partisan issue in modern America; at most there's a mud-slinging match about which side is trying harder to make something non-partisan.

I don't want that crap here in Australia, Miranda. But I can feel it coming. The state of politics at the moment is deplorable, the behaviour, the tone of debate – *everything*. But this is the time when the public needs writers like you, and Andrew Bolt and David Marr and Piers Akerman and Michelle Grattan and Paul Kelly and Lenore Taylor and Gerard Henderson and Janet Albrechtsen, to *make it better* and *make us smarter*, not to just revel in the apocalypse. I don't want blowhards in my newspapers who try to compete for who has the most dramatic point of view and who can phrase it in the most outrageous way; I want thinkers. I want people who aren't fighting to twist every weekly event in the country to fit the ideology they signed up for. I want people with compassion who think about the effect their writing might have on reinforcing prejudices and whipping up fear; on how it might affect the young silent gay kid in the back of the classroom or the grieving family member or the partner of the politician.

And I believe you're fully capable of doing that, Miranda.

I had a couple of jokes about you in my stand-up show this year. When I was in front of a Victorian audience, I said the best way to explain who you are is to imagine if Mr Devine and Mrs Devine had a baby, and that baby grew up to be a cunt.

Was it a cheap shot? Sure. But KFC chips are cheap and they're still fucking delicious.

Demonisation is really easy. You just flick off that switch in your brain that tells you all human beings have feelings, cook up some good imagery, throw in a joke or two to use as a defence when people get offended, and off you go. It's easy, and I've been doing it throughout this letter because it gets laughs.

I think you can be better than that. You're clearly an intelligent person who is passionate about public debate, moral dilemmas and the challenges facing this country. You're extremely well read, you're fluent in Japanese, you're a patriot, I've seen you be downright funny on *Q&A*, and the small piece you wrote about the Salvos a little while ago was lovely and worthy without being mawkish.

But you write a lot of shit, Miranda, and it's poisonous. You changed my life with your writing because you made me want to be so much better than both it and what it represents. I'm trying to be a better person and not give in to the fear and the petty malice that bleeds through a lot of your work; the fear and petty malice that I see everywhere and that I know is within me.

I'm not trampling on your freedom of speech. Of course you have a right to have an opinion, to express that opinion. And you clearly have a huge readership and you get paid very well and you'll continue your career for as long as you want to, probably.

I just want to remind you that strong, evidence-based, compassionate, soaring commentary can truly make a difference to conversations and beliefs and lives. You are privileged to do what you do, as am I, as is anyone who gets to float and discuss ideas for a living. It's a job to be treated seriously. Through your bad example, you've taught me to respect that.

I saw you once, Miranda. In the flesh. That sounds creepy, but hear me out. I was at the *Daily Telegraph*, in the foyer, waiting to go in to do an interview. And you walked out of the hall and used your swipe card and the automatic doors whipped open and you just kept walking, straight ahead, stone-faced. A real human being just going home to her family after another day at work.

Please write back, Miranda; it'd be great to hear from you.

Yours in love, not hate,
Tom

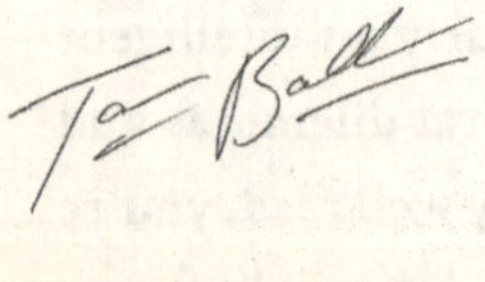

To the moment the lights came on

TRACEY SPICER

Dear Mr Misogynist,

I'd like to thank you for everything you've taught me over the past twenty-five years.

Why, I had no idea I was so fat, ugly and stupid. I thought being a size twelve was perfectly acceptable. But when you yelled across the newsroom, 'I want two inches off your hair and two inches off your arse!' suddenly a light went on.

Of course! The size of my posterior is directly related to the content and credibility of the stories I'm reporting on for this network. Silly me. You're right. I'll never make it as a TV journalist.

Those wise words of yours from 1986 are still ringing in my ears. 'That's why you don't see blonde newsreaders,' you explained patiently. 'People don't take them seriously.'

It reminded me of another sage piece of advice, from a radio boss during a job interview. He put it simply yet eloquently. 'There's a reason you don't hear women on commercial talkback radio,' he said, all those years ago. 'No one wants to hear the whiney sound of a female voice. Us blokes get enough nagging at home!'

It's true, isn't it?

Really, in retrospect, it was foolish to think I was worthy of such a role. Like all women, I only have two areas of specialisation: shoes and handbags. And we all know high heels are a patriarchal construct to disempower us by constricting movement.

Oh dear. Must stop having thoughts like that. Sorry, I have no idea where that came from.

Anyway, through some quirk of fate, I managed to land a news reading job.

I know what you're thinking: I finally decided to speak into that flesh-coloured microphone you were always pointing in my direction.

Oddly enough, though, I was offered the job by a woman. Who would have thought?

Initially, I was wary. You always said you'd never work for a female boss because, 'You can't trust anything that bleeds for five days and doesn't die.'

Hilarious! It's a good thing I was wearing a corset or my sides would have split.

Fortunately, there were enough blokes around to keep me on the straight and narrow.

On my first night, the station manager came down and said, 'You need to stick your tits out more.'

Once again, my brain wasn't working properly. In between the raging bushfires, the political crises and savage cuts to welfare, I'd forgotten to flirt with the camera.

A couple of years later – I'm ashamed to say this – I 'porked up', according to one of the producers. Frankly, I was unsightly. I stood out like a bull in a china shop, around those fragile lollipop ladies with their skinny bodies and massive heads. My new boss quickly raced out and arranged sponsorship from the local gym.

Then one day I got a nasty shock when I looked in the mirror. Wrinkles around my eyes *and* on my forehead. Too much thinking? Surely not.

I remember you reviewing a videotape of one of my colleagues – clever girl, Walkley Award winner, as I recall – and saying, 'The problems seem to be here and here,' pointing to her ghastly crow's feet.

However, as it turns out, wrinkles were the least of my worries.

I'd gotten myself knocked up.

I wanted to go back to work when bubby was three months old. But, once again, it took a man to show me the error of my ways.

'Women should be at home with their children,' my news director said. 'Or the fabric of society will be rent asunder.

'Anyway, Trace. You're getting a bit long in the tooth. Why don't you give some of the younger girls an opportunity?'

Suddenly, *all* the lights went on.

And it was so bright – it made *your* light look like a limp, insipid flicker.

This is difficult for me to put into words.

But if I had to, it would sound a bit like this: *Fuck you.*

Fuck you, you misogynist bully with your archaic beliefs, intellect of a pygmy, and tiny dick.

Fuck you, and all who sail with you.

The reason I am writing this letter is to thank you. Among others – too many to mention – you lit a fire in my belly that's become an inferno. These days, I don't cop shit from anyone.

When I was sacked by email after the birth of my second baby, I fought the fuckers. I use the term 'fuckers' advisedly, having checked with my attorney. After all, truth is a defence in this country.

I do hope you receive this correspondence. I had trouble finding a forwarding address after you lost your house due to that unfortunate sexual harassment case.

(I'm sure the bitch was asking for it.)

Yours in emancipation,
Tracey

LEIGH SALES

Dear Amanda,

I'm not sure if you'll remember me. I was the tall, freckle-faced Queenslander who came to your school in grade seven. You were the girl with no friends.

I know that sounds harsh. But if you're to understand why I'm writing, we'll have to be frank and agree that it's true. You were that kid who seems to haunt every school, that lonely shadow hunched on a playground bench at lunchtime, intently concentrating on eating a sandwich so as to not seem bothered that everyone else is playing and running and whispering secrets. You were that odd sock left over when the class paired up.

There was no obvious reason why you were the un-chosen one. You had very wild, woolly dark hair. Was that it? Or was it some obscure ethnic thing? When I arrived as an eleven year old at our Melbourne school, I was mystified by the hostility between the Serbian and the Croatian kids. I once called one of my new friends Yugoslavian and she hissed in fury, 'Not Yugoslavian – Croatian!' In Brisbane, exotic qualified as a Nutella sandwich in your lunchbox. The political overtones of a Melbourne schoolyard were well over my head. Maybe you were somehow caught up in that? With that hair and your olive skin, I'd guess you were Greek or Italian, but I never thought about it at the time. The notable thing about you wasn't your ethnic background; it was your friendlessness.

You might remember that the two of us used to go off alone together to an instrumental music class once a week. We learned cello from Miss Spark, who I once spied kissing her boyfriend in the botanic gardens. In that one period a week, I would chat to you as a regular friend, about what we thought of our teachers and our cello practice and boys in our grade. But the second we rejoined the regular class, I went back to acting as if you didn't exist. I never bullied you. I simply joined the other kids in acting as though you were invisible.

Almost thirty years later, this causes me great shame, and two things about it puzzle me. The first is why I was so two-faced. The second is why you never called me on it.

There is really no excuse for my cowardice, so the best I can do is apologise and try to explain what my eleven-year-old self was thinking.

I think my behaviour was based in feeling that I was perilously close to suffering your isolation. I didn't know the first thing about fitting in at this new school. All the Melbourne kids said 'grouse', but in Brisbane we said 'unreal'. 'Will you go with me?' was how a Brisbane boy asked someone to be his girlfriend, but in Melbourne it was 'getting on' with somebody. In Brisbane, we were all still playing red rover at lunchtime and learning square dancing. In Melbourne, we were smoking behind the toilet block and graffitiing the walls.

Miraculously, I'd managed to make some friends at school. But to hold on to them, I felt like I was faking it the whole time: faking that I knew what they were talking about, faking that I was cool with their worldly behaviour, faking that I wouldn't have traded the whole lot of them in an instant to be back riding my bike in the sweltering Queensland summer, pretending that my best friend and I were Trixie Belden and Honey Wheeler on the trail of smugglers. I felt as if these hip Melbourne kids would abandon me the second they figured out who I really was. The prospect of being 'left out' terrified me and you embodied it.

The uniform at our school was a grey-and-green tartan dress in summer and a navy duffle coat and grey corduroy pants in winter. One of the worst days of my life was the day my mother sent me to school wearing a pair of shapeless, baggy grey cords when all the other kids wore skin-tight pants (and, Amanda, I know that speaks volumes about what a cruisy life I've had, that a bad pair of jeans qualifies as an earth-shattering moment). To not wear tight jeans was the greatest social faux pas you could commit. I never saw a single kid at that school whose cords didn't look spray-painted on. Even you wore the right cords, Amanda. For some reason, my mother was vehemently opposed to letting me wear fitted trousers. To this day, I have no idea what she was thinking. Maybe she had some theory about over-sexualising her pre-adolescent daughter, or maybe she just couldn't afford the cool pants. Whatever the reason, I thought the baggy trousers would be the last oddity my new friends would tolerate. I was already lugging a cello around the school, for God's sake! How much more would they take?

I still recall the misery of wearing those pants for the first time, walking through the school gates and clocking the incredulous stares in my direction. I remember the way I stood pressed up against a wall, wretchedly folding the material behind my calves and pressing them into the bricks in the futile hope they'd look tight. I remember walking to school in the rain and the way those flappy pant-legs would get soaked and damply cling to me all day. I remember the way my big feet would catch in the hems of the trousers when I walked quickly, making me stumble.

Almost as inexplicable as my mother's opposition to tight jeans was my friends' decision to overlook them. There were a few questions on the first day I wore them, but after that they were never mentioned again – or at least not by anyone in my immediate social group. You might think, Amanda, that my fear of having no friends might have given me some empathy for your position. But it did just the opposite. I was worried that whatever you had was contagious.

Why did you go along with my duplicity, allowing me to be your friend only when it was convenient for me? I can only imagine it was because you didn't want to risk that hour a week when you had a mate. How you must have longed for that cello lesson to come around, when, for just one hour and the walk to and from the music block, you chatted and laughed and had a friend. Then we'd return to class and you'd go back into your protective crouch, lest you do something to provoke the kids into worse than merely ignoring you.

It is to my great embarrassment and shame that it was well after leaving that school that the lights came on for me regarding my behaviour. I don't even know that I bothered to say goodbye to you when I was going home to Brisbane. What a self-absorbed little shit I was. I wish I'd had the guts to be more than somebody who held out friendship only when others weren't looking.

Anyway, Amanda, I think of you often and hope that grade seven was the only bad year in your life.

Kind regards,
Leigh

Leigh Sales

JENNIFER BYRNE

I was sixteen years old when I walked into the buzzing newsroom of *The Age* for the first time, and I can still remember what I was wearing. There was the short, kicky lavender skirt. A white cotton tank top, with stripes – including toning lavender – tight across the chest. And, at the end of my somewhat pudgy schoolgirl legs, skyscraper-high cork-wedge shoes. I thought I looked a million bucks. Then one of the old-time reporters called out, 'It's Minnie Mouse!', serving notice that my fashion sense, cultivated over four years at boarding school, was going to have to be pretty quickly recalibrated. Everyone around me – and there seemed to be hundreds of them – looked like derelicts, ties and collars askew, smoking furiously, as they closely appraised the five new cadet journalists reporting for duty. Of which I was one.

It was the early seventies. *The Female Eunuch* had just been published and the little man with the big ears, Billy McMahon, was our prime minister. Not that I knew anything about either of these: feminism hadn't made it to our country boarding house, and as for politics, I had never troubled myself with reading a newspaper. I'd just finished my HSC and like most students then – and pretty much all of them now – believed the next logical step after finishing school was to hightail it to university and study something which might one day add up to a career. I'd seen enough episodes of *Perry Mason* to think that law looked interesting, and had visions of myself striding around the courtroom in black fish-net stockings, solving crimes and showing up the police prosecutors for the weaselly clods they were. I'd scored a place at Melbourne University, but since I was so young, my mother – nervous about how her innocent teenage daughter would deal with the dangerous activism and raffishness of university – had persuaded me to defer and take what would now be called a gap year, which was what I was doing in the *Age* newsroom. Just filling in the time before my real life started.

Journalism wasn't an obvious choice for my year off. I'd been quite good at English at school – and Lois Lane was my second-favourite TV character – but we'd never had a journalist in the family. We'd never had a salaried woman, actually. Unlike my mother, who thought a year's cadetship would be a soft landing, my grandmother declared the whole idea appalling. Journalists were vulgar people. And, she'd heard, they drank. I visited her on the night before my lavender outburst and her core advice was never to drink gin, as it gave you ulcers. Also, gin made a woman's face hard. I will go to my grave believing this.

As to what *I* thought, well, my expectations were minimal. I was chuffed to have been hired – even then cadetships weren't easy to get – but really didn't know why they'd bothered since my future lay elsewhere. My instructions were to report at 2 p.m., and I thought how nice, how thoughtful, to ease us in with a gentle half-day's work, discovering only on arrival that the main shift on a morning newspaper ran from 2 to 11 p.m. Getting home became an immediate problem. I didn't drive, of course. Was it safe to get a tram home that late? Would they even still be running? And forty dollars a week, the princely sum earned by a first-year cadet, was not going to stretch to many taxis – especially as I was paying all of ten dollars a week for my share of a bedsit. We five newbies spent the afternoon and night faffing about, making nuisances of ourselves and taking turns 'monitoring the news' – which involved walking over to a radio every hour, turning on the ABC, and writing down, in order, each of the stories covered, to be sure the paper hadn't missed something.

I kept worrying about how I'd get home and when, as it approached knock-off time, a rather wolfish-looking man with the title of Chief State Political Reporter offered me a lift (he lived nearby, he said), I was quick to accept. A bad step. Because as we headed out of the bustling newsroom just after 11, we caught the eye of the editor – a fierce, craggy man called Graham Perkin, a legendary figure who looked and sounded like a big lion. He was the one who'd hired us cadets, but he'd been ignoring us all day – until now, sadly. He put down the copy he was working on at the subs' table and stared at us.

Lest you think I'm exaggerating, here's an eyewitness account of what happened next from journalist Ben Hills.

'Perkin, red-faced with anger, half-stood from his chair at the head of the table and rested his fists on the desk, glowering around. "That," he roared into the sudden silence, "is a sixteen year old who has come directly from school to join our staff. She's not just young, she is the governor's grand-daughter"' – which I was, making things worse – '"and, more to the point, the first man that lays a hand on her loses his job."'

And that was my first day of work. Obviously he meant well but, frankly, he may as well have slung a big fat target around my neck reading, 'Virgin! Opportunities available!' Which was clearly how it was interpreted by the entire newsroom – this being the priapic days before sexual harassment laws. But I was a girl who was desperate to grow up, and the fact is, after eleven years of all-girl education, I was so desperately ready for some heady doses of testosterone. There was only one other female cadet and we were, shall we say, very busy girls.

When we weren't monitoring, we cadets took turns on the daily shipping round, a painstaking listing of the arrival time of every single cargo ship into the Melbourne docks, their names and wharf assignments. This was the dinosaur age, technologically, but it was supposed to teach us accuracy – and in a weird way, it did. There were captains and old salts at various vantage points around Port

Phillip Heads, their binoculars trained on the sea, for whom shipping reports were holier than the Bible. And I mean this literally. If the *Omar Maru* bailed up at 14 North Wharf at the wrong time, it was a serious offence.

We learned that what happened today must of course be reported in the paper as yesterday, and tomorrow's events become today's – which one of us forgot when reporting a state funeral, triggering hundreds of complaints from would-be mourners. I think they may have been sacked for that. A few afternoons a week, we were sent off to RMIT to attend journalism school. The sessions on landmark investigations and wrongful court convictions were fascinating; lessons on how to use the telephone book less so. We shared the classroom with cadets from other newspapers, like our morning rival, *The Sun*, plus a wannabe group who'd so far missed out on cadetships – and the dividing lines couldn't have been clearer. They were students. We were trainee journalists. No matter how mundane our duties, how incompetent our efforts, we were in the club. Which was when the light started to flicker. How I adored being a working girl. It didn't matter the feebleness of my pay packet; I got one, I was making my way, I was free. And the preoccupations of my student friends started to seem very dull and tame.

A few weeks went by and we started being rostered out with the senior reporters, tagging after them on their rounds and scribbling our version of what we saw and heard into little red and white notebooks. We pecked the stories out on manual typewriters and were told all the reasons they were hopeless. Instruction – and seduction – continued at the local pub, The Golden Age, to which we retreated around 7 p.m. every night, in a mob, to drink vastly and eat huge, crumby veal parmigianas while the old hands told tall stories, inducting us into their seedy but glamorous world. Very occasionally the great Perkin would join us, and we listened, rapt, as he expounded his theory of journalistic success. All you really needed, he believed, was rat-like cunning, a slight literary ability and a plausible manner. This was nothing like what we'd learned at school.

The lights were switching on everywhere, fizzing like fireworks, but the moment they all came on together was about seven months in, when I had to decide whether to commit to the full three-year cadetship – or take up that place they'd kept warm at Melbourne Uni. Abroad, the Watergate scandal was slowly unravelling; at home, Labor leader Gough Whitlam was holding election rallies, urging the Men and Women of Australia to call 'time' on twenty-three years of Liberal Party government. I was seventeen by then, writing my first feeble articles – and so in love with my job and my life as a journalist, it shone out of me. Maybe that was where the light came from. Or maybe it was just the harsh ugly neon over Perkin's desk when I told him I'd be staying.

It's all different now, of course. Newspapers are on their knees, we all know this, and on a personal level, many fine colleagues have been among those to lose or leave their jobs in both Fairfax and Murdoch newsrooms. There are very few journalistic cadetships available, and only the highest-marked graduates are considered. I sometimes wonder what would have happened if the light hadn't gone on, if I'd chosen differently, but not often. It set my whole life's course.

I do wonder if in the push to improve Australia's national educational standards, to encourage everyone into tertiary study lest they never get a decent job, we may be overlooking the obvious. There are other ways through. I'm not saying work makes you free – that would be a bit creepy – but it was powerfully true for me. And, in fact, it proved to be exactly where heaven lies.

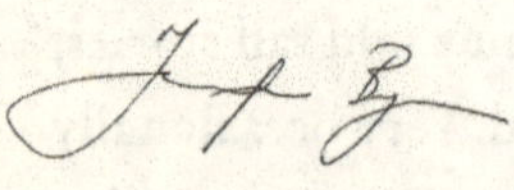

CHARLOTTE DAWSON

Dear Miraculous Dating Agency,

I write to you today to seek your help. Like a taxi full of people, a flat torch or a fridge when the door is closed, my light has gone out.

You see, Miraculous Dating Agency, when I am in love, my light goes on. I can ignite my light, no problem. I assure you, my wick is dipped in a mixture of kerosene and gunpowder, and I have a full box of matches. My difficulty lies in keeping the bugger lit. This is where you come in.

I would very much like your assistance in keeping my light lit for more than a couple of years, a couple of months, a fortnight, or a revolutionary afternoon.

I thought my light was on for good when I, as a moderately successful media personality who didn't crack too many mirrors, met an Olympic swimmer with a golden future and fell in love. We were youngish. We looked nice in clothes. He was a bit of a sort. We got engaged, we got married, and our lights were burning so brightly we could have lit cigarettes on the other side of the country.

Of course, when those old, nuggetty chestnuts arise, like cheating, like a husband's career taking precedence over keeping a baby to term, and furniture getting thrown, and management getting involved in matrimony, and one half going to a magazine with made-up stories about violence and the other half slinking back to New Zealand with their tail between their legs and a winner of a defamation suit – you know, the usual stuff – one's bulb does flicker a bit.

It may be that my switch is faulty. It goes on, the dimmer is cranked up to full, and then the whole mechanism pops and fizzles like a cherry tomato on a hotplate.

Light goes on: I fall in love with an old friend, a man I've known for a decade plus change. It's swoony. It's passionate. His dog likes me.

Light goes off: He's arrested for bank fraud.

Light goes on: The best-looking man on a dating site shows an interest and takes me out. Maybe he'll say those three words every girl wants to hear?

Light goes off: He says those three words no girl wants to hear – 'I've killed someone.'

Light goes on: I meet a handsome young man who can't get enough of me, has dimples to Christmas and doesn't seem like a douchebag.

Light goes off: He wears a screenplay he's written on a thumb drive around his neck. Suddenly seems like a douchebag.

Light goes on: A Kiwi tennis coach of extensive education, worldly experience and quite impressive thighs has me on his arm around New Zealand for a while.

Light goes off: His sister tells him that going out with me will give his mother coronary problems, as for a while there in the land of the long white cloud, I was generally regarded as about as appealing as a wet towel on the floor of Kyle Sandiland's bathroom.

Light goes on: An outrageously wealthy, well-connected man pursues me for a few years, takes me out on his suburb-sized boat, calls me five times a day and tells me I look pretty at the Logies.

Light goes off: After dinner one night he tells me I should probably sleep in the spare room because he's met someone else and it's serious.

Light stays off: I try celibacy for a couple of years. I really get quite a lot done.

So basically, Miraculous Dating Agency, you can help me in a few ways.

You can match me with a man with no past (or future) criminal record.

You can match me with a man who places me higher than number ten on his list of priorities, particularly if none of the higher items are the names of other women.

You can match me with a man who has the right equipment for the bedroom but none of the equipment for making notches on the bedpost and no getaway car.

You can match me with a man who needs a maximum of three menu items explained to him and read out phonetically.

I would like all the lights to go on.

And I would like to gaffer tape the switch in place.

ANNABEL CRABB

Dear Moment,

You're a tough bugger to identify, I'll say that for you. On reflection, it turns out the vast majority of my life has been comprehensively, not to say stubbornly, counter-epiphanic in nature.

The penny has dropped many times – I'm sure it has. It's just that I never hear it. And as for the moment the lights come on – well. To be frank, they could be flipping rhythmically on and off, accompanied by a $2-million firework display, atop the Sydney Harbour Bridge, spelling out 'Annabel Crabb! The Right Man For You Is, In Fact, As You Have Often Half-Suspected, 1938 Jimmy Stewart, And A Time Machine Will Be Here For The Next Fifteen Minutes Ready To Take You To Him,' and I would certainly still miss it.

Take a few weeks ago, when I got head lice. You'd think I might have been on the lookout for that one. You'd think the warning bells on lice infestation might have been vaguely audible. I have two children under six years of age. Ding-a-ling!

I have a head of hair in which an agoraphobic hamster could live a comfortable life, entirely unmolested by contact with the outside world, so it stands to reason that any louse would find it more than agreeable real estate. Ding-a-ling!

Most damningly, there was a nit outbreak at my daughter's school, which meant my sweet little child – the one who crawls into bed with us at about five o'clock every morning – DING-A-LING-A-LING! – was all of a sudden a crawling nest of microscopic bugs, requiring nightly applications of some kind of vile DDT substance with cute cartoon figures on the box.

I felt a little scratchy, sure. But I subconsciously assumed it was psychosomatic, like the other phantom symptoms I pick up from my children: an unaccountable affection for processed cheese, for example, or the deep and atavistic suspicion, in moments of conflict, that slapping might help.

So by the time I worked out that I too had been included in the infestation, there was a community of nits in my hair so established that they had a land titles office and their own currency.

And if you think there's anything more humiliating, by the way, than having nits as an adult, you can think again. Whole aeons of human civilisation and advancement melt away; all of a sudden, you have direct attributes in common with a dog blanket or a shipyard rat. You may as well just live in a cave and fight other nit-infested people with flaming rags on sticks. In vain do you howl your protests at the unfeeling cosmos: 'I can't have nits! I'm thirty-nine! I've written books! I've been interviewed by Margaret Throsby, you filthy teeming little bastards!'

And then, the shame comes.

And you start to wonder what, exactly, the obligations are on a moderately socially interactive woman with nits. Is there a mandatory notification deal? Did I try on any hats in the last few days? Oh God – do I need to have an uncomfortable conversation with the ABC hair and makeup department? Should I be tolling a bell before me wherever I go? Is this turban a bit obvious?

It's all fine now. I don't have head lice any more. But you get the point. I have trouble picking things up. Apart from nits, that is, obviously.

But if I scroll back through the points in my life at which the penny has dropped and I've actually heard it clang, a couple do spring to mind.

I remember the moment at which I first became conscious of being badly dressed. I was in grade four. I was wearing black Clarks lace-up school shoes, a pair of khaki fleecy-lined tracksuit pants with a patch pocket at the front on which two strawberries had been embroidered by my mother in cream thread, and a stripy velour top belonging to my elder brother James. No one alerted me to the problem; I just recall surveying the situation in the playground and thinking it was probably, as a look, less than ideal.

And then there was you – the moment to which this, let's face it, ridiculously haphazard missive is formally addressed.

And you are located somewhere in, I think, November of 1987; a fleeting moment, and in the whoop and warp of things barely significant at all, but all the same undeniably a *moment*, nonetheless.

You are the moment at which I realised I would never be a scientist.

Now, to be fair, the idea that I would ever be a scientist was probably just as risible back then as it seems now. And nature had already, by means of various amicable little hints, done its best to hasten your progress towards me, Moment, but of course I ignored them all.

The not being all that good at science, for instance. The lack of any firm idea of what science even was, really, beyond some romanticised biographical material I had consumed on Marie Curie and some entirely unconnected but – at the time – despicably orthodox stirrings in the direction of marine biology.

Undaunted, I ploughed on, and in year ten arranged to do work experience in a scientific lab – at the Waite Institute, a branch of the CSIRO in Adelaide's south-eastern suburbs.

It took me an hour and a half to get there from the farm, by car, train and bus, but I was drawn by the cool flame of knowledge so I didn't mind.

I didn't mind that I spent the whole first day cleaning out rat cages and didn't talk to a single person except the lab supervisor who showed me where the rat cages were.

I didn't mind that I spent the whole second day cleaning out rat cages. On the third day, there was a change of pace when I cleaned out some spinifex hopping mouse cages. I tried not to think about what spinifex hopping mice might be doing in a laboratory.

On day four, the lab supervisor reappeared, slapped me heartily on the back and said something about how tomorrow I would be able to sit in on a proper experiment.

And so as my fifth and final day of laboratory work experience commenced, I finally entered a laboratory. The procedure underway was the dissection of a giant ram's testicle into hundreds of little pink meaty cubes, and the careful tweezing of one cube into each of the rows upon rows of test tubes that had been thoughtfully laid out upon the lab bench. I maintained, as instructed, a clinical distance, and watched.

It was not yet noon, but already it was a warm day, and in the stuffy laboratory the air seemed thick and unyielding. I had started the day with fairly nasty period pain and had forgotten to bring the painkillers on which I generally depended in such circumstances. As the dissection proceeded, there seemed hundreds of test tubes that now had little testicle cubes in them, but the actual main body of the testicle seemed magically undiminished, like some sort of insane, giant, enchanted *Alice in Wonderland* bollock. I tried to focus on a clock mounted on the far wall, as the waves of back pain gave way to dizziness and my vision swam. A fly settled on a stray chunk of testicle. Its compound eye met mine, as it rubbed its legs together with evident satisfaction.

How long did that moment last – your predecessor, in point of fact, dear Moment in Question?

I cannot be sure. All I know is that when I woke up, one cheek pressed to the delicious coolness of a tiled laboratory floor, the lights had definitely come on.

And sure, maybe the actual lights were prosaic in origin: a horrified laboratory supervisor checking my pupils with a pocket torch. But a light bulb moment is a light bulb moment is a light bulb moment, and you, Moment, were mine.

I never became a scientist.

Love,
Annabel

LUCY CARTER

Dear Rob,

I'm sure you know the saying, that you can choose your friends but you can't choose your family.

But what of step-parents? The family that is chosen for you. Selected on your behalf without much consultation, and then somewhat awkwardly brought into your family, one step at a time.

Even the word, 'stepfather', sounds weird. Is it a step back? A step down? Is there an implication that someone has stepped aside, leaving a vacant space for someone to just . . . step into?

Let's backtrack a little to the year 2000. You came into our family at a pretty tough time. You know the context: Dad had died barely a month after I turned thirteen, and before that there had been plenty of unhappiness. Separated parents, infighting and long periods of silence between people who were meant to love one another unconditionally. Teenage years are hard enough but then suddenly there was this huge gaping hole in the family, one that my brother and I didn't really want filled.

Then, within a year, there was you. Sure, you were making Mum happier, but with typical thirteen-year-old girl logic, all that did was make me angry. Weren't we enough? Was I doing something wrong?

I remember the night Mum brought you over for dinner to meet us. Introductions were made, everyone was extremely polite, and

I think we all sat and watched a movie afterwards. I didn't really know what to make of it all. I didn't think it would last.

But pretty soon you were a regular fixture in our lives. I'm sure you remember how fantastic Mum was during this period; she was always checking to see if Danny and I were okay with everything that was going on, making sure she was including us and basically walking on eggshells to make sure we were coping with these pretty big changes. Nursing the relationships as they crept forward. Baby steps.

A few months down the track, I realised you weren't going anywhere. In what has to be the crappiest rebellion in history, I started offering to make you cups of tea and coffee after dinner and adding food colouring to dye them blue. Che Guevara I was not. It was literally all I could think of to do to show my unease at you stepping into this role.

To your credit, you took the caffeine sabotage quite well. I think you quietly looked at the normal-coloured coffee I made for Mum, sipped at the fluoro muck I presented you with and then just got up and poured it down the sink. Eventually you stopped accepting my night-time offers of hot drinks. Probably a step in the right direction.

After maybe a year, you moved into an apartment at the top of the street. Another year or two after that you were living in our house. There was never any animosity between us – in fact, quite the opposite. We got on well. You put up with my truly spectacular teenage tantrums and meltdowns, and, more importantly, propped up Mum when I lashed out at her again and again. You never tried to parent me and you gave me lots of really solid advice through those years. But no matter what . . . You just weren't my dad.

It took over a decade for the lights to switch on for me. For me to realise. And looking back there were so many things that should have tipped me off, clues that you were pretty okay.

I remember you and Mum visiting me at uni in Bathurst one time. You slipped off with my car and told us it was to check if the tyres were flat – but it came back with a full tank of petrol. As a student, that was like someone had slipped me a million dollars.

Another time, Mum was overseas and it was just you and me at home. You got a slightly wild look in your eyes and sent me off to buy Baileys and butterscotch schnapps because it was your 'last night of freedom'. We stayed up until 2 a.m. doing cowboy shots even though we both had work the next day. Sorry, ABC. Also, I heard some pretty hilarious stories about my mother that night. Sorry, Mum.

We've shared road trips, hotel rooms and a ridiculous few nights in LA when we thought 'light beer' in America meant low alcohol. I still don't know how you didn't die, accidentally plastered and on the wrong side of the freeway.

We worked well as travel buddies, seeing the sights for a few hours and then mutually, wordlessly agreeing to find a bar where we could watch sport and eat popcorn shrimp until it was dinnertime. In San Francisco during fleet week, you showed your colours as a truly excellent wingman, attempting to set me up with almost an entire US naval fleet.

Over the years you've taught me how to drive, helped me put together my first professional résumé and steered me towards creating the perfect roast lamb. In response I introduced you to *Game of Thrones* and became an acceptable person to take to rugby union games, and I'm slowly coming to accept that I will never be able to sneakily add vegetables to your spaghetti bolognaise. Old dog, new tricks, and all that? It's clearly a step too far.

But it wasn't until this year that I got the message properly. When I heard you were in hospital after a heart attack and I fell apart. For a minute it felt like one of my best friends had died.

You were completely fine, to the point that you pretended to be dead when I visited you in hospital and then jumped up at me. But in that instant, standing outside my house, when Mum got that first phone call? That really was the moment that the lights came on.

You aren't my dad and you never will be. But that's totally okay. What they say is true – you can't choose your family but you can choose your friends. And as cheesy as it sounds, I'm very happy to step forward and say I've chosen you as a friend.

Love,
Lucy

xx Lucy

PS Please don't pretend to be dead again, or I *will* kill you.

ANITA HEISS

Dear academia,

It's been a long time since we first met way back in the Dreamtime of 1987. I was a fresh-faced, hopeful eighteen year old, wearing a stone-washed denim drop-waist skirt and a jacket with shoulder pads. You, dear academia, greeted me with dark, stale theatres and mostly male lecturers who often read from their own textbooks.

It was an overcast day in March when we started our journey together. I walked the campus in naive awe as you promised me clubs where I could learn how to surf, or become a young socialist, or a food lover, or a fitness freak. In my head there was also the promise of being noticed by spunky male undergrads who would fall in love with me on the library lawn, as bands played lunchtime sets. None of the above happened, dear academia, but it's neither here nor there now.

For the first leg of our journey we had a reasonable relationship, you and I, but we were never a perfect fit, were we? I was always nervous, intimidated and perhaps not serious enough for you, who often looked down on me from your ivory tower, or so I thought. Perhaps if we'd talked more at the uni bar or at the Golf House on Botany Street, we may have found we had more in common.

But I do want to thank you, dear academia, for without our time together as an undergrad, I would never have learned about Orientalism or the Westminster system or why I really, really don't enjoy Chaucer. You taught me not only the skills and knowledge of what

I would *apparently* need to get through life, but more importantly, you opened my eyes as to what I *didn't* need to know. As if learning trigonometry at school wasn't waste of time enough, you made me sit through brain-draining economics subjects. And what good did they do, dear academia? My BAS is still nearly always late and, without doubt, incorrect. Oh, and please don't show this letter to the ATO.

I'd like to take this time now, though, dear ostracising, often-alienating, too-far-removed from the real-world academia, to acknowledge that you taught me a whole new vocab. Words and phrases like 'shifting paradigms', 'expressionism' and 'philosophical optimism'. It's a language I find particularly useful when working with kids in primary schools or in remote Aboriginal communities. I think of you fondly at those times.

But of course my favourite term remains 'post-colonial'. Yes, dear academia, we are going to have to agree to disagree on that one because I stand by my view that Aboriginal Australia *is* still being colonised. Perhaps you haven't heard of the NT Intervention or Stronger Futures. Or perhaps you have and *still* maintain your position, because to admit you were wrong would be – well, it would never be.

I know what you're thinking, dear academia – that I should at least thank you for my major in political science, for making me so political today, but my sense of politics is different to what I was taught at uni where I learned the intricate details of the British, American and Australian systems. You didn't teach me about grassroots politics like the reconciliation movement. You didn't teach me the power of politics through poetry and song and theatre. I experienced all that *off* campus, with people you didn't deem bright enough to join us where the 'intellectuals' gathered.

And apropos of the above, and to not ignore the concept of post-modernism, can I say I'm post-academic now? Would you roll your eyes at a dinner party with other faculty members if I said that in front of you? Would you be ashamed of the failure you may see me as? Well, don't be: I'm doing just fine, thanks. I've published chick-lit novels. I know you don't rate them, but some people do, because stories *about women actually do matter*. Don't believe me? Well, why don't you google it? Apparently that's how some Australian journos do their research today. But I digress.

Back to the topic of language. Dear academia, did you know that I really loathe the word 'discourse'? Don't look so shocked. And every time you used it in my presence or in my textbooks I wanted to scream. I really wish you could just learn to yarn – that's what I call community discourse. Ah, but you don't give a damn about community discourse, do you? Not unless there's an ARC grant involved, or you can add it to your publications list, or maybe use it when you're on sabbatical.

Oh, don't get shitty with me now, academia, emotion doesn't suit you. Let's be honest with each other. You were never the emotional one. You were the practical, business-minded, theoretical one. I, on the other hand, cried all the way to visit you in my Honours year as I hated studying the industrial revolution with a room full of students doing theses on topics like eighteenth-century Scottish architecture and other similarly useful research. Yes, you taught me sarcasm as well.

I admit there were a few good times. In the early days, when we partied together, we danced at BnS balls at the Roundhouse and played pool at the pub down the road, and had theme nights when I ran the social club of the Aboriginal Students Association. I still look at the photos and smile. But, of course, we got older and the parties became fewer, and of a much more official variety. At these times you showed interest, you gave me credit, you even called in the marketing office to get some 'brownie points' – and yes, that *is* a pun.

In 1992 you made me wear a black gown and a flat black hat with a curtain tassle on it. It gave me hat hair but I didn't complain because I'd still prefer it over a fascinator. I said goodbye to you after the pomp and pageantry of the graduation ceremony, willing myself to have a relationship with the real world. I took my skills and got a job pulling beers in an RSL club. That's right. You can imagine how proud my parents were after six years of private schooling and four at uni and I ended up behind a bar. But rest easy, it wasn't for long. I was out of the door pretty much the minute I entered it, after a patron asked for a schooner of 'nigger' – you know, a schooner of black beer. Unfortunately, dear academia, you taught me about Keynesian theory and the history of industrial relations in Australia, but you didn't teach me how to react to racism in the workplace, which I learned from having to deal with ignorant patrons.

But then I got what some might term a 'proper job'. Oh, dear academia, it wasn't down the high end of town in pleated skirt and court shoes like I'd imagined I'd get, you know, after our relationship. Oh, no – it was in a warehouse in Glebe writing comic scripts dressed in boots and jeans. But it was right for me. I was going to make some changes for young people with low literacy skills and this new relationship made me promises that it kept.

In that place I never imagined going back to you again. It was over; we were over. You were my past, I was my own future. But after a visit to the Mohawk community in Canada, I was inspired and I could see some attraction in you again, and there *was* chemistry still between us, as there often is with the one you shouldn't be with. And, with promises of faculty support and interest in my PhD topic, we were in bed again. But this time, we were on a more even level. And you were proud when I finished. Hell, *I* was proud. You having your first Aboriginal doctoral graduate, me having finished my research and wearing a floppy hat this time. My dad wore a three-piece suit and bought me every bit of graduation paraphernalia possible. I thought he must have won the lottery. I'll never forget that day, dear academia; it was probably the highlight of our relationship.

I still wear my graduation dress today, and I smile when I put it on because it still fits. And for a woman with body issues, that reality is almost as much of an achievement as the degree itself.

We parted ways again in 2001, but by 2003, you were patting the side of the bed and saying, 'Come, sit down, let's talk,' and I knew at some level you cared about me. You used words like 'peace' and 'justice' – I was immediately yours again. We were on the same page of a book that was fast becoming a trilogy. To be fair, I wanted a salary and super and believed that this time you would keep your promises and we would indeed change the world. But maybe you just can't change the world unless you are part of the Group of Eight – maybe when you're in a relationship with one of the left-over group of thirty-one, then you have to settle for the best you can do in your own little patch. We found our own groove and as I powered along and taught hundreds of students and marked thousands of essays, and sat on committees even though I was never really sure of their purpose, you kept banging on about publication credit points and quotas and black bums on seats.

I'm sorry, academia. I started this letter as a gesture of healing, one of peacemaking between you and me, but the more I think about our relationship, the more I recall why it ended so abruptly.

Do you remember that moment? Probably not, because you would consider that to be a female, sentimental thing to do. I know, I can't make sweeping generalisations like that. I need to back it up with research, but that would require an ARC grant application, and quite frankly I'd rather do another PhD than have to write one of those.

What I want you to know now is that the last straw was in 2006 when I attended a conference in Fiji on epistemologies. I should have known before I left Sydney that it was a bad idea. When every time I mentioned the conference to my Koori friends, they would say, 'Epista-what?' Epistafuckingwhat indeed.

But I went anyway, and as I sat listening to scholars from around the Pacific speak in their foreign academic language about themselves while alienating members of their own communities – well, dear academia, that's the moment all the lights came on. And my reality was as illuminated as the hub of Times Square, as bright as a thousand suns. It was blindingly obvious that you and I were *not* meant to be – at least, of course, until you seduce me again.

I'm signing off now, dear academia, albeit with an acknowledgement that, without you, I wouldn't be who I am today, and I wouldn't be reading this letter out loud in Marrickville.

Until the next time,
Yours sincerely,
Dr Anita Heiss, the girl from the burbs

Anita

To that thing on my body

JILL SINGER

Dear hair – plural – hairs,

I've never quite known whether to defend you as being just part of my natural landscape, of my DNA – part of that which defines me.

Or should I fight you, hairs? Or view you as my own personal cockroach, sure to survive after the rest of me starts to rot?

Don't you find it funny that in the singular – hair – you sound attractive? Desirable. A girl can wear her hair up or down. She can flick it, swing it, do it, have it done.

But there can be no glamorous swinging and flicking of *hairs*. As soon as we speak of you in the plural, hairs, you become dangerous. Our thoughts take us to manky drains clogged with soap scum, cockroaches and you, hairs, tangled and matted.

Do you remember when I was a fledgling? God knows I actually looked forward to your arrival. Girls in my school were split into two camps, the deserts and the forests – and no little girl wanted to belong to the desert brigade forever.

Remember that mother-and-daughter night at school? A picture of a baby came onto the screen. Pink, smooth and innocent. And then we girls were told that grown-ups such as our blushing mothers were not just very big babies underneath their corsetry – they had hair in new places. A graphic showed us where you would appear to signal our transition to womanhood.

It became clear that to have a bush was a badge of honour. A badge I didn't have but yearned for.

I started scanning every inch of myself, checking for your arrival. Like a watched kettle, you didn't boil – until one day, when I mustn't have been looking, you suddenly boiled over. And didn't you cause a frenzy when you arrived?

Not that anyone else but me knew about your sprouting from what my mother called 'down there'. No, it was your lush embrace of my legs that caused a particular stir. Overnight I went from being called 'lucky legs' by my brothers – lucky they didn't break – to 'the girl with the mohair stockings'.

Mum would lower her voice while she was on the phone to her mates talking about you – as though you'd transformed me into something troubling. There was mention of hormone and chromosome tests and something called 'electrolysis'. Poor Mum. After two boys she'd been desperate to have a girl to decorate, and instead she found herself with a little ape on her hands. I could see the problem. Everybody could see the problem.

When I was in year twelve, a gang of boys held me down on the main street of town while I was on my way home from school. These were boys from my class. They wrestled me to the ground yelling instructions at each other – *grab her arms, hold her legs*. There was one boy sitting on my chest. Two more were holding my arms splayed back while the others were pulling the legs of my jeans up and my socks down. Look at it look at it, they screamed. White skin and black hairs – she's a dog.

I didn't tell Mum. Why share the shame? Instead I started dealing with you little bastards.

I always made a hash of shaving you. You were so stubborn that by the time I'd scraped you from my legs, blood would be oozing and trickling down them.

The summer between school and university I decided on a

strategy to deal with you that struck me as very practical. During the warmer months I'd do everything short of napalming myself to be free of you, but come winter you could have your own way, and stay happily hidden beneath my jeans.

Unfortunately, news spread among my peers about my special underwear, my mohair stockings. Again, another gang of young men decided I should be taught a lesson. They dragged me into a small college room, held me down and this time, you, my hairs, were shaved from me.

Actually, hairs, I'm sorry, I need to pull myself up here. I teach journalism. I should stop using the passive voice when I document the battle involving your existence.

You were not 'shaved from me'. The men shaved me. Much as I have also come to despise you I have to admit you've always been the innocent bystander in this war.

And my role? Well, I guess I've become the equivalent of the UN, proudly declaring your right to exist, free from attack – but I stopped defending you long ago.

Instead, I became complicit in your destruction. I've plucked at you for hours on end, one by one, as though, if I know each and every one of you, I can beat you.

I've set fire to a house, heating a wax pot on a gas burner – going for the big kill. And I've paid a not-so-small fortune for allied assistance in the war against you. Do you remember the German sisters who ran the Salon de Beauté in Albury? Hilda took one look at you on my legs and ran off screaming, 'Helga, Helga, come look! Zere are three hairs in the one follicle!'

I've gathered a veritable cache of weaponry to fight you. Tube upon tube of Nair – Christ knows what's in that stuff, I never dared read the label. A Philips Ladyshave. Five tubs of Agent Orange. And perhaps the most brutal of all weapons lurking in my arsenal – the Epilady.

As soon as I had a buck to my name, I invested it in having lasers turned upon you. I remember the smoke coming from my kneecaps as you frizzled down to the follicles, and the smell of your mass slaughter – like a dog thrown upon a barbecue.

Your numbers have sure taken a whack, but still I see you creeping back on my thighs, springing from my upper lip and even sprouting from the tops of my big toes.

One day my body will become a forgotten territory where, because of you, wars were fought and battles lost. I wonder about our futures. The worst I imagine is that one day I'll end up stuck in a nursing home and be incapable of fighting you – and there'll be no one else left who thinks it matters.

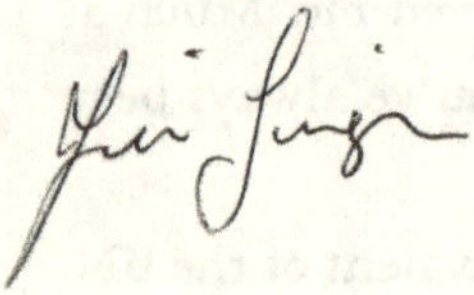

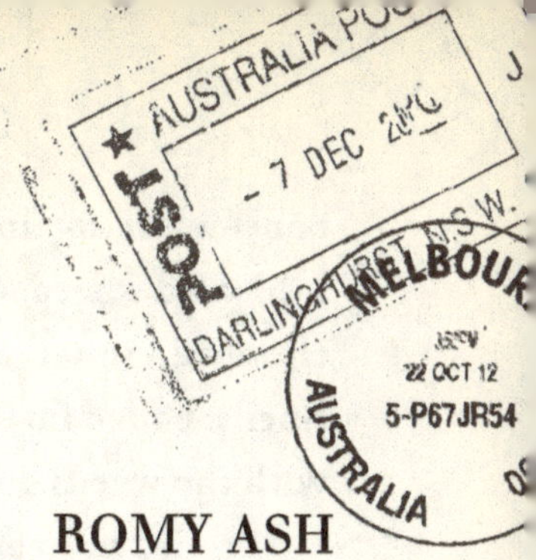

ROMY ASH

Dear Skin,

I don't have many scars, or stories to go with them. There's one from when I was five and tied my legs together with a dressing-gown cord and walked around as a gag. I split my chin open on the lounge-room floor. One, a shiny cross on my stomach, is from the removal of a benign mole. Not exactly riveting stuff. It's the things that don't show that are more interesting. The stories that are held inside. Experiences that should give a new skin, but don't.

This summer past I went canoeing in the Whanganui River in New Zealand. A guest of my boyfriend's family, who have farmed the banks since the forests were cleared and land parcelled. Luminous redheads, they look like they were all poured into and turned out of the same mould. I'd been joking for months about it being a spiritual journey.

We drove up the mountain, close to the birthplace of the river that gouged a way through deeply forested cliffs. Early the next morning we slipped the canoes, our *wakas*, into a tributary as the sky threw rain at us. Our life jackets were clipped over raincoats and jumpers. We were puffed up and waddling. Rain dripped off hat brims as if off awnings. As my feet left the silty floor, the river took us fast. Part of the bank crumbled into the muddy water.

Days before we'd driven to the river mouth. The beach was black sand and the driftwood clumped in tree-sized tangles, dried bone-white against the black. Caught among the branches was a bloated sheep carcass. On one side of the river the factories clumped, squat as barnacles. Their tops opened with different smells: boiled fat, blood, metallic burnt toast. These smells mingled with the weeds and salt.

I rolled my jeans up and walked to the water. The waves brown as the river. The water changed abruptly past the breakers from brown to deep blue. As if the ocean refused to have the river. The black sand clung to my feet for hours.

I understand how oceans move. I can read a beach. Tell where it's safe to swim. Waves are usually predictable; they come in patterns. But as the brown river took the *waka*, I realised I didn't understand this water at all. An eddy can take a canoe and hold it upright, and that morning our canoe gulped water.

Our guide, Charles, a Maori man who drove trucks for a living and whose smile opened him up like a split in a plastic bag, said every day it's a different river. The belly of a river shifts. What looks soft can be hard and sharp. Sometimes the river runs green. If there's no rain, it clears like the sky after a storm.

'A little *fresh* makes a great deal of difference,' he said. Rocks are immersed or bared in a snarl of foam. The water beneath the fresh is old, it's tidal for a long way, and the fresh water sits above it, like a hat. Each rapid has a name. As if in the naming they can be controlled, tamed.

When the rain stopped he told us stories, of war canoes that could fit 100 men, of missionaries who lost themselves by the banks of the river, of his grandmother who was watching us pass from her burial ground high atop a cliff. 'Around every corner is a *taniwha*,' he said. A mythical river dragon that shifts shape from story to story. With a shark's teeth and a dragon's body, it had always lain in wait in the river. Trees swept past, dark and wet, leaves stripped from the branches by the force of the water.

The man who drowned had a baby face and he was a joker. He was part of a large family group, relations of Charles, and they were half an hour in front of us on the river. When we landed at the *marae*, the meeting house where we would be welcomed and sleep, the man teased us and helped us carry our stow bags and barrels up the steep, muddy tracks. He sang Bob Marley's 'Zimbabwe' from beginning to end. His deep voice absorbed by the damp forest.

We walked slowly and carefully, placing our wet river shoes firmly on the mud. None of us fell. Later, his cousin told us that they were all waiting for us to fall, knew that we would fall. Because this was their land and we were *honkies*, whitefellas, stepping onto it for the first time. This was before we'd been welcomed and before the terrible thing happened.

The mud at the centre of the path sucked my feet. I tried to skirt its edges, stepping on the moss, apologising to the moss. I turned the moss to mud.

The path up the hill opened out onto a clearing. The forest standing up around it. During the *pōwhiri*, a ceremony to welcome us, a storm threw its weight, howling through the trees, drenching us to our already damp, creaking bones. We all stood there in the rain as voices were lifted through the forest with the wind.

When we were welcome, the wind ceased abruptly. Sunlight dripped off ferns. Tender tips unfurling. 'There's a doorway here,' said Charles, and he meant to the other side. But he cracked a smile and it was sunny and he took the children, and me, back down to the river to set an eel trap, a *henake*. The water looked thick as juice.

'There are three types of eel. The little ones are like caviar, caviar eel, and they run at a certain time of year. Then two larger eels. We're after the big eels. Going to deep fry them,' said Charles. He had a way of talking that went right up at the end, like his words were trying to outrun him.

One of the younger boys, his name was Judge, had the *henake* under his arm. The cage slung over his shoulder with rope. He wore white gumboots, camo-print pants and shirt, and a fluoro pink beanie.

'I've got my purse,' he said and everyone laughed.

The canoes were staked into high ground with rope, but still bobbed on the surface of the water. Judge clambered to the tip. Dropping the trap into deep water. The rope ran away, fast.

'Too deep,' said Charles.

Judge hauled the rope back up, river water streaming down his arms, and dropped it closer to the bank.

'Good.' They knotted the rope tightly to the canoe. I watched the ribbon of the river, all one piece, running faster and higher.

In the morning the *henake* was still empty. 'This river's not giving nothing,' said Charles and shrugged. We readied ourselves for the day's paddle, tying bags to the ribs of the canoes.

The river had risen metres in the night. A waterfall spouted joyfully from the cliff opposite the bank.

We didn't see him go under; just the canoe full of men catching us up and then chasing the shadow of him down.

Our canoe shifted on the water. We were out in the quick. I pulled my paddle through the water. But it was as if the water was him now. I pulled through his skin, his bones, into a corner of his smile. Water dripped from the paddle as I pulled and plunged it back through the surface. I imagined him grabbing a hold of the paddle and pulling it in, pulling me in, and then I'd be under the water too. It was like we all belonged there. I didn't know what we were playing at, bobbing there on surface.

In the beginning a body is heavy. It's only after a week or so that we lose our weight, that we begin to float. The river gave him back eventually, weeks later, when the water was green and clear. His cousins found him right down near the river mouth, snagged on a submerged log, long after the official search party had been called off.

It took us days to paddle out. We paddled with him and with the river. Mud coating us in layers, drying and cracking, giving us each new skins. But when the river spat us out, we left him. The river cleared and our skins washed clean.

Romy Ash.

CLAIRY BROWNE

This letter topic to me speaks of flesh and gender. The body, and its natural shape and structure and the physical accents and attachments that we place on it. What we make of it against a backdrop of social pressures.

We are, as women, talking about a landscape worth looking at but also an intricate and complex mask worth studying and understanding. So all the little tributaries and spider-vein roads and curves and mountains have a story. And each part of our bodies affects our relationships with ourselves and the world. When I received this topic, I immediately thought of women I have known throughout my life and their relationships with their bodies, both empowered and tarnished, and the way that this places them in a world full of judgement and criticism. I thought of the female body in two ways: the natural form and the adornments and accessories we don to further make an impression of our identity on the world. I think the relationships with both these 'things' on our bodies, the things that naturally 'are' and the things we choose to put on, are so deeply entwined.

And then I thought about my body. With its thirty-one years of making statements. You would need a map and a good compass to navigate my body. She is scarred and pillaged, primped and preened, adorned with false decorations, and has seen joy and evil in the same breath. She has been through a lot. As a child she knocked elbows and made scabs, lost balance and broke teeth, got bumped and bullied, did competitions where her knees were tied to other kids' knees, got sick, got better, grew a little, got drunk, danced, ran, sat very still and cried in a crumpled heap. She has, in her time, fucked, frolicked, held kittens and babies, and been bruised by battle and burned by the sun. Been pierced and prodded in places unseen, been content with food or yearned for touch. She grew fat, grew thin, grew fat again, acquiring stretch marks like river lines on a map, each one with a history of its own. She has been girl and she has been adolescent and she has been woman. Changing shape and taking on different decorations throughout her years. She is a testimony to my travels.

I want to address my letter to that thing on my body that makes me woman, naturally and courageously, that thing that makes a statement boldly about my journey from self-loathing to empowerment, in all its robust glory.

Dear Arse,

When I was a child we were estranged; you meant nothing to me. You were just one of a joined-up bunch of parts, sewn together by sinew and muscle. You were indistinguishable from other arses until I hit thirteen. Then, after that, you found a way to speak and be heard.

You grew. Not just out to the sides but through all angles and dimensions – your proportions changed, like a morbid growth upon teenage misery.

So I hated you. I sincerely despised you. You made me feel bulky in the '90s, when all I wanted to do was drown in an ocean of cocaine chic, looking exactly like Kate Moss in a Calvin Klein ad.

I tried to hide you under big jeans or oversized shirts but you still remained prominent and unfazed. I stood in front of the mirror and pushed you down to try to flatten you out, but still you held your ground. You were a mystery of genetics to me. Nothing like you had presented itself on my mother or my mother's mother. I trawled through family albums to find the guilty predecessor who had cursed me with you. My mother's mother looked like Elizabeth Taylor, with glorious full breasts and beehived hair. But no booty. You were an orphan, with no visible roots. I learned from that reliable cornerstone of our misogynist television generation, Al Bundy in *Married with Children*, that big arses make you unattractive. I remember distinctly an episode where he was assessing a whole lot of ladies underwear hanging on a clothes line and when he got to the larger pairs he shook his head and screwed up his face. Comical. Perhaps. For me at the time it was like discovering I belonged to the not-hot club.

Not that I take Al Bundy's word for gospel. I could never understand why he didn't want to have sex with his wife. Peggy Bundy was, in my mind, totally hot. She later became a fashion icon of mine with her tight leggings and big hair and overt femininity. Her body was whole and real and she had an arse. Which, in Al's book (along with being his wife) made her unappealing in the sexy stakes.

And it wasn't just Al – other little birdies also told me my arse wasn't a good arse. In magazines and movies, the buzz word was 'waif'.

You became well acquainted with my jumper, tied carefully in a knot around my waist and hanging over you to shield you from the eyes of the world.

In high school, there were these mirrored doors that you could see your reflection in when you were walking towards them. I knew just the right lines in the pavement to walk within so I couldn't see my mirrored self or you beneath that jumper. And in bed at night we were worst enemies. I would lie with every limb outstretched so that no part of my body touched you, because if they did I would be reminded of your existence.

Our coexistence was so toxic. Mind and arse at war. No room for a peace talk.

And then something changed.

I started listening to hip-hop. I found solace in the sweet, dulcet rhymes of Sir Mix-a-Lot's 'Baby Got Back' and Wreckx-n-Effect's 'Rumpshaker'.

Meanwhile you were developing a poise of your own, one I had no control over. You would wiggle your way down the supermarket aisle even if no one was watching. I hate to say it, but you became braver than me. You would shimmy behind me even on those days I had no confidence and had to work. And as I got older I realised that all these women around me I knew – sister, mother, friend, lover – all of us have these warped and tenuous relationships with our bodies. And I began to think: Who are we beneath this and how on God's earth did we get to be so far removed from it?

My sister and I tripped on acid one night in Tokyo. And she held up her legs as if seeing them for the first time and said, 'Are these my legs? How embarrassing!' We laughed about it many times. And how telling it is. To all those like me with a bad relationship with their arse, thighs, breasts, skin, hips, knees, whatever earns your relentless scorn – I would like to ask sincerely: 'Is this our relationship with our bodies? How embarrassing!'

I realised there must be a way to right this wrong, for me to make friends with you for the first time, and hold you with pride, and work you like you should be worked. Unveil you and shake you and celebrate you in a crowded room or alone beneath the sheets with a lover. So, after reflecting on what got me to the point of repulsion and utter disgust with you, wishing and hoping you would change, I came to understand that if I bounced you with my strut with self-acceptance and attitude, then you were immediately my ally rather than my enemy.

So I took a simple three-step program to help me love you.

Step one: Hang around big-butt enthusiasts to show myself good examples of women-to-arse relationships.

Finding big-butt enthusiasts wasn't hard. Candy Bowers' show

Australian Booty was a great beginning. I figured everyone in the audience was sure to love arse, and if they didn't before the show, they surely would after. So I loitered in the lobby after the show and looked for kindred spirits.

I began to dress to show you off and let you lead the dance. Friends of arse just came out of the woodwork then, and I saw that my initial shame of you paled in comparison to the glory you render.

Through finding friends of arse, I began to mend my broken relationship with you and see you as not only glorious for your size but a loyal assistant to me when impressing my proud femme identity on the world.

Step two: Embrace hip-hop culture. Hip-hop has been telling me to love you since before Tupac and Biggie's mothers were growing them in their bellies. Hip-hop gave me many pet names to call you adoringly: booty, jelly, junk, honky Tonk badonkadonk.

LL Cool J's 'Big Ole Butt' challenged the idea that skinny women were the ultimate object of desire and beauty. In his own words he praises the bigger buttocks without shame and it gave me hope. There are folks out there, albeit probably complete dickheads, who were prepared to leave their girlfriends just for a big booty. So it made me look at you differently. You and I could work as a team. To be empowered and feminine and desirable and proud. Even try our hand at a bit of home wrecking. If that's what we wanted, of course. Really, we could do anything.

And the ladies want to celebrate their own junk. Lady is twerking, Missy is working, and Nicki Minaj sets the standard, showing us what a healthy and loving relationship between a woman and her butt should be. She and her arse have the best relationship ever. I want us to be like them. Walking hand in hand into the sunset. Taking on a history of denigration and self-punishment and turning it into power.

It is undeniable that embracing hip-hop culture made me think that perhaps I should give you more credit than I have.

You and I together, I realised, could take on the world.

Step three: Reconcile with my body by being outwardly proud of you and wearing you with confidence and sass.

Reclaim the prowess that I denied you for so long. These days I like to use you to slam car doors closed, to open the door of a local restaurant with a 'Whoomp! There it is!' and make a goddamn entrance! You are my queen and I herald it for the world to take heed. I'll cover you in sequins and let you sway under the lights.

So I'm writing you this letter. Forgive me for taking so long.

Forgive me for all the names I called you, the hoodies I tied around you to mask you and the times I starved you in hopes that you would just shrink away. I ask that you allow me to love and honour you from now on, because you make me a woman. Allow me to shake the shit out of you on every dance floor until I just can't shake you any more.

I sincerely hope that, through my open healing and overt appreciation for you now, other women will start from the tips of their toes and little by little attempt to make the most of their attributes, and try and make amends with their loathing. Make little less burden, make most of flesh.

I still have days where you piss me off. Days when I allow the dark seed of comparison to sprout.

On those days, I dig out my short shorts, bundle you up nice and tight and take you once around the dance floor with LL Cool J.

And by the end of it, we are tight again.

Clairy
Browne
xxx

To my U-turn

TRACEE HUTCHISON

Dear Tom,

I suspect you're long gone to the highway in the sky now.
I'm not even sure you'd recognise the nickname I gave you.
It's a name I've ascribed in rose-tinted retrospect.
And I've come to love you more and more,
As the years put more distance between us.

Like many profound loves, I didn't recognise it at the time.
And I didn't think to tell you. Yes, I took you for granted.
Too busy with my preoccupations to really appreciate you,
Or bother to let you know.

But I loved you. And the flights of fancy you afforded.
The way you hugged my body in all the right places – from behind.
That first taste of unbridled freedom – to be what I wanted to be,
It still gives me goosebumps.

You were no-nonsense, functional and pragmatic.
Just sleek-lined efficiency.
I loved your smell and your ability to take me places I never thought possible.
The U-ies and the hook turns that seemed to defy logic.

One eye on the journey ahead – and the other on the road just travelled. Clear and demisted. Even when it rained.

I loved how you shimmered for me,

In your trademark 1970s metallic-green coat.

And your three on the tree –

None of that fancy four on the floor for you and me.

I loved the power under your hood.

And the way you responded so willingly at the slightest touch.

And those nights of sexual gymnastics amid the gear stick and the handbrake and the bucket seats.

But I was ruthless with you.

And, once you'd taken me where I needed to go, I traded you for a younger model.

I had eyes on other prizes.

Another man. Another city. Another life.

Highway 31. The Deadly Hume. Sin City.

I packed you up and pointed you north.

And you carried me away from all that I knew – like a Paul Kelly song all yearning and lovesick.

It all started off innocently enough.

You drove me to my fate like a spring lamb to the slaughter.

A rock and roll adventure.

A roll of the dice . . . The night that changed my life.

And a U-turn that took twenty years of painful stop-starts to complete.

Looking back, it would have been the little things that gave the game away.

The radio flicked from AM rotations to FM alternatives.
Access all areas passes in the glove box,
'No Nukes' stickers on the rear window,
As I traded suburban safety for the bright lights of harm,
And lost myself in the temper of the times.

But I had to go. We both knew that.
Had to be in the world and find whatever it was I was looking for.

Had to understand how a love so intoxicating could be so cruel.
Had to feel my heart shatter like glass and withstand it.
Had to find my way back to myself and trust in love again.

It seems a hundred lifetimes ago now, Tom.

But when I see myself there – side of stage – the crowd in a zealot-like frenzy – I can almost touch it.

Wondering what I might have been.

But you were solid as a rock, patiently cooling your treads.

There, when I found the courage to walk away.

There, as I picked myself back up and courted your replacement as a symbolic gesture to draw a line . . .

You must have been indignant when I drove you to that wreckers' yard on Sydney's northern beaches,

A sporty, bright-yellow Toyota sitting in your place at home.

But you went quietly and stoically.

And I just walked away.

Left you there to be crushed as brutally as the memories you contained had crushed me.

That cheery canary was just the first in a string of infidelities and vehicular peccadilloes.

I left her in Darwin with all the other broken hearts and misfits after she blew a head gasket when I wasn't thinking somewhere between Darwin and Katherine.

I slunk ashamedly into a Pulsar for a while.

But the Pulsar was sluggish and I upscaled to an Alfa.

Yes. I got some tickets on myself for a while there.

But the Alfa was pure folly. It spent more time on a hoist than on the road, so I ended up in a Datsun that looked a bit like you . . .

That's when I started turning for home.

The first attempt at a U-turn was in a car that felt a bit like you.

I pointed south.

And found myself in a battle of wills with the me I left behind.

Up and down the Deadly Hume I travelled,

Lost in a highway limbo.

Forever stuck in that halfway place between Gundagai and Holbrook. Never quite leaving or arriving.

Until finally I did. Just found the courage one day to be.

And so I came home. In a brand new Toyota.

Four-cylinder. Japanese. Pragmatic.

Not flashy – despite her name.

She's a Starlet. Yes. A Starlet.

Gleaming silver for visibility.

I've still got her. And I think you'd like her.

She handles well and responds to the slightest touch.

And she completed that U-turn for me –

The one we started all those years ago,

On that fateful October night at a rock and roll gig in 1981.

That day we packed up and headed out on the Hume,

Just you and me.

Tommy Torana. My 1970 SL.
My prized – and once precious – very first car.
Four doors, sleek lines and three on the tree.
With your body-hugging seat and powerful bonnet.
In shimmering metallic green.

We shared some history, and some miles, you and I.

You showed me how to see the world with one eye on the road ahead and one eye over my shoulder.

I still see the world that way.

It's helped me put my heart back together.

And I wish I'd kept you,

Just so I could thank you in person

For not taking me home on that October night in 1981.

And for lighting the path of the journey of my life – that day on the Hume when we set off on a twenty-year U-turn – that finally brought me home.

Tracee X

JEN CLOHER

On 4 March 2007, I moved to Auckland at my father's request. A year earlier, my mother had been diagnosed with Alzheimer's disease. Although both my parents grew up in New Zealand, they'd moved to Australia before I was born, returning twenty years later when Mum was offered a position at the University of Auckland. I didn't really know anyone there aside from a few relatives, so it was with some trepidation that I found myself sixteen years later, at the age of thirty-three, once again living under their roof.

The move came at a difficult time. My first album had just been nominated for an ARIA and after many years of hard work, offers were beginning to come my way. It felt like a missed opportunity to be relocating to live in Auckland, but as their only child I didn't have a choice. I knew I had to be there.

My parents lived in a two-storey house along the Eastern Bays of Auckland overlooking the Hauraki Gulf. In the distance you could see Rangitoto, a now-extinct volcanic island. The neighbourhood was quiet and conservative, consisting of families or professional retirees like my parents. I lived downstairs, so each morning I would go up to say hello, make coffee and then come back down to Mum's study. For the remainder of the morning I would sit at my mother's desk, staring out the window, trying to write a new album. Her study, once a hub of academic achievement, was now a mess of scrawled notes to self and handwritten instructions furiously underlined with red pen:

1. Turn power on at the wall. 2. Push ON button below desk. 3. Wait for computer to load. 4. Type in username 'Dorothy', password 'Nunky'.

A couple of years earlier my mother had written a book about the famous warrior chief Hongi Hika. It caused controversy among certain Maori factions but received utmost praise from New Zealand's most accomplished historian, the late Michael King. Mum told me she was writing the book as quickly as she could because her memory wasn't as strong as it had been. We never suspected the diagnosis that was around the corner; Alzheimer's only happened to people who didn't do crosswords enough.

Although Mum had been diagnosed with dementia, she was in heavy denial. At the Alzheimer's Association support group, Dad and I were told this was a normal reaction, that in many cases the sufferer never fully comprehended their condition or the toll it took on those around them. Mum would spend most of the day in her favourite armchair with her cat, Pushkin, looking out to sea and dozing. On brighter days, she would scan the headlines of the newspaper or look at old photo albums of her family.

Mum was the youngest of a family of ten, five boys and five girls born to a Yugoslav father and a Maori mother. Raised in the far north of New Zealand, they had a windswept wildness about them. Handsome, dark-haired and lean. As Mum's disease progressed, she would speak more and more of her childhood, recounting fond memories of her father, Jim, placing ceramic jugs of homemade wine on the dinner table which the children were allowed to drink.

One day, as I was listening to Mum, it occurred to me that it would be a good idea to take her back to her childhood stomping ground. The plan was to catch a thirty-minute flight from Auckland to Kaitaia, pick up a hire car at the airport and drive to my cousin's motel at Ninety Mile Beach. We would spend two nights there, take a look around at some of Mum's old haunts, and then fly home. The first part of the plan went well. Mum enjoyed the flight in the twelve-seater plane and in the car out to Ninety Mile Beach she recognised a lot of the little towns and landmarks, pointing them out to me as we drove by. It wasn't until dinner with our cousins that she began to grow tired. I could see Mum wasn't really sure who they were or how she knew them, but kept up a polite front, smiling and going along with it.

Seeing her exhaustion, I excused us from the table early. We walked back to our room, brushed our teeth and went to bed. As we lay in the dark I could hear Mum was finding it difficult to sleep, moving around in the bed restlessly and sighing. Then, in a tiny voice: 'Tom, are you awake?'

'No, Mum, it's me, Jennifer. We're in Kaitaia for the night having a holiday, we'll see Dad on Friday.'

'Oh,' she responded.

Then, five minutes later: 'Tom, are you awake?'

'No, Mum, it's me.'

'Oh, where's Tom?'

'He's at home in Auckland.'

'Why didn't he come with us?'

'He didn't want to. Besides, we're having a girls' holiday, just the two of us.'

'Oh, where are we?'

'We're in Kaitaia, Mum, where you grew up.'

'Oh.'

And then a minute later: 'Tom, are you awake?'

'No, Mum, it's me, Jennifer.'

'Where's Tom?'

'He's at home in Auckland.'

'Why?'

'Because we wanted to take a holiday just you and me together, mother and daughter.'

'Oh . . . I want to go home.'

'But you are home, Mum. We're in Kaitaia where you grew up.'

'No. I don't remember this place. I want to go home to Tom and Pushkin.'

'We'll go home in the morning, Mum. Just sleep now, you're safe. We'll see Dad tomorrow.'

Just as I was falling asleep, the light came on. Mum stood there in her nightie like a frightened little girl. 'I don't know where we are. I want to go home.'

'But we can't right now, Mum, we're up north and it's very late. We'll head home in the morning when we've rested.'

Mum turned out the light and got back into bed but I could hear by her breathing that she was starting to panic. I lay there feeling entirely overwhelmed and helpless. In that moment I wanted more than anything in the world to magically teleport us back home. I hated hearing my mother's distress and not being able to do anything to comfort her. I looked at my phone. It was only midnight. The thought of spending the next six hours this way felt like an eternity. So we got up, packed our bags and got in the car.

The drive back to Auckland was five hours of winding coastal road in the rain and I had moments of feeling insane. Mum stayed awake for the whole journey home, asking every five minutes where we were going and then, on receiving the explanation, apologising for not being able to remember where we were. 'What's wrong with me, Jennifer?' she asked at one point.

I realised after that trip that my mother was no longer capable of long journeys away. My romanticised pilgrimage, having failed miserably, helped me see that all Mum wanted was my company. The past Mum spoke about was in her heart. All I needed to do was to give her my full attention. Mum was happiest when I sat with her on the balcony, in the moment, just being.

Last year on my birthday, Dad died suddenly from pneumonia.

He'd been living with Parkinson's for over two years and was exhausted. I was in Melbourne but took the first flight out when I heard about the diagnosis, arriving just a few hours before he went. I sat next to his hospital bed, stroking his forehead and singing 'The Longing Song', his favourite of mine. As I sang, I saw the pained expression on his face relax and his breathing slow. 'You can go now, Dad. I'll take care of Mum, don't worry.'

Mum had moved into full-time care a year earlier when things had become too unmanageable at home, and Dad would go to visit her each day. The staff at the Alzheimer's ward said they would often find them sitting together in the morning holding hands.

On Christmas Day, Mum and I had lunch together at her care unit. It felt strange not having Dad there. After a rather lacklustre pudding we sat in the lounge room and I played some songs on my guitar. I sang a song I had written for Mum a few years ago, one of her favourites called 'Mother's Desk'. Halfway through her eyes lit up with recognition: 'Now I know who you are! You're my daughter, Jennifer.' That evening around 8 p.m. my mother suffered a massive heart attack, dying in her bed just three months after Dad.

On 4 March 2007, it had seemed like such a step backwards to be moving to Auckland. I would never have guessed that in just five years so much would change. To care for my parents, to earn their complete trust, to be a daughter and to witness the transformative power of music right up until the last moments of their lives, is the greatest step forward I could have taken.

Love
Jen xxx

EVA DE JONG-DULDIG

Eva's U-turn
Poste Restante
The Outernet

My dear U-turn,

Henri and I were really sorry you couldn't join us to celebrate our fiftieth wedding anniversary, especially as my friendship with you was at the heart of our decision to marry in the first place. This letter will remind you of how we met, though, when I think about it, my parents and I had been fortunate to come across other members of your family much earlier.

I was born on 11 February 1938, in Vienna, and Hitler marched into the city one month later. Austria became part of Nazi Germany with disastrous consequences for Vienna's 200000 Jewish citizens. At first my artist parents, Karl and Slawa, went about their normal routine, focusing most of their energy on their new baby. At this point surely one of your relatives intervened, for a bizarre accident thrust my father into imminent danger of arrest by the Nazis, and my mother urged him to leave Vienna immediately.

Your relatives played a substantial part in our story for the next four years. First Karl was lucky enough to get a tourist visa to Switzerland. There a friendly immigration official, Mr Ernst Speck, in return for Karl modelling his portrait, issued my mother a visa so that we could join my father in Switzerland. Then a telegram reading 'Opportunity Singapore' arrived, which prompted us to leave Europe.

My parents adjusted quickly to life in Singapore, their new refuge. They established a successful art school and Karl also received some fantastic commissions, including a contract to execute four life-size sculptures in bronze for the multi-millionaire manufacturer of the Tiger Balm ointment, Aw Boon Haw. They would have stayed happily in this tropical haven for the rest of their lives.

But in September 1940 your Singapore relative came along to spoil the fun.

Because we held German papers, we were classified as 'enemy aliens', so the British authorities deported us to Australia where we were interned in Tatura. In Internment Camp 3D I had lots of playmates and wandered freely within the barbed-wire compound, but for my parents it was a traumatic experience.

As it turned out, however, it seems that your Singapore relative knew more about what was good for us than we did, for in February 1942 Singapore fell to the advancing Japanese army. A disastrous military setback for the Allies, this nevertheless prompted the Australian government to offer 'enemy alien' internees the opportunity to enlist in the Australian army. Soon Karl was peeling potatoes for army kitchens in the 8th Employment Company in Royal Park, and Mum and I came to Melbourne.

We became 'Australians' in 1946. My parents re-established their shattered lives and rebuilt their professional careers. At school it was my sporting ability, rather than my brains, that gained me the acceptance I craved among my peers. With dozens of tennis courts in the immediate vicinity of our house and encouraged by my father, I soon became a leading Victorian tennis player. However, with no opportunity to pursue a viable sporting career, I went to university, became a teacher and only played tennis at weekends and during school holidays.

After more than three years of teaching, I decided to pursue a long-held dream to play at Wimbledon, so in 1961 I took six months unpaid leave, bought a return airline ticket with Qantas and travelled alone to the other side of the world. With a respectable Australian record and good pre-Wimbledon form, I was accepted straight into the main draw in the singles, doubles and mixed doubles.

Watching Wimbledon on TV last week reminded me again of the feverish excitement, the crowds around every court, the ivy-covered, perfectly proportioned and intimate centre court, and the players who came from all over the world to compete on its hallowed lawns.

Today Hawk-Eye watches the lines, there is a retractable roof over the centre court and security is everywhere. However, the players still wear white, the game is still played on grass and the fans are as enthusiastic as ever. Back then, though, in all our wildest dreams we could never have imagined the prize money on offer to first-round losers today, let alone the £1.15 million earned by Serena Williams, this year's Ladies' Champion. In 1961 each competitor received £50 and a silver pen to commemorate the seventy-fifth anniversary of the Championship!

On the first day of the tournament, the children of my host family, wide-eyed with awe, watched as the limousine flying the distinctive purple and green Wimbledon flag picked me up. As we drove through London's streets, people stared at me as if I were royalty. The wrought-iron Wimbledon gates opened to more peering eyes and, once out of the car, I was besieged by autograph hunters intent on getting signatures from every single competitor.

Tall and athletic, the top-ranking German player, Renata Osterman, expected little opposition from her first-round opponent – an 'unknown' Australian. But she had no inkling of the adrenaline that accompanied me onto Court 5 that day. Playing for my country and my heritage, I had travelled a long way to fulfil a dream and had nothing to lose.

I won the first set comfortably. Renata's friends, who sat on the grass alongside the umpire's chair, talked to her at every change of end. Soon I had lost the second set. It was one–love to me in the decider and as we changed ends I walked over to the group and said, *Wir spielen diesen Satz ohne Hilfe bitte.* (*We'll play this set without help please.*) Their mouths gaped but not another word was uttered for the rest of the match. Renata was thoroughly unnerved and I won comfortably. Next day a telegram arrived. *Congratulations! Parents.* My parents had heard the result in the daily Wimbledon report at 6.45 a.m. on ABC radio. On a high, I won round two in straight sets and offered spirited resistance in the third round before bowing out of the singles to the eventual winner of the tournament, the American player Karen Hantze.

In the ladies' doubles, together with my South African partner, Marlene Gerson, I reached the quarterfinal. The match was played on Stadium Court One where the applause from the adjacent Centre Court was clearly audible. We knew full well that, if successful, we would play the semi-final on that court. But it never happened. On day ten I was out of the tournament, having achieved far more than I ever expected, with lots of impressive newspaper clippings to add to my scrapbook, and resigned to the fact that I would never play at Wimbledon again.

But at that point I had not counted on meeting you, my dear U-turn.

My last scheduled tournament before returning home was in the 6th Maccabiah Games in Israel.

I had been travelling for five months and was feeling a bit homesick. Harry Stanton, my Australian mixed-doubles partner, hand-delivered a letter from my parents. Inside the envelope, wrapped in blue airmail writing paper, was a small balsa wood clog. The clog had been lovingly carved by the skilled hands of my mother. I wondered about its significance but my mother was too far away to ask, so

I popped it in my red travel bag as a lucky mascot.

Competitors from all participating countries shared the few available tennis courts in Tel Aviv. One day Harry introduced me to Henri, a member of the Dutch tennis team, whose surname I could not get my tongue around. A charming, good-looking young man, he offered to carry my bags.

Five days later Henri and I were sitting beside the swimming pool in the athlete's village when we decided to spend the rest of our lives together. I knew this would mean that life as I had known it would never be the same, but at the time I had a lot of faith in you, my dear U-turn, in your friendship and in your wisdom.

I drafted the following telegram to my parents:

5 Sept 1961

To Duldig Caulfield East Vic
Fly Holland September 10 with prima Dutch boy.
Meeting his parents. Should like permission to get engaged.
Friends managers family think it wonderful like me. Return
Australia end September. Express letter follows. Love Eva
Henri

My parents telegraphed back:

Eva Duldig Maccabiah Ramat Gan Israel
Very happy awaiting anxiously express letter love parents.

Henri's parents were on holiday and could not be contacted.

My opponent in the final in Tel Aviv was none other than Marlene, my doubles partner from Wimbledon. We battled it out for three close sets on those hot clay courts in the middle of the city before I emerged victorious.

Marlene and I embraced across the net and she said, 'You had everything going for you today.'

'What do you mean?' I asked.

'You could not lose – you're in love!'

I was nearer to Holland than Henri to Australia so it was decided I would travel to Holland to meet the 'de Jong' family. (By this time I at least knew how to spell and pronounce my future surname!) My return London/Melbourne ticket did not accommodate a Tel Aviv–Amsterdam detour, so the Dutch team manager suggested I join the team's charter flight back to Amsterdam. Without a ticket, and wearing the wrong uniform, I walked onto the plane in Tel Aviv and four hours later walked off the plane in Amsterdam without any problems whatsoever.

After a couple of weeks in Holland, I flew back to Australia and returned to my teaching job. Henri and I exchanged letters for five months and in February 1962 we were married in Melbourne.

I went to live in Holland and contrary to my earlier expectations I competed at Wimbledon twice more. I learned the Dutch language, became Dutch National Tennis Champion and represented Holland in the first Federation Cup in London in 1963 as well as in international matches throughout Europe.

The little balsa wood clog carved by my mother still sits on my bedside table. I often look at it and wonder how much influence it and you, dear U-turn, had on the momentous decisions I made in 1961 – decisions which undeniably changed my life.

Affectionately,
Eva

PS You have been there for me ever since 1961 and I am so glad we are still good friends. Together we have achieved a great deal and I hope this will continue for a while yet. Enclosed is our fiftieth wedding anniversary brochure, which I think you will enjoy. And by separate mail I am sending you a bottle of Faith. The label reads: 'It was a leap of Faith that combined the vines from Austria and the Netherlands to be planted in Australia in 1962. In the ensuing fifty years a perfectly balanced blend was developed in a friendly climate, and it is anticipated this will further mature with careful ageing.' Enjoy.

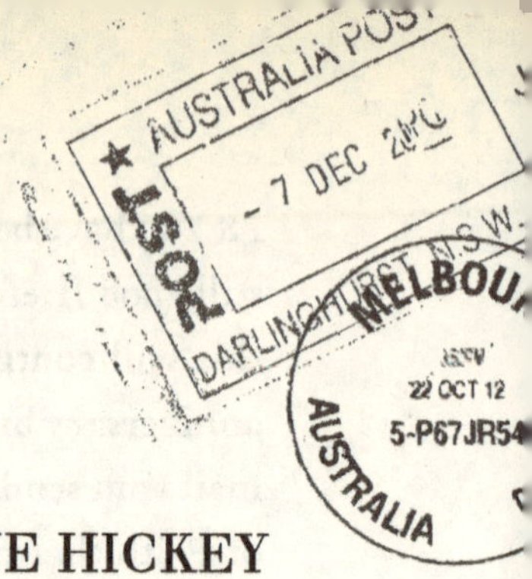

GERALDINE HICKEY

I remember when we first met. I was sitting at home one day and I was quite bored so I thought I would go to Kmart to buy a book. Sure, most people would go to a bookstore to buy a book, but to be perfectly honest I had been making my way through the Tomorrow, When the War Began series and I knew Kmart had them on sale for $12 each. Yes, I am probably too old to be reading a book you are required to read in Year Eight English, but I have the attention span of a fourteen year old, so I like books aimed at teenagers. I like them because shit happens and that shit happens without the use of big words. I do not care for struggles with postmodern existential existence; I just want to know who dies and when. I also really like books about sharks and crocodiles. Especially crocodiles – I don't know how to convey to you how much I love crocodiles, but trust me when I say it is a lot. In fact, it would require another letter altogether to express it.

However, Kmart did not have any of the books I was after, so I had to resort to plan B. I made my way to the entertainment section and stood in front of a wall of DVDs. That's when I met you. I had heard of you, people had said good things about you, and you were wearing an enticing red sticker that read 'Sale $25'. I took you off the shelf and made my way to the checkout. The girl at the checkout picked you up, looked at you and said, '*The L Word*. I've heard this is a good show.'

'Me too,' I replied.

I handed over my cash and made my way home. Once I was there, you and I went to my bedroom. I didn't want to share you with anyone else. I wanted to lie on my bed and watch you with my laptop resting on my belly, then, when it got too hot, to move it to the left of my head. Never on the right side, though. I don't know why but it just doesn't work.

I was hooked on you from the first episode. I found your lead character to be highly relatable, the other characters were entertaining and the cheesy storyline kept me wanting more. Before I knew it I had watched, to paraphrase Crowded House, 'A whole season in one day.'

You were my first step in realising I was gay. You didn't make me gay – you made me acknowledge it. I guess it's the same as when a fat person realises they are obese after they see themselves eating a pie in slow motion on the big screen at the MCG. They always knew they were fat; they just hadn't acknowledged it. I did start compiling a list at that stage of 'signs I may have missed'. Little things, like that I look good in purple, or the fact I don't wear makeup. Or that I don't own a hairbrush but my fingernails are always well groomed. Or that I own only three pairs of shoes, all of them sneakers. Or that time I had a cock in my mouth and did a tiny vomit. You know, just little things.

Days turned into weeks, weeks turned into months, and pretty soon you were forgotten. I stopped wondering if I was gay and started wondering how many deaths in the world crocodiles are responsible for every year. It's roughly 3000, but as a lot of deaths in Africa and Asia are not recorded, it's hard to say. Sorry I have gone off topic but, like I said, I have a short attention span.

I was in Adelaide for the Adelaide Fringe Festival, and a good friend of mine, Hannah, was organising a late-night gig. She asked me to do a spot and I said I would be delighted. The night before the gig, Hannah rang to tell me there was a theme for the night.

'It's very loose,' she said, 'but if you want to do something with it you can. Anyway, the theme is "boy or girl".'

I hung up the phone, shrugged my shoulders and thought to myself, Well, I guess I'll just come out then, and that's what I did. I didn't put too much thought into it. It was like someone had come up to me and said, 'Excuse me, would you like a piece of cake?' and I thought about it and went, 'Yeah, I fucking love cake. Hey everyone, I fucking love cake, can somebody please bring me a cake so I can munch on it?'

I soon started telling more people that I was gay. Telling strangers was easy as I was constantly doing it at gigs and tweeting it, and I wrote a comedy festival show about it. However, when it came to telling my parents, I didn't know how to do it. I didn't want to make it a big deal but at the same time it *is* a big deal. It wasn't like I was worried what their reaction would be – I was pretty confident they were going to be cool with it. This was mainly due to a brief period five years ago when my father went around telling everyone I was gay. I denied it when I found out and told Mum to make him stop saying it. I know, you'd think I would have realised then. I mean, my dad had worked it out and he doesn't even own a gaydar. But I wasn't going to come out because someone told me I was gay. I'm Geraldine Hickey and no one tells me what to do.

Six months went past before I told my parents. Then one day I was sitting in a beer garden with one of my best friends, Harley. He pointed out that I really needed to tell my parents. I agreed but was still at a loss as to how to do it. We discussed different scenarios, none of which I was happy with. An hour later my phone rang. Harley looked down at the name displayed on the screen: 'Oh, it's your mum.'

I picked up the phone and said, 'I guess I'll just tell her now then.'

Harley looked at me wide-eyed and asked, 'Really?'

'No,' I replied. I saw Harley's shoulders relax when he discovered

I was joking. Then I thought, Hang on a minute, this is probably the perfect time to do it. It didn't matter how it would pan out, since I knew that at the end I could hang up the phone and get a big hug from my best friend.

Mum had called to give me the Kris Kringle list for Christmas. Once we had that sorted I said, 'So, Mum, I'm just sitting here with Harley doing some work on the show. Do you want to know what the show is about?'

'Oh, yes,' she replied.

'All right then, Mum, you might want to sit down for this one, it's a big one. The show is about me coming out and telling everyone I'm gay, because I'm gay.'

There was a slight pause before my mother replied with, 'So is this true or is it just for the show?'

'It's true. So how are you?'

'Well, I can't say that I'm that happy about it,' she answered, 'but as long as you're happy.'

'I am happy. I'm very happy'

She then asked if I wanted to tell my dad. I asked her what she thought I should do and we decided that she would tell him just so he could hear it from someone face to face. I agreed to have my phone with me in case he wanted to talk or ask any questions. I hung up the phone, got a big hug from Harley and then we celebrated the momentous occasion with glasses of Coke.

I didn't hear back from my parents that night so I figured all went well. I woke the next morning with a text from my mum that said: 'Have not told your father, felt it wasn't my place. By the way, who have you told? And I can't say that I'm that happy about you putting it in a show.'

That was the moment my heart broke. To put it into perspective, the first show I ever did was about a week I spent in a psychiatric unit. Mum was cool with that. She was fine with everyone knowing

I was a loony but didn't want anyone to know I was gay. My mother was ashamed of me and that was a horrible, horrible feeling.

Not wanting to react with too much emotion, I left it for the day, and then the next day I wrote my parents an email.

I've included the email to make this a babushka letter. Get it? Because I have put a letter inside another letter. Never mind.

Dear Mum and Dad,

As much as I would like to sit down and tell you this news in person, I didn't know when the opportunity would present itself, and, to be honest, this way will probably be easier on all of us.

I'm gay. While this is not really news to me, I understand it certainly will be to you. However, you need to know that the only choice I've made here is the choice to accept that I'm gay – I haven't chosen to be gay. I feel extremely happy and comfortable with my decision and it feels like a large weight has been lifted off my shoulders. This may take some time for both of you to understand and that's okay, as long as you try. Maybe focus on the 'I'm really happy' part.

Feel free to talk to whoever you need to. Talking helps. And you don't need to be worried about who knows and doesn't know – I am not ashamed that I'm gay and I'm hoping you won't be either. I'm not saying you should go out and shout it from the rooftops; I'm just saying don't think you can't talk to a friend about what you are going through because you are worried you'll have to tell them I'm gay. Sally, Pauline and Therese already know so if you like you could start with them.

Also I will be talking about me being gay in my next

show. My comedy has always come from a place of honesty and I have no intentions of hiding who I am either onstage or off.

Please take some time to let this all sink in and know that I have not changed and am still the same daughter you always had.

Love,

Geraldine

PS No, I am not seeing anyone.

Later that afternoon I spoke to my father.

'I got your email,' he said.

'Yep,' I replied, terrified of what he would say next. Having one parent being disappointed and ashamed in you is bad enough.

He continued, 'And I just wanted to say that nothing has changed and you're my daughter and I love you no matter what.'

The relief I felt manifested itself in tears rolling down my cheeks. 'Thanks, Dad, that means a lot,' I said.

'I don't really know what I'm supposed to say,' he continued.

'Dad, what you just said was perfect, that's all I needed to hear. I know this is hard for you.'

'Yeah, it is a bit, but at the end of the day I love you. Always have and always will.'

'Thanks, Dad, I love you too.'

'Righto, talk to you tomorrow then.'

'Righto.'

We then hung up.

I didn't hear from Mum that day. In fact, I didn't hear from her for two weeks, which on the face of it is not that big a deal – there have probably been other two-week periods when my mum and I have not been in contact. But this was two weeks of my mum not talking to me because she was ashamed, and that made me feel awful.

She did make contact eventually. I was on Facebook one morning and the chat box popped up and it was Mum saying, 'Hello, Geraldine.' I know, I couldn't believe it either. She was all in the dark ages about me being gay but manages to nail social media. What the fuck?

Our relationship is fine now. At the end of the day, I can see how tough it was for her. The thing that I had forgotten to factor in when coming out to her was the fact that she is a conservative Catholic living in regional Australia – and not just any part of regional Australia, I'm talking the birthplace of Margaret Court. So two weeks is pretty good, really. My mum now carries a printed-out copy of the email to show everyone. What started out to be a source of shame is now something she pulls out to show people how proud she is of me.

I guess I wanted to write you this letter to thank you for this U-turn you have sent me on. It has been quite the journey. Sure, some of it wasn't easy, but this pretty rainbow road full of glitter feels like the track that will take me home and for that I thank you. I would also like an apology for the next five seasons of you. They were rubbish.

Geraldine
Hickey

To the woman who changed my life

ANDY GRIFFITHS

Dear Margaret,

It's been a long time since I last wrote – almost nineteen years, in fact. Things have changed a lot for me since then and that's in no small part thanks to you. Back in 1994 I was a struggling young writer with a crazy dream: a dream to create a book full of prank complaint letters, and any replies I might get. But your response to the very first letter I sent out set me on a completely different – and ultimately far more rewarding – course.

I'm guessing that you remember the letter but if you don't, it doesn't matter, because I have a copy.

29 May 1994

To whom it may concern,

I am writing to complain about an unpleasant experience that I had in one of your stores last Saturday morning.

After waiting for a long time in a checkout queue, I finally reached the cashier, who was working very slowly and seemed rather white in the face. I asked her whether she was feeling all right. She told me that there was nothing wrong and to mind my own business. I was surprised at her rudeness, but even more surprised when, a few moments later, she suddenly exploded, covering me and my three-year-old daughter in blood, flesh and guts. Immediately after the incident I complained to the manager who simply shrugged and said that it happened all the time and that it wasn't his fault.

This is simply not good enough! My daughter, who has never experienced this sort of thing before, had to be taken to hospital and treated for severe shock. It was also very inconvenient for me as I was wearing a hired suit for a wedding that I was attending that afternoon, and I not only had to return it to the hire shop to acquire another suit, but incurred the full replacement cost of a new suit as the first was too stained and damaged to be cleaned.

I do not seek reimbursement. All I wish to know is whether it is your company's policy to allow your employees to explode, without warning, in front of the customers. Surely there are rooms provided for your employees to explode discreetly without inconveniencing and upsetting the customers, and if not, why not?

Please lift your game! Unless I receive a full apology and explanation I will be taking my business elsewhere in future.

Yours sincerely,
Andy Griffiths

I made copies of the letter and sent them out to a number of department stores and supermarkets but you were the only one who replied. And quite promptly, too.

Target Australia Pty Ltd
31 May 1994

Dear Mr Griffiths,

We have received your letter, and were concerned to read your comments.

If at all possible, we would appreciate you contacting us so that we can discuss your comments with you. Our toll free number is 008 814 788, and we look forward to hearing from you shortly.

Sincerely yours,
Margaret Healy
National Customer Relations Manager

I was amazed! My complaint had gone straight to the top! I would have been happy with a reply from a state, or even regional, manager, but *national* customer relations manager was beyond my wildest dreams. And you were *concerned!* Clearly I was dealing with a company that took the potentially combustible nature of staff–customer relations seriously.

I guess I should have been happy, but to tell you the truth I felt kind of uncomfortable with the idea of wasting the time of somebody so important. Especially somebody who seemed so nice and so *concerned*.

The more I thought about it, the more it became clear to me that I had to abandon my prank. To have continued any further in this deception would have felt like taking advantage of your good nature and compassion.

But how? I couldn't just admit I'd been lying. It would have felt cheap and mean and you deserved better than that. It took me a while, but finally I hit on the perfect way out – one that has, throughout the ages, helped many a desperate writer extract themselves from a tight fictional corner.

2 June 1994

Dear Ms Healy,

Do you ever get the feeling that you are going insane and can't tell the difference between dreaming and real life? I do.

Please accept my apologies for my letter (29/5/94) in which I complained about an exploding cashier in one of your stores.

It was just an exceptionally vivid dream most probably caused by my habit of sleeping with too many blankets on my bed.

It took me a few days to realise that the incident in question hadn't actually happened, but by then it was too late and I'd already sent my letter.

Regards and apologies,
Andy Griffiths

I thought that would definitely be the end of it. But it wasn't. A few days later, this arrived:

Target Australia Pty Ltd
6 June 1994

Dear Mr Griffiths,

Thank you for writing to us and advising us that your letter of 29/5/94 was based on an incident of an ethereal rather than extant nature.

As a company that is totally committed to superior customer service, we want you to know how very relieved we were to learn of this.

Wishing you restful sleep and sweet dreams.

Sincerely yours,
Margaret Healy
National Customer Relations Manager

Bravo, Margaret. Bravo! 'Ethereal rather than extant nature' was a nice touch. So was wishing me 'restful sleep and sweet dreams'. You didn't have to do that. It was a business letter. But you went that extra step. Well, a *few* extra steps, actually.

I know you didn't *really* believe that a cashier had exploded in your store, but nevertheless you engaged with and responded to my letters in a lighthearted and playful way. And in doing so, you changed my life.

I found I liked having this sort of relationship with a reader and I wanted more. I began to wonder, what if, instead of piss-farting around wasting people's time, I wrote to amuse and entertain them? What if, instead of writing prank letters about exploding cashiers, I wrote *fiction* about exploding cashiers? And not just about exploding cashiers, either, but about lots of other exploding things as well: exploding cats, exploding dogs, exploding cows, exploding butterflies, exploding nativity scenes, exploding bums and even exploding explosions.

Which is pretty much what I've spent the last nineteen years doing, thanks to you, Margaret. Because of you – and your enlightened responses to my stupid letters – I am now an author who is totally committed to superior author–reader relations, and I want you to know how very grateful I am to you for this.

Wishing *you* restful sleep and sweet dreams,
Andy Griffiths

MERV HUGHES

I treasure letters I receive. I had 10000 letters sent to me by family, friends, fans and critics during my playing career and I kept them all. The bloke who wrote the one beginning, 'You're an overweight, disgusting prick and a disgrace to the Australian cricket tradition . . .' got a bit of a shock when I tracked him down in his local pub and asked him to explain himself. A good letter is worth keeping because you get something extra from it on the second reading. I hope that is the case with my letter today. I have written to three women who have had an enormous impact on my life. The first two are women from the past and the third is, well, I think you will work her out.

Dear Christina Willes, Florence Rose Murphy
and You Know Who You Are,

Thank you for changing my life.

Christina, you got roped in to playing backyard cricket with your brother John, and the result was my most potent weapon. When you were playing, bowling of course because your brother wanted to bat, you had difficulty delivering the ball underarm, the only way to do it then. Those hooped dresses can be a bugger. It was early in the nineteenth century and you invented overarm bowling.

Imagine cricket without overarm bowling! The game would be filled with boring little bowlers with no imagination and less personality. And batsmen who never experienced fear. But because of you, I played cricket knowing that the only good batsman was a scared batsman.

You gave me the tools I needed to play for Australia. I was already an overweight, disgusting prick, but you gave me overarm bowling. I let the ball go from a height of better than eight foot. I was always trying to take a wicket, and I never deliberately hurt a batsman. Sometimes I just got lucky.

Overarm bowling changed my life. When I started my first-class career, I was employed at the same time packing diaries into boxes at a printer's warehouse. I ended up pounding the cherry into batsmen's boxes as they tightened their sphincters in fear. I went from a diary packer to a date puckerer.

Florence Rose Murphy, you were born in Beechworth, in the same neck of the woods as me. I have admired you for a long time, because the ashes of the burnt bails that you presented to the England captain in 1882 became the most important trophy in Australian sport. You told Ivo Bligh when you gave him the urn that they represented the death of English cricket after his team was thumped by the Aussies in England. I admired you because you knew how to take the piss, and you ended up marrying the bastard as well. Can't blame him. Who doesn't love an Aussie woman with a sense of humour?

The Ashes became much more than a joke. They became the most revered trophy in international cricket. They became the name of a test series. They are how all Australian cricketers define themselves.

It is one of the greatest honours imaginable to be selected to represent Australia on the sporting field. But if you are an Australian Test cricketer, you are measured by your performances in Ashes

Tests. The day I was picked for my first Test match, I was as happy as a dog with three balls. But the day I was selected for my first Ashes Test was something else entirely. Words cannot illuminate the sense of excitement, of disbelief, the pure adrenaline rush of that moment. Some people say that playing in an Ashes Test is a matter of life and death. It's much, much more important than that. Playing in the Ashes changed my life.

Finally, to You Know Who You Are,

I was too young to understand when I first met you. You captivated me instantly. How you looked, how you smelt, how you felt when you went down. And at first I think I loved you most because you were forbidden. It was always furtive. We would get together when out with friends. At my place if my parents weren't home. In the park, the back seat of cars. When I became old enough for us to be acceptable, we tried to act sensibly. But I could never get enough of you. Remember that night when we just kept on going and going and going? I passed out. And in the morning you tempted me again. Just to get me started. So often after a night together, I could smell you on me all day, as though your essence was leaking from my pores.

We have been together in the most exotic of locations. The Caribbean, Paris; in hotels, in changing rooms, in restaurants. On planes repeatedly, and more than anyone will ever know. You were what kept me going on those hot, hot days when the pitch was a freeway and those bastards were batting with doors. You were my reward for a hard day in the field. You were with me after success but you never deserted me in failure. You were my commiseration and my celebration. You were what cajoled me to strive to be better.

You have been so much a part of my greatest days in cricket, my greatest days in life. You have always been the prize, the reward. You are the one I have gone to when the weapon given to me by Christina has been used for the purpose given to me by Florence. Yes, you changed my life and made me who I am, beer.

Christina, Florence and beer, I thank you.
Merv

Merv

ROBERT MANNE

Dear Margaret,

You probably don't remember me. We were both members of the stolen generations taskforce established by the Victorian government. But even though our acquaintance was fleeting, because of one small incident, I will remember you for as long as I live. To understand why this incident had such meaning for me I need to explain to you something about the woman who brought me to the stolen generations taskforce and who truly changed my life by opening my eyes to the distinctive evil of racism – the great German-Jewish philosopher, Hannah Arendt.

When I was a little boy growing up happily in Melbourne, I discovered that the Nazi state had wanted to murder my people, in its entirety. The discovery so shocked and astonished me that my soul was scarred – forever. My parents had fled Europe as refugees but had lost their own parents in that mysterious event called the Holocaust. They were so wounded by all this that they did not talk about it much. Perhaps they wanted to protect me. Their silence only made me more curious to learn whatever I could.

The image that first haunted me was a photograph in a book from my father's collection. It showed a young Jewish boy in a cap, about the same age as me, with his hands in the air surrendering to a German soldier. To discover how such a thing was possible, when I was a little older I sought understanding from the work of historians. The facts, however, were not enough. I wanted to comprehend the nature of the crime that had been committed. The word for the crime was clear: genocide. But what did that word mean?

When I was at university I read a famous and controversial book about the trial of one of the architects of the Holocaust. The book was called *Eichmann in Jerusalem*. Its author was Hannah Arendt. Arendt believed that Eichmann deserved to die for what he had done. Towards the end of her book she composed a speech that she thought the judges ought to have delivered to the man in the dock. These were the words she chose:

> It was when the Nazi regime declared that the German people . . . wished to make the entire Jewish people disappear from the face of the earth that the new crime of [genocide] appeared . . . And just as you supported and carried out a policy of not wanting to share the earth with the Jewish people – as though you and your superiors had any right to determine who should and should not inhabit the world – we find that no one . . . can be expected to want to share the earth with you.

With these words I thought I understood finally just what it was that the crime of genocide entailed. When I lectured on the Holocaust I always quoted this passage. As it happens, these words changed the trajectory of my life.

I had always been vaguely aware of the tragedy that had befallen your people, the Indigenous people of Australia. I am, however, not proud of the fact that it was very many years before I truly turned my attention to your people's fate. I can in fact remember the exact moment when that happened. The ABC was showing a documentary called *Frontier*. The final episode quoted the West

Australian chief protector of Aboriginals, AO Neville – the main non-Indigenous character from the film *Rabbit-Proof Fence*. These were his words: 'Are we going to have a population of 1 million blacks in the commonwealth, or are we going to merge them into our white community and eventually forget that there were ever any Aborigines in Australia?'

The program made clear that Neville's words came from a 1937 conference of Aboriginal protectors. Because of Arendt, when I heard them they struck me with the force of lightning. Neville had spoken unambiguously about an ambition to merge the Aboriginals into the white population. He obviously believed that the world would be a better place if the very existence of the Indigenous population were to be forgotten by future generations of Australians. It was obvious, then, that he thought that he and the other protectors had the right to determine whether Indigenous Australians ought or ought not to inhabit the earth.

I went to my university's library and discovered a verbatim transcript of the 1937 conference where these words had been spoken. I learned that Neville had not been quoted by *Frontier* out of context. I learned, too, that his words had excited no indignation among his fellow protectors. Like other delegates, he believed that 'full-blood' Aboriginals were destined to die out. Like them, he believed that the really menacing Aboriginal problem facing Australia was the growth in the number of the so-called 'half-castes'. There was, however, he believed, a solution to the 'problem' of the 'half-caste'. The 'half-caste' children should be removed from their mothers. They should be educated in special institutions. The girls should be forbidden to marry 'full-blood' Aboriginals and encouraged to marry lower-class white males. The policy was known at the time as 'breeding out the colour'. Once colour was bred out, in three or four generations, even the fact that an Indigenous population had once inhabited Australia might be forgotten. Eventually, through the policy of breeding out the colour, the Aboriginal people would be removed from the face of the earth.

I knew the passage from Arendt about the nature of Eichmann's crime by heart. It had alerted me to the terrible meaning implicit in the *Frontier* quote from Neville. In turn, this led me to the discovery of the existence of a kind of racism in interwar Australia of which I had previously been almost altogether unaware.

I became intensely interested in the politics and history surrounding the question of the Indigenous dispossession in general and the stolen generations in particular. What I learned led me into conflict with two right-wing Australians – the faux-historian Keith Windschuttle and the faux-journalist Andrew Bolt. It opened the possibility of meeting with some wonderful Indigenous Australians – Lowitja O'Donoghue, Pat and Mick Dodson. It also brought me onto the stolen generations taskforce, where I met you.

To be perfectly honest, Margaret, not much seemed to be achieved at the meetings of the taskforce. But for me the conversation was utterly absorbing. Most people serving on the committee had been removed from parents and communities. I was deeply impressed and deeply moved by the way you and the other Indigenous members of the committee talked about these sad experiences and about the vital task of rebuilding your stolen lives and your broken families.

I come now to the point of my letter. At one meeting of the committee, held in my university office, you took me by complete surprise. You were aware that I had listened with attention and indeed fascination to the stories of the Indigenous families. Out of the blue, you asked me to speak about my grandparents. I answered that they had all been murdered by the Nazis. I will never forget your response. You burst into tears and had to leave the room for several minutes.

Our paths crossed briefly. But I thought you might be interested to know that what happened that morning will stay with me for as long as I live. Your life experience and my own could have hardly been more different. Yet at that moment I understood that at the most important level – in what we shared, in our common humanity – we were linked.

With warmest wishes,
Rob

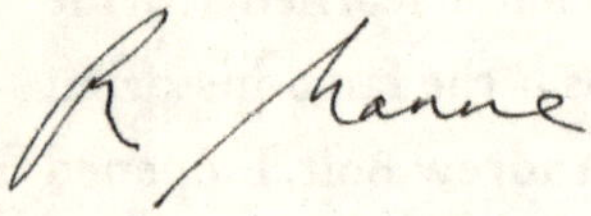

STEVE VIZARD

It's coming up to fifty years, a long time between drinks, I know, but I will get this off my chest.

It's summer, the '60s, always summer in our street of Inverness Way, and the days are long and the skies are blue and the world is vast, calibrated only by our scooter rides to Liam McCall's cubby and the lulling soundtrack of cicadas and Kennedy speeches. Remember? It's the age of Play-Doh and plane trees, of Super Balls and hula hoops, when any grazed knee can be healed by the panacea of Vegemite on Tip Top or the miracle of Mum's chocolate Quik. Remember?

And there you are, you curly haired vixen. You, all of six and beaming. Me, blue-eyed, innocent and seven. You smile, you dance, you sing, you steal my seven-year-old heart, and I am yours, hook line and sinker.

Shirley Temple. Curly Tops. Little Miss Broadway.

It is true, Shirley, I've only seen you in the movies on the good TV on Sunday afternoons after World Championship Wrestling, your warm-up act Professor Tanaka and Brute Bernard and the Golden Greek, Spiros Arion, and their cast of musclebound racial misfits fit to fuel any immigration debate. Amid the flurry of sleeper holds and half nelsons, my little brother, Andy, and I wait by the TV for you, Shirley; hanging from the rafters, jumping from the turnbuckles, we wait for you.

And then you come, Shirley, in black and white, grainy as a NASA transmission, as though you're tap-dancing live from Cape Canaveral.

And from your very first 'Polly Wolly Doodle', I love you.

I want to run away with you, Shirley Temple, to Sunnybrook Farm and Aunt Becky and Bill 'Bojangles' Robinson, where the men are Brylcreemed and moustached, and a ninety-piece orchestra springs from every bush, and every passerby knows the lyrics and croons like Crosby, and every older sister finds a millionaire fiancé, and all our woes are resolved in three acts, final song, close-up Shirley, roll credits.

And for three infinite months in that infinite golden summer, I am yours, Shirley Temple.

I try to teach myself to tap-dance. In the car, on our way to school, at dinner, cleaning my teeth. Ratatatat. My feet are flying like a broken rivet gun; I'm like a midget with Saint Vitus Dance. I experiment with different footwear and discover the best noise comes when I wear my leather footy boots with the metal studs in the bathroom. And now I'm in the bathroom in my footy boots every spare minute: ratatatat. I'm Ben Cousins after a big night on the town. Ratatatat. I'm Buddy Franklin with Parkinson's. Ratatatat. Tapping like there's no tomorrow. Until Mum and Dad can take no more

Shut the fuck up! Enough already, Stephen!

Mum, driven to despair, consults the Yellow Pages and locates the only tap-dancing teacher within a 20-kilometre radius of Inverness Way. One grey Saturday afternoon she carts me to Mrs Mitchell's grandly named Eltham Ballet and Movement Academy, a sad extension at the rear of her ramshackle brick-veneer bungalow. A seven-year-old boy in an Academy/ kitchenette full of five-year-old girls jumping to a tuneless piano manned by a purple-haired, chain-smoking harridan thumping out 'The Sunny Side of the Street'. But there's nothing sunny in Eltham on this Saturday. Between the smell of burning eucalyptus leaves and the faint drone of Norman Banks on a distant transistor, even I can find little hint of Hollywood here. I skulk from the Eltham Ballet and Movement

Academy never to return, tap-less, Sunnybrook Farmless, *Animal Crackers*-less, Bojangle-less. Shirley-less.

Undeterred, back home, I now pronounce to the family over dinnertime fish fingers, I want to hit the stage. Big time. Just like Shirley. My bewildered father enlists Andy and me in the local Anglican Christ Church nativity play. We are to be the three wise men. Just the two of us. The numbers don't add up, I can see that, but there's a shortage of primary school thespians, or at least Anglican ones. Mum's got to make the wise men costumes. Time is short, Mum's Singer is rusting in the garage and, anyway, Andy and I have already got costumes. Although mine is a Superman costume: a royal blue, Kardashian-esque clinging body suit with a scarlet cape and a giant red and yellow 'S' embroidered on the front. And Andy's is a Samurai outfit, complete with sword.

I don't remember much about the nativity play, other than this: the newly born baby Jesus is being held aloft by Mary, a mean-tempered, freckled nine year old somehow related to the vicar, flanked on either side by a supporting juvenile cow and camel.

Cue the Vizard boys. Go wise men. Now. Enter wise men. Now.

Andy and I reluctantly nudge our way towards the manger, bearing gifts.

And then it happens.

The audience start laughing. Not just a bit. But uncontrollably and then hysterically.

Andy starts crying and takes out his sword and waves it at the guffawing naysayers as though they are money changers in the Temple.

And they laugh even more.

Nearly fifty years on, still humiliated and still trying to make sense of it, I can see how the sudden arrival at the birth of our Lord Saviour of a miniature Man of Steel and Shintaro might represent an unpalatable departure from the scriptures. Especially one wise man down and bearing two presents wrapped in red Myer Emporium Christmas paper.

Despite the setbacks, Shirley, you need to know that, even then, Andy and I remained committed. Still we basked in your all-singing, all-dancing Sunday reverie. Still, Shirley, I was yours.

Until that day. That fateful day. As black and haunting and inexpugnable as Lennon's death or Princess Di's demise.

I'm seven, it's now school holidays, and I'm playing with Silly Putty and talking to my mum in the kitchen. Mum lets slip that she too grew up with Shirley Temple.

What?

Says my mum, 'I loved Shirley when I was about your age too, Stephen.'

Hang on – are you crazy?

Mum, my mum, old as Methuselah, Mum grew up with you, loved you, had her hair in curlers and sang 'On the Good Ship Lollipop' and danced her way through the Ballarat South Street Dance Competition?

'Here's my tap-dancing blue ribbon to prove it,' confides the crazy woman.

Surely not my beloved Shirley Temple. Surely, Mum, you mean some other six-year-old, chubby-cheeked, curly-haired, tap-dancing freak called Shirley. Surely another Shirley.

But she doesn't.

And it dawns on me, rudimentary though my seven-year-old maths may be, limited by fingers and Cuisenaire rods, if my Shirley and Mum's Shirley are one and the same, our Shirley can no longer be six. Nor even sixteen. She must be . . .

And that is the precise moment my world falls apart. That is the exact second of the gut-wrenching realisation that I will never dance or sing or escape with you, Shirley; I will never 'S-M-I-L-E to be H-A-double P-Y' with you; I will never do anything with you, on the sunny shores of Peppermint Bay or elsewhere.

And I pine. And I ache. And I am angry.

Shirley Temple, you floozy. I have given you my everything; when you were Little Miss Broadway, the Little Colonel, the Little Princess, the Littlest Rebel. And in reality you are nothing but the Littlest Cocktease.

And not even that little, you two-faced tap-dancing Tori Spelling. Little! Me seven and you forty-three! Your roly-poly legs by now as veined and sun-spotted as Mum's. Your careworn world now an unreachable world away, a World War away, kids and cut lunches away, with no time left for impromptu barnyard concerts. Your tap shoes rusting and cobwebbed, the leather as parched and brittle and broken as my seven-year-old dreams.

Shirley, you have let me down. Faithless and fickle.

But the real culprit here, it dawns on me, is not Shirley.

The real malefactor is Time. Not the wasted Time of my own making, the Time I've squandered on a couch or in a bar, the frittered Time that killed my potential career as a concert pianist or my chance to open the batting for Australia.

No, a different sort of Time has flattened me. Big-picture Time, Stephen Hawking-sized Time, way-out-of–my-hands Time, the Time that divides me from a generation before. The mocking, inarguable Time that separates aeons like continents and stands between me and Ancient Rome or Sunnybrook Farm, denying me the togas I might have worn, the Last Suppers I might have consumed, the tap-dancing showstoppers you, Shirley, and I might have sung.

Time is the life-changing bitch.

There is a coda.

It's 1999. I'm in California with my friend Mark. As we drive through Woodside, he says, 'See that street there? That's where Shirley Temple lives.'

And I ask him to pull over. 'No reason,' say I. And I walk to the front fence and there in the garden I see a woman, an old woman, the same age as Mum, on her knees turning the soil with a small trowel.

And it's her.

It's you.

Shirley.

And though we never speak, on this day, in this garden, all I hear is an orchestra swinging in crackly syncopation and the sounds of tapping feet.

And all I see is a mop of blonde curls and a smile that lights up the world and Bill 'Bojangles' Robinson tapping down your front steps. And I'm flying again and the world is bright and anything is possible.

So I write to Time, of the nagging hourglass and the mocking hands. Let it be known, Time, that fifty years on, despite your trickery and tomfoolery, I'll have none of it.

Let it be known, Time, you can stick your nitpicking seconds up your arse. I've had it with you.

Let it be known, Time, as far as I'm concerned, and from hereon in, the plane trees are in flower, my red scooter is polished, Killer Karl Kox is jumping from the turnbuckle, I'm wearing my Superman costume – yes, with the big S embroidered on the front. Anything is possible and somewhere in the near distance an orchestra swells, cue the wise men, cue Shirley, cue close up, roll closing credits: The End.

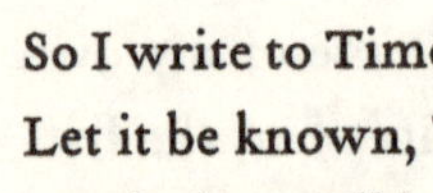

QUAN YEOMANS

Dear You,

To say you are *the* woman who changed my life does seem a little disproportionate, not to mention premature, but for the purpose of this event and for the benefit of romance, I will suspend all reality checks and defer my self-esteem for the next few pages.

I could pretend to be calm. Throw in an aphorism about people entering our field of gravity, drifting far and wide upon their elliptical orbits but nonetheless being bound to us in some way forever. But I doubt it would help.

In truth, I am shit scared.

I can feel the terror strangling my tongue and coagulating the blood in my hands. So what do I do to allay these fears? I agree to bare my terror in front of a large group of people I don't know at a public speaking event. I feel like I may have been making some questionable life decisions lately . . .

I'm sure it is because of you I find myself in such situations. I'm normally good at avoiding this sort of thing. I keep maps open. I know where the exits are. I think about nutrition. I use a dictionary. I always shave before leaving the house. I guess at some point my science failed, though, and you managed to slip through the rigour of my methods.

You know how in that Cronenberg film we all learned that flies throw up on their food to liquefy it so that they can casually suck it up through their straw-like proboscises? Well – I think you did that to my heart.

I've wanted to tell you that for the longest time but I could never quite frame it romantically enough. Something about a fly vomiting on my heart seemed a tricky image to present with any sweetness.

So I'll avoid this metaphor and instead stick to bland seasonal verse. You've taught me how to loathe October. I never noticed how fucking long and dreary it is before. How dull and impotent spring can really be. It is only now, as I lie in parks softly moaning, that I notice how doleful the new flower buds seem. How lifeless trees bristling with fresh green actually are.

Everything and everyone is in cahoots.

All the birds that flit by seem to hiss at me like snakes. Overhead, clouds coalesce into erotic scenes of delight to taunt me. Butterflies pair up and flutter sweet 'fuck you's in my general direction. And small children covered in ice cream smile knowingly at me, silently praising the success of their parents' coition.

Though my eyes are closed, I am not at rest.

I grow tired of trying to picture your tendons tensing and drawing your muscles into taut poses on squash courts; anxious attempting to recall the slight, oddly attractive in-turning of your eyes; frustrated with not seeing your teeth pop out like blank score cards from under your lips when you snigger at my poor attempts to entertain you with crappy anecdotes; absolutely terrified about some immaculately dressed corporate fly boy cutting in on our dance before I even get to the ball.

I want to pretend that I'm Stephin Merritt and sing gravelly odes to my despair and desperation, but I can't find the energy to go sit in gay bars all night and pen clever rhymes among the glistening muscle.

I would tell you I miss you all the time but perhaps it would be more accurate to say that I struggle to remember you constantly. It seems absurd but after so long my memories of your physical presence appear to me like a bunch of dodgy-looking characters in a police line-up. Me trapped on the outside of the one-way mirror, forcing myself to create believable stories to incriminate the version of you I pick out.

Last time you wrote you didn't ask me anything specific, so here are some random factoids about myself to get you up to speed.

I was born at the age of five. I know this because I don't remember anything else before that.

At eight when my parents finally divorced, I listened to Fleetwood Mac's *Rumours* on vinyl almost constantly for a year. As a result, it has taken me a long time not to be instantly traumatised by indie music.

When I was nine, my hair was straight, then it went wavy. By thirteen it was completely curly. At this point I started feeling fairly certain one of my parents wasn't genetically connected to me but I could never decide on which one had been driven to fornicate with the postie.

At fourteen, after three years of torturous piano lessons, I stole a guitar from my high school's music department storeroom and found my 'calling'. Well . . . I guess technically I stole my calling.

At sixteen my virginity was handed nervously over to a tall, smart, confident girl called Tessa. When I first tentatively put my fingers into Tessa's vagina, I remember thinking it was like a 'bucket of slime'. Later that week I took her to the 'prom' but left alone after about half an hour because it just felt awkward being there with her, knowing full well that my hand had been inside her only days before. We only ever 'did it' once.

Two weeks after graduating from high school, my mother put me on a plane to Europe and America and I went travelling on my own for six weeks. I think I may have been a little too young to really appreciate it.

The highlight of travelling across the entire United States ended up being getting mugged in Memphis. I was so bored of being in the back of the Greyhound, listening to white trash talking shit while swapping alcohol for Valium, that I got off, went to a 7-Eleven and bought a six pack of beer for a random snaggle-toothed gentleman loitering suspiciously around the bus terminal. I wandered into a seedy part of town with him, 30-kilogram backpack slung over my shoulders. It was 11 at night. I thought we were getting along great, casually walking around drinking together for about half an hour. Then he pulled a knife on me. I don't think it was something I said. I think he was just doing his job. At least he worked pretty hard for the twenty bucks, which was all I had in my wallet. Poor guy.

Listen, I could go on, but the only thing that writing this letter makes me want to do is sleep through this cursed month like a princess under some spiteful stepmother's enchantment and then have you wake me with a kiss, a high-fibre breakfast and some light pillow talk involving the promise of everlasting cake. Is that really too much to ask?

Forgive me; I am trying my best not to get ahead of myself this time, as I am prone to do.

Normally by this stage I would have sent you a kind of standardised assessment survey involving copies of my two favourite books: de Saint-Exupéry's *The Little Prince* and *The Story of the Eye* by Georges Bataille. The test is designed to simultaneously alienate and eliminate the heartless and the squeamish, both of which I decided to waste no more time upon a while ago. But I will admit that the cocktail of pornographic violence and childlike transcendental enlightenment is sometimes a little confusing even for the good ones. Those few who don't come away from this test thinking that I have the self-image of a deranged sex addict trapped in the plot of an adorably poignant children's fable are clearly the type of girls I am looking for.

I got halfway through the assessment with you, though, and thought better of it. Some part of me realised that the test is fundamentally flawed, because it reveals way too much of my psyche, and everyone knows that romance is in the 'not knowing'.

Fortunately I have engaged another far superior character-assessment test in the last few years. It's called 'cold sores'.

I keep telling myself that I've been good. That I've not let romance infect my past letters to you too much. That I've restrained the rogue agents of desire commissioned by my genes to do their wet work, and carefully kept my hands from penning their sinister plots.

And yet here I am.

The timing of the event that I am in fact reading this letter out at couldn't really be much better. Not three hours after its conclusion, I will be hopping on a plane bound for you. There in that sealed aluminium tube, hurtling through dark space at frightening velocities, my brain will go through the final stages of maddening doubt and blind panic, culminating in something like a cross between a SWAT team's mission briefing and a Woody Allen film script. The two main protagonists and subjects of direction being your lovely left hand and my clammy right.

Both Mr Allen and the SWAT team are hoping for a witty but bloodless scene but neither really know whether it will cut seamlessly into *Annie Hall* or *City of God*.

In not three hours the fantasy begins its downward spiral into the brutal depths of reality where the secret language of pheromones, saliva, vocal timbre and fashion sense take the wheels of our sports car chassis and make hollow puppets of our heads. At least in the fantasy bubble of this missive I still have control of the plane, even though the engines are on fire, the hydraulic pressure feeding the wing flaps is dropping alarmingly, fuel tanks are critically low and the navigation computer is definitely on the blink. It is really a freefall dressed as flight.

And as my plane careers towards its fate, what can I do but gently remind myself that no one else ever breaks your heart? It is always you that makes an anvil of another's and moulds, tempers and sometimes cracks your own heart upon it.

Yours possibly,
Quan

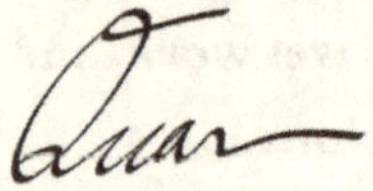

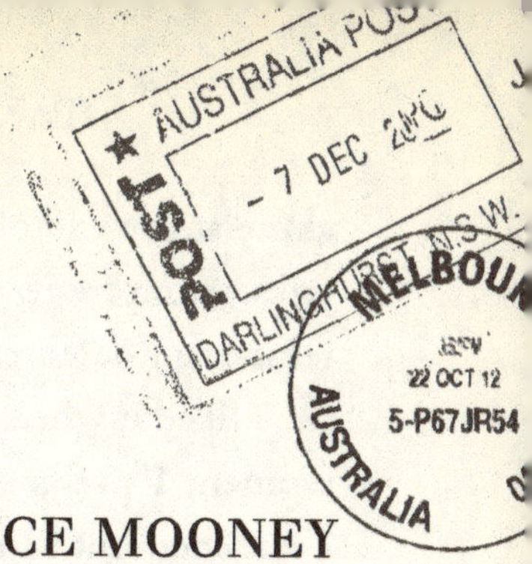

LAWRENCE MOONEY

I write to you as one, collectively, for you are the craziest bitches I have ever been out with and I'm writing to tell you how much you changed my life.

You may baulk at the term 'crazy bitch' but it's a linguistic coupling that's hard to deny, like 'weak prick' or 'dumb cunt'. Plus I don't think crazy bitch is a pejorative, it's a genre, and all women are in fact to a greater or lesser extent crazy bitches.

You taught me what normal looked like because our relationships weren't. Our relationships were shit, they were exasperating confusion; life could be serene and beautiful or it could be the most abject hell any two people have ever had to sustain in the name of love. The areas in between were Pinteresque in their tension, and never dull.

You all taught me that one can't find self-esteem in a relationship. If you want to be loved and be able to love in return without picking at the thread until the whole thing unravels into a mess, you need to arrive at a relationship with some sense of self.

Let's talk sex. Thank you for teaching me cunnilingus. Before that I was taking a bit of a lick and a munch like a kid with a gelato – you taught me that the idea was to make a woman orgasm. It was a big shift in my consciousness, it really was. That lesson also included things being thrown, cups smashing and a Coke bottle hitting me in the head. I was really shocked and slightly amused but when I suggested you were a domestic violent, you really went bananas and I could still hear you screaming abuse, my name and then some more abuse at the end of Delbridge Street. After the fights came the peace talks. Sumptuous feasts, favourite films and long embraces in the temporary detente.

I liked it when it really got crazy. I love stomping, demonstrative women; I prefer screaming to angry silence, silence is torture – I searched until I found a woman who doesn't do silence. Silence is the most hideous form of manipulation. None of you were silent and I love that about you all.

Besides, a real donnybrook is so cleansing – when things got thrown and smashed, something inside me was thrilled and excited. I know these things supposedly have no place in sane, well-balanced relationships, because everybody gets a tad spooked when stuff gets broken, but I loved it. To see the passion and the madness affected me greatly: I think it improved my self-worth.

I'm not going to abrogate my responsibility in the madness. I can be infuriating, and loose with the booze, the truth and my pants. But the more you refused to accept my bullshit, the more I loved you. When you screamed down the hall at Clyde Street, 'You can't treat me like this, you weak prick – is that fucking clear?' and held your finger millimetres from my nose, I thought, Finally. Because men love women to set the boundaries.

I learned that only one person in a relationship can be the drinker, because if we were both pissed it was only good to a point and then it got ferocious. Then it got bad.

Amid your incredibly messy rooms – a luxury I couldn't afford myself because I was always way more uptight than you – you all taught me to aim higher. All of you repeatedly told me I underestimated myself, which was such a contradiction coming from people who were running on empty when it came to self-esteem. Your contradictions were what made you fascinating to me.

You were all so driven, creative and productive. The urgency wasn't just about perfecting relationships; that frisson would create fashion and accessories, films and soundscapes, articles and books – it was amazing how much you created, and so was the busyness of your lives and the boldness you employed to ask for what you wanted. It might sound like a rankly mercantile thing to say but you helped me put a price on what I did.

Maybe *Macbeth* isn't about a woman's murderous lust for power but is rather just another tale of a woman sick to death of a man's indolence, indecisiveness and inability to see how much he's got to offer. You're all right, Lady Macbeth, you're all right.

Let's go back to the sex, because you all loved your sex. The maxim that crazy women go off in bed is completely true and that changed me. You were unbridled – it was probably the only time when you appeared freed of the burden you were dragging around. And it helped me become a crazy bitch too; that kind of intensity is contagious. Maybe it's an attempt to fill the existential void, or maybe you just love sex. The scratching is a bit much though, really, cut that shit out.

One night I tried to have sex with you and you spat at me, 'Get that disgusting little thing away from me.' The adjective was more hurtful than the rejection.

You were capable of such tenderness and the shabbiest self-obsessed behaviour – you rode life with brilliance, toxicity, corrosive self-doubt, joyous celebration and a hunger. There is not much you don't love but if there is you fucking hate it. You are the best haters and I love that about each of you.

As memory lets me set aside the exasperation and confusion, the final farewell of, 'You'll regret this, you fuckwit,' when I dumped you on the phone when you were in New York, I want to thank you all for teaching me so much. The above is but a few of these things.

You're never far from my thoughts.

Love,
Lawrence

LAWRENCE.

FRANK WOODLEY

Dear Mary Anderson

I never met you and I know very little about you, but nevertheless you've had a profound effect on me. In fact, if it weren't for you, I'd never've been born, which, I imagine, would've had a significant impact on my life.

Yes, over the years you've periodically changed the course of my life and I'd like to tell you how.

Three stories. Three stories, spanning two generations, connected by one unremarkable activity . . .

On 16 November 1957, a young man and a young woman both attended a dance at Melba Hall in Royal Parade. When he was introduced to her by a mutual friend, he took a deep breath and complimented her on her dress. She thanked him with the kind of strained smile you give a nurse just after she's said, 'Done.' He was sensitive enough, or cocky enough, to interpret this pained expression as shyness rather than disgust. It was actually a little bit of both because he had a haircut that, in 1957 – it was difficult to appreciate. He was trying to look

like James Dean, but he didn't. Not even close. Due to exuberant, unruly frizziness, his hair was . . . Sort of . . . Put it this way: if this story was set not in the late '50s but instead in the late '70s and he'd found himself in the company of the New Zealand band Split Enz at the height of their theatrical powers, it's possible that Noel Crombie would've glanced at his head and thought, That's a bit over the top. But in spite of his being way ahead of his time and having something growing out of the top of his skull that looked like an upside-down electrocuted octopus dipped in pubes, when he invited her to dance, she agreed.

His left hand held her right hand. It felt good. His grip was not too firm, not too wimpy. The young woman rested her left hand on the young man's shoulder, and that felt pretty good too. But the element of this ritualistic coupling that was really setting off all sorts of chemical chaos in both of them was his right hand touching her waist. The placement of his hand on her curvature, was really, really, *really* erotic. He'd placed it in the perfect spot: his middle finger resting snugly into the little crease caused by her slightly swayed back and plumpness, and his third finger and pinky sitting on her hip bone at the point on her body where her bottom half started expanding in a woman-y way.

He asked her to promise that the last dance would be for him, and him alone.

And it was – she'd left.

But twenty minutes later, when a car pulled up alongside the young woman standing at a tram stop in the rain and the man leaned across from the driver's seat and wound down the passenger window, there was something kind about the eyes staring out from under that ridiculous mop of nonsense, and when he asked, 'Would you like a lift?', she got in.

For me, family camping trips have two integral parts. Firstly, a wonderful connection with nature. Stars, surf, dirt, fire, bugs, birds, and all that stuff. And secondly, they must include at least one memorable traumatic experience. These can range from the least serious – like when for a minute I got caught in a rip at Torquay – to middling-level trauma – like when at the age of thirteen I went on a trail ride and was bucked off by a massive black horse. The guy running it said, 'If you don't get straight back up, you'll never ride again.' I didn't and I haven't.

But without a doubt my most traumatic family camping experience was at the Cathedral Ranges when I was eleven. We'd been for a bushwalk and were all muckin' around having fun. My dad had this pamphlet about the local flora and fauna and he goes, 'Okay, it says, "Look out for the following plants".' My cousin goes, 'Following plants! What do they do after they follow you? Do they attack you?' It started to rain and we all ran back to camp screaming, 'The following plants! Run for your lives!' I had a smile on my face as I crawled into my tent on all fours. As I put my weight on my left arm, something flipped up and wacked me on the hand. It was a tiger snake. It'd bitten me.

It was weird. It didn't hurt much, and I wasn't overly upset 'cause I couldn't really comprehend what had happened.

I remember it like a dream.

Rain's bashing down on the car roof and my brain's pounding. They mingle into a sort of thunderous throb. I've got my head on my mum's lap and I'm lying on the back seat of our EH Holden. I lie there staring at the ashtray that was built into the back seat. It has a silver metal faceplate with stripes cut across it, and on the right-hand side a handsome little lion is sitting with his paw resting on a ball. It annoys me when Mum flips the plate down so she can drop a butt in. I quickly reach up and push it closed so I can see the lion again.

I don't remember being frightened. I was too scared to be frightened.

I don't recall anything else, but they must've got through the rain to the hospital, 'cause I'm here to not remember.

I'd got home from a gig at about 11.30 and put the kettle on. I was feeling quite tense, 'cause there'd been a little incident when I was signing things after the show. Two boys came forward and handed me a DVD. I said, 'Hello, there. Who should I make this out to?' and one of the boys said, 'Luke.' I started signing and an elderly woman standing to the side said, 'And Andy.' And I said quite loudly in front of a big queue, 'You're lucky, Andy, that your grandma's looking out for you,' and she said, 'Mother.' And, as one, the entire line went, '. . . Oooh.' And I said, '. . . Sorry,' which is where I should have left it, but for some reason I pushed on with, 'I don't know why I said that. I saw you out of the corner of my eye and you looked older than you look. Now . . . that I look at you . . . more directly . . .' And she said, 'I'm thirty-nine.' And I said, 'I heard about a woman who became a grandma at thirty-two.' I was vaguely aware of the entire queue anxiously shaking their heads in horror. She said, 'So you glanced up and thought, She looks about thirty-nine but like a 39-year-old grandmother?' And I said, 'Sorry, I made an inappropriate assumption, 'cause of the grey hair.' And she said, 'It's platinum blonde.'

And I said, 'Out of the corner of your eye, Marilyn Monroe looks a bit nanna-ish.' And the woman selling the DVDs leaned over and said, 'You need to stop speaking now.'

So I'm at home after the gig, feeling mortified, and I start prowling the kitchen for a sweet snack. I was rapt to discover that on the bench were about a dozen muffins sitting in a baking tray. There was a piece of A4 paper sitting on top of them. I lifted it off and gazed at the muffins with exhausted relief. It was gonna be okay. I'm not a bad person. I'm a homemade-choc-chip-muffin-eating person. I sat, sipped tea, ate muffins and played the scene over and over in my head. I emerged from my reverie after about twenty-five minutes. There were three muffins left but I couldn't fit in another bite.

I was still holding the piece of paper I'd lifted off the muffins and my attention slowly focused on some black markings on it. They were shapes, but not a reoccurring pattern. They seemed to be a series of symbols. Writing! It was writing! In English!

'PLEASE DO NOT EAT THESE MUFFINS.'

What?

'Please do not eat these muffins. They're for Mark's birthday tomorrow.'

What? Oh no! That's right. Our neighbours, Mark and Claire, are having a party tomorrow, and my wife has baked these muffins for that. Oh my God! Not only had I eaten the muffins, but I'd picked up, in my hand, a sign that said 'PLEASE DO NOT EAT THESE MUFFINS'! So that I could eat the muffins! I was fucked! Seriously, seriously fucked!

Because this wasn't an isolated incident. You have to understand . . . My wife is an extremely, extremely tolerant person. But this moment of thoughtlessness wasn't just the straw that broke the camel's back. It was more like – stretching across the desert floor to the horizon the sand is littered with twisted camel carcasses and there's straw everywhere. I'm not gonna go into the details, but trust me. Fucked. Seriously. You know when you're playing Jenga and you're sure that the next block is going to send everything crashing down? I'd just gorged myself on Jenga muffins and my marriage was definitely quivering and wobbling.

There was only one thing I could do. I had to bake more muffins. I'd never baked anything in my life. So I baked something. They weren't muffins. They were something. I thought they tasted quite good. They were sweet and chocolate-y. They weren't muffins. I tried again. I burned the bejeezus out of them. I was fucked. I called my sister. I woke her up. I explained; she understood; I drove through the rain to her place with a baking tray and a single choc-chip muffin as an example of the currency to be counterfeited. We drove through the rain to the all-night supermarket for ingredients. We drove through the rain back to her place. Kate baked. I thanked her many, many, many times. I drove through the rain, and at about 4.30 a.m. tucked the imposter muffins in under their little white blanket that read 'PLEASE DO NOT EAT THESE MUFFINS'.

So Mary Anderson,

Had my father not picked up my mother from that tram stop and driven her home through the rain . . .

Had our EH Holden not driven through the rain towards some antivenom . . .

And had I not driven through the rain to get some marriage-saving proxy muffins . . .

My world would be inconceivably different.

So thank you, Mary Anderson. I can never sufficiently express my gratitude to you for that day in 1903, when you invented the windscreen wiper.

Frank Woodley

BOB BROWN

Dear Hypatia,

I first got to know you in 1977, on page 365 of Bertrand Russell's 789-page tome *A History of Western Civilization*. You rated one paragraph.

There are very few women in that three thousand years of history, drawn from the annals of men. But there you were, the world's greatest mind on mathematics, astronomy and philosophy in 400 AD.

The last sentence of Russell's paragraph on you is etched in my brain. After you were killed by Christian terrorists, he observed dryly, 'Alexandria was no longer troubled by philosophers.'

When I read about you in 1977, the campaign to save Tasmania's Franklin River from a brace of dam-building engineers was getting underway. I was in the thick of it, as the odds in favour of the destruction of the Franklin River wilderness grew.

The Tasmanian governor joined the premier in declaring that it was a crime against mankind to allow the Franklin's waters to run unharnessed to the sea.

By 1982, both the Labor and the Liberal parties were pro-dam, both houses of the Tasmanian parliament were pro-dam, all three Tasmanian newspapers were pro-dam, big business and the Chamber of Commerce were, of course, pro-dam. Australia's High Court threw out our first challenge. The prime minister told us to take our pleas back to Tasmania, as the dam was a state government matter. We were trounced in the state elections and Premier Gray sent the bulldozers rumbling into the pristine Franklin Valley, dismissing the wild river as a 'brown, leech-ridden ditch'. But through all of this, in my beleaguered mind, your resolution, to stand for the truth as you saw it, was aflame.

When the clouds menacing Alexandria's last days as a great city of learning gathered, you stood firm against hypocrisy and religious mythology – including the concocted myths and inventions about the good, non-magical man Jesus – and you continued to espouse your philosophy to the crowds of Alexandrians who came to hear your logic.

But over at the cathedral, Bishop Cyril, having evicted the Jews from Alexandria, had you firmly in his sights. You were labelled a witch and a heretic. You were dragged through the streets to the temple where Cyril's men in black robes stripped you and cut up your body with the razored ends of broken tiles and oyster shells.

After your murder, the Pope made Cyril a saint.

As a Green philosopher and activist, people have asked me over the years, 'How do you put up with the nastiness, the threats and insults?' My answer is always, 'I read history.' Whenever the going's tough – like being menaced in Salamanca Place late at night by a man with an iron bar; like being hunted by a carload of men with dogs, guns and gelignite in the Picton Forests; like reading an editorial about the Greens in *The Australian* – I think of the Suffragettes, or those who fought to abolish slavery, or, quite simply, Hypatia, of you.

In reality, I know this letter won't ever be read by you. It is a paeon to your optimism, intelligence and defiance – characteristics which have been there in all those human beings who have stood firm against the powerbrokers in hopeless times in order to make the world a better place.

But letters like this allow for dreams. This letter is my way of thanking you, Hypatia, for encouraging me, in much easier circumstances than yours, fifteen centuries later in a world of greed, needless destruction and short-sightedness, to stand strong for the logic of the Greens' philosophy of peace, democracy, social justice and protecting the Earth's biosphere upon which all life, and all of us, depend.

Thank you for helping me stand strong for the Franklin River, even when its cause seemed utterly hopeless.

It has been said, Hypatia, that I saved the Franklin River. That's not true. The rescue depended upon the locals who loved the river, the thousands of people risking arrest in the blockade against the bulldozers in those rainforests in 1982, and the even greater number of Australians who voted to elect the Hawke government and save that sacred river in 1983.

Three decades later, in 2012, American experts have declared the Franklin River the world's best white water rafting adventure, ahead of rivers in Tibet, Peru and Chile.

In so far as I did play a part in saving this global treasure, and if pushed to declare who most inspired me and sustained me through the Franklin River's darkest days, I'd name you, Hypatia of Alexandria. It may sound a little absurd, but it's true: because of you, Hypatia, the Franklin runs free to the sea.

Yours in admiration,
Bob Brown

SAM PANG

Dear Mrs Janovskis,

I'm glad you're dead.

Actually, I'm not sure you are, but seeing as though I've had nothing to do with you since 1983, you might as well be.

Let me start by acknowledging that you are a very boring choice for the woman who changed my life. That's okay. You were a very boring woman.

A boring, humourless, stern disciplinarian who went within an inch of sucking all the fun out of life and specifically out of my primary school experience. You were Nurse Ratched in the form of a grade four teacher.

I must admit that an earlier draft of this letter was in fact addressed to Lisa Bonet. But I wondered if anyone in the room would even know who I was talking about. By the silence in the room, I was right to choose you.

Or I could have written to Samantha Fox, Princess Leia, Susanna Hoffs, Martika, the old girl in *Titanic*, the woman in the film clip for Daryl Braithwaite's 'The Horses'. The list goes on and on, but what's done is done, and when I really thought about it, it was you. It had to be you. You miserable old cow.

Entering grade four filled me with excitement, enthusiasm, anticipation and a number of other words recommended by the thesaurus tool in Word. I was into footy. I had learned swear words in both English and Greek to the point where 'shit', 'dickbrain' and '*na fas skata*' were rolling off my tongue in an almost Shakespearian way. Oh yes, grade four was going to be crazy, because, I assumed, it was going to be exactly like grade three. I was wrong.

If grade three was like the movie *Stripes* – an irreverent, undisciplined celebration of the recklessness of life – then grade four was like *Platoon* – a suicidal symphony to the futility of war and death.

Although for the sake of this letter, I could say that grade four was like *Stripes* as well. Which would make you Sergeant Hulka. And after grade three, it was obvious to all except me that Sergeant Hulka was what I needed.

My grade three teacher was Mr Flatley. You remember him – a man who was multitasking before anyone knew what it was. Mr Flatley, who taught grade three, served in the role of vice principal, and was in charge of the canteen, house sports and drama class, all the while gambling away to his heart's content. Mr Flatley, whose teaching methods included taking the roll at the start of the day, setting us some work to do that didn't require his supervision, then going downstairs to his office and punting on everything from thoroughbred racing at Sandown to the trots at Harold Park. It was only later in life that I realised that if you are betting on the Harold Park trots, all is not well in your life. Although I will say that with all the numbers involved in the art of racing – form guides, horses' odds, daily doubles and quadrellas – it did mean that our class was well ahead of the curve when it came to mathematics.

Sometimes Mr Flatley wouldn't even make it back to class for the 3.30 home-time bell – leaving ten-year-old Paul Shepartanis to call an end to our school day. Which he often did at 2.45.

Yes, it was safe to say he was one of the worst teachers in the history of education. And I loved him.

I hated you. In preparing for this letter, I asked my mum what she remembered about you. Her reply: 'She was a smart, warm person who cared about her students and was recognised by staff and parents at the school as one of the best teachers in the education system. And you hated her.'

Why? Well, for some incomprehensible reason, you didn't allow me to do exactly what I felt like whenever I wanted. You couldn't just let me play with my wrestling figurines during class. You wouldn't let me cut and style the other kids' hair. You never let me glue Lyndal Gordon's ear to the desk.

Oh, no. You had other plans for me. You were going to set me straight. Yes, I was cute as a button, but that wasn't going to stop you on your quest to ruin my life. You told me the truth. And that silly, stubborn, adorable nine-year-old boy didn't like it.

(Right now I'm trusting that my description of myself as 'cute as a button' and 'adorable' has been received in the ridiculous manner it was intended.)

You told me and the rest of the class that grade three was about fun, and grade four was about truth. And you would administer it all year, in your own way.

Take the incident involving the class's pet yabby, Winston. My best friend Russ and I were first to class one morning and I noticed that Winston wasn't moving in his tank with the vim and verve that we had become accustomed to. In fact, he wasn't moving at all. Russ, the smart one, noticed that not only was Winston not moving, but that there was now another yabby in the tank moving with the exact same vim and verve as Winston was known for. As you can imagine, we were in shock. We had gone from having a tank with one living yabby in it the day before to a tank with one living yabby and one dead yabby in it the next. Of course, Russ and I came to the only conclusion we thought logical: another yabby had snuck into the tank during the night and eaten Winston. Not only that, but this new yabby was arrogantly prancing around the tank in a fashion that seemed very disrespectful to its slain foe.

When you got to class and found us crying, were you concerned? Were you sympathetic? No. You were truthful. You explained that the yabby in the tank was Winston, that Winston was a growing yabby and all he had done was shed his exoskeleton, and in the next couple of days Winston's new exoskeleton would harden and everything would be back to normal. Russ and I both had the same reaction to your explanation. *Bullshit.* I didn't believe a word, and didn't talk to you for the rest of the day.

In hindsight, I should have realised that your truth-telling was good for me when it paid off big time after you convinced me that throwing Caroline Roycroft's books out the window was not the way to get her to like me. No sooner had I stopped combining her books with aerodynamics than I was tongue-kissing her behind the toilets. I may have even touched her breast. At least I hope that's what it was. Winston would have been proud.

More truth came when you refuted my claim that George Peppard's work in *The A-Team* was the best he'd ever done. You explained that Peppard had enjoyed many highs in his career and that *The A-Team* was not one of them. You told me it was a mad grab for cash, a superannuation job from a desperate ageing actor in his twilight years, and recommended I watch some of his earlier work like *Breakfast at Tiffany's* or *How the West Was Won*. My response: *na fas skata*.

This went on all year. You kept it up. Day after day. Month after month. Until grade three was so far in the rear-vision mirror that I couldn't see it any more. Much like many of the horses Mr Flatley bet on. By the end of grade four, my knowledge of maths had extended to times tables and long division, I had learned that yabbies shed their skins, and I'd accepted that George Peppard'd had a career before *The A-Team*. And I still didn't like you. When the year was over, I wasn't upset that you wouldn't be my teacher the following year. I never went back and visited you when I was in grades five and six. But as

I stand here now, reading this letter, the impact of my grade four year with you is undeniable.

Of course, this could all be revisionist history on my behalf. Maybe you were just a mean, bitter old cunt who delighted in stealing joy from the souls of children.

But you and the truth are what I needed, for one school year anyway, and you changed my life.

Thank you, Mrs Janovskis.

Sincerely,
Sam

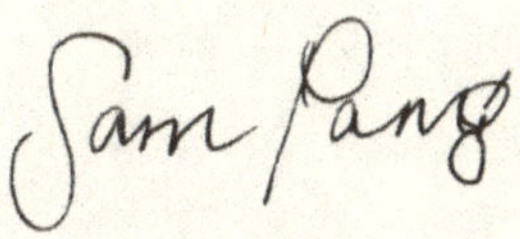

To my biggest sacrifice

RUBY J MURRAY

I want to introduce myself, because you might have heard of me. I enjoyed a brief, breathtaking summer of fame in the late 1980s, a summer when I was the star guest at every party, when the brim of my plastic cup overflowed, when girls in pink taffeta party frocks and boys in Batman suits hung off my every word.

Yes. I was the girl who saw the real Father Christmas.

I was seven that Christmas. I watched him out of the corner of my eye, in his torn red suit, tricking me while I was tricking him. I remember, so clearly, the hot night and the feeling as he shucked the pillowcase off the edge of my bunk.

And then, the fame that followed. Oh, the high times, the envy.

He's not what you expect, I told my adoring fans at the time. Much thinner, full of cunning and glee. Strange, and strangely beautiful.

I was understandably annoyed when Jack Berryman began telling everyone in our home-schooling group that Father Christmas was, in fact, our parents. And I did what you do to all liars: I punched him in the face.

That was my first blood sacrifice to stories. I was more than happy to offer up any chunk of Jack Berryman that I could tear off to the higher power, the higher ideal, of Christmas. In the end, I was lifted off him before I could get a good chunk out, and locked in the car.

In my defence, I blame my mother. Who, in turn, would not blame her mother – because she is scared of setting bad precedents – but might point out that, as the child of one of the most conservative Catholics in Melbourne, she liked a good story.

My grandmother left the Church of England because they wouldn't ordain women. My mother's rebellion against her own mother's Catholicism took an interesting form. My mother became a sort of syncretic, fucked-up Catholic. She got married in a conservative white dress, sure, but she wasn't no virgin, and her mohawk was growing out in feathery tufts. And she brought up her own children to believe not in one god but in all of them.

So, I believed everything. They were not all happy stories, but they were all true. I believed that Shadrach, Meshach and Abednego walked into the fiery furnace; I believed that Rumpelstiltskin flew through the night in a rage on his cooking ladle; I believed in the children who slept in the woods; and, for the longest time, I believed my father when he told me that the active cleaning ingredient in shampoo is made from the poo of shams – small animals that live in your hair and crawl into your ears if you aren't careful, and which are harvested by corporations and kept in factories on big nets which they shake the shit through like a sieve.

These days, while I no longer believe Dad's story about the shampoo, I've remained in careful awe of the power of the shit you rub into your head, and what we will do for it.

This letter is to myself, a long time ago in a real galaxy far, far away.

When I was eleven, in my last year of primary school, the boys got sent next door to watch a video – *Cliffhanger*, I think – and the girls went with Miss T, who drew a woman's reproductive system on the whiteboard and labelled the bits: labia, vagina, cervix, fallopian tubes, ovaries. The uterine parking space Miss T claimed was inside us all wasn't too disturbing to me then. I knew those things only happened to adults, and to adult women at that, and I was going to grow up and be a boy.

It was a bit deranged, how sure I was that I would one day be a boy. I already had my period, after all. But, see, I didn't think periods were about being a girl, not really. My period had arrived a few weeks before that first sex ed class, the week my Aunt Joy died of breast cancer, and the blood was intimately linked with her and my memories of her removing her fake breasts at night when I slept over, placing them on the bedside table. Breasts were something you could take off. Blood was only a sign of grief.

So while it might seem like I should be writing this letter to my eleven-year-old self, since that's when sex ed officially started, I'm not sure she'd understand its importance yet.

We'll go, instead, to my twelve-year-old self. To my second sex-ed classroom, in my first year of high school, where once again the boys have been asked to leave and the girls are being prepared for the real world, and every girl's seat has sitting in front of it a plastic show bag full of condoms, tampons and pads courtesy of the lovely people in the marketing department at Libra. A room where a story is being whispered.

I go back to that classroom all the time. I go back and I drag myself out of that class, and I take twelve-year-old Ruby down to the park. I give her a cigarette, because she's going to smoke anyway, and I make her a whisky sour. And I say: don't start fucking smoking.

And then I say: also, by the way, you will not grow up and be a boy.

In ten years, you won't even recognise yourself.

When my twelve-year-old self becomes defensive, I say: come on, Ruby. You know how, this year, you've been trying to hide the whole breasts thing? You know how it feels when men begin to look at you, just sometimes? You know that feeling. As if you are lost in your own flesh.

You'll be a girl, and then a woman. You'll grow pubic hair, and I mean it, not like what you're trying to cover up right now with those sun-smart bathers with the arm caps and boy legs; you will *grow* it. It will sprout out of your skin like a goddamn beard.

And you know what? That Brazilian you get at sixteen in the Ivanhoe Plaza's beauty salon for your boyfriend's formal? Don't. It will make you feel like you have a steak slapping down there between your thighs, you'll be walking to school with your legs crossed for days, it'll grow back with ingrown hairs like grilled cheese. Girl, you will have pubes. You are Scottish, wench. There are some things you cannot escape.

When I do this in my head, go back, this is the point where it gets difficult. Where I tell her that there are amazing, wonderful things about being a girl, and then a woman. But that it will take us over a decade to start working out what they are.

Because first, I tell her, there will be a story. Only one story; not the many. A whispering story, told quietly, in fragments. But it's a classic, it has the weight of the ages, and we'll pick up its thread everywhere we turn, over and over. We'll accumulate it for years, without even realising it.

I tell her about the man we will fall in love with when we're eighteen, in Paris. It will sound romantic. I tell her that he will be thirteen years older than us, and he'll be American, just out of his first marriage, and sort of broken, but we won't be sure, yet, what broken feels like, and we'll be crazy for him.

This is when the story will begin to hang off our arms and our legs, I tell her, wind its way around our neck at night, crawl into our ears like shams, whispering for our blood. It will become the only thing we can hear; it will become the grown-up story, the right one, the one with the happy ending. At dinner parties in Paris, we'll stop interrupting when the men are talking, our jaw heavy with fatigue while we listen to the story's low murmuring in our chest.

We'll begin to do every dish, wash every load, his correspondence will become our life as we walk behind him with our arms out, and it will feel right. The story will demand it; it won't be his fault. He will love us for it.

After six years together, standing alone in the cutlery department at Myer with a gift registry list, we'll be crying while we try to make choices he will like, because the idea of having to fight about the forks again, come back, return them, is too much. At twenty-four, all we will want is for our wedding to be over, so we never have to worry about love again.

Because at the end of the story, after the wedding, that's when we think it will all stop, that's when we think we can rest. And the story will be so heavy, we won't be able to carry its weight much further.

In the wedding boat on the way up the Yarra, with our reception looking down on us, he will elbow us and say: smile for the camera. And when the story demands it, we will.

I say to my twelve-year-old self: you will not recognise yourself. Six months after you get married, you will have an affair, smash every idea of ourself in our head, and every idea of ourself in his. The night before we finally leave him will take us another six years to understand. Which means that, right now, while we're here under this overhang, smoking our cigarettes and drinking our whisky sours, I still don't know how to explain to you exactly how bad it got, or how we got there.

After this, I will say to her: remember our kaleidoscope? The one that Father Christmas gave us. It was covered in a faded green paper, and the end was full of bright, shifting beads.

When we held it up to our eye and pointed it towards the sun, the beads shone and glowed, tessellating into crazy symmetrical patterns.

And each turn or shake of our wrist produced a new constellation, equally complex, equally beautiful. The same elements but the slightest movement and we had a completely different picture. We found patterns that were there before, that had always been there, but that we hadn't been able to see.

I will take some chalk out of my pocket, and together on the ground of Princes Park, while we should be in sex education, we will draw a woman, and while we draw, I will tell my twelve-year-old self that everything is always moving. I will tell her that the ends of the woman on the ground are not steady, but porous, shifting all the time, each atom vibrating against the next so if we get close enough we won't be able to see where the chalk ends and the air begins. We will promise to fight for the chalk woman even when we don't know what she means. (My twelve-year-old self and I will be a little drunk by this stage.)

We will agree, together, on what we will give the chalk woman, on what form our sacrifices will take.

We will give the chalk woman the many. We won't whisper them; we will scream them. We will give her Boadicea riding across the plains of England with her horde; we will give her Baba Yaga crouching in her chicken-legged hut; we will give her Rosa Parks on a bus in Montgomery, Alabama; and Ada Lovelace in front of the difference engine. We will give her enemies and failures, children and lovers and mothers and friends, mistresses and more. Margaret Mead in the jungles of Samoa, Marie Antoinette with cake on her face, Virginia Woolf with a pocket full of stones and Sylvia Plath with her head in the oven. Walyer the warrior of Van Diemen's, Gertrude Stein and Alice B Toklas in their Paris salon. We will shake our kaleidoscope again and again and give her the child of Hermes and Aphrodite, give her Pope Joan, and Scheherazade, sitting at the windowsill.

We will not whisper our stories, we will scream them. They will be so bright and so unlikely that they will float away into the hot sky and take us with them. With all our thousand stories sacrificed up to her, our chalk woman will tessellate and dissolve.

And my twelve-year-old self and I will remind ourself to doubt.

SACHA HORLER

Dedicated to my gorgeous boy of eight and divine girl of five, and my accomplice in dance.

To my biggest sacrifice,
or
Farewell to my old partying ways.

Hey, how's tricks?

I was just remembering that night, that rooftop party. Do you remember? It was a cracker! Over a hundred people squashed into that small square of roof, backs to the crumbling concrete walls, arms dangling, gripping the edge, holding ciggy butts, beer bottles, plastic cups, stained by cheap red. Looking down, down, for the third time that month, on irate neighbours.

The rooftop should have only held a third of us, but what did we care? We were buzzing. Me and all those happy people, we were glistening, we were dancing and drinking and offering ourselves to that glorious summer night.

Remember parties of wonderful summer sweat? Singlet stuck to my back as I danced and turned and drank and smoked and screamed. Bodies pressed up against mine, straining towards the music, diving into its sound. The music, sweet baby Jesus, the *music*. I could feel it in my mouth, swarming around my cheeks, spilling out past my lips onto the warm breeze of the night. I quickly sucked it back in and the music ran hot down my throat, mixing with the vodka and the cigarette smoke and my sweat, and it felt good and strong and alive.

'I never want this to end.'

Arms around my waist. I turned my face to see which whirling dervish of a boy had me in his grasp. It was so loud, we had to smash our faces together to hear, his lips hard against my ear.

I slip, I'm laughing, his grip tightens, and he is laughing, and as the neon light from some nearby building falls on his face, I look at this heavenly face and think, Beautiful. You are so beautiful.

Happiness surges up my thighs and into my chest, but somewhere there is pain. I close my eyes, flick them open – he's still there. But where am I?

The pain slides up and down and out of my body. I'm here, but not here. I can feel, but not feel. The surge begins.

Up goes my hand, my eyes rolling, neck straining, back arching, my fingers red and white, clenching and unclenching. My breath rasping against my throat. Then nothing.

'Come on.' A voice cracks through.

Where? I think. Downstairs? Leave the party?

'Come on.' The voice urges me on.

Ha! I laugh. This must be a stupid game. I must be more shitfaced than I thought. I close my eyes again and I can almost ignore this pain searing through me.

But then I look at my hand and there are knuckle bones straining against the skin, and they are gripping a crisp white sheet, on a bed, in a room. Not a rooftop. Not dancing.

Owwww. Fuck – I'm giving birth!

'Come on!' he says. 'You can do it!'

His fear is so present, so clear, his eyes so full of love. The boy from those parties so long ago, still here.

His hand gripping mine. I *can* do this. 'Come on, push, push!' His eyes catch me and hold me, swollen with love.

And my baby is beautiful.

My love, my perfect pink little divine delicious heart-bursting joy, is in my arms and that guy's here, the one from the rooftop party – next to me, holding my hand, holding our baby, crying tears of love.

Hang on, hang on! This baby/husband thing is cool, it's great, but I want to go back, just for a bit, just for a while, to that rooftop party, to all those great parties, because I was the life of the party – I was! No bullshit – really! I was the chick who you'd just met, and one vodka shot, one race onto the dance floor later, you were turning to your friend and saying, Who is that? Wow! She's great!

But don't worry about me, I can do it, I can transport myself back to long, long ago.

I'm back on the roof, voice hoarse from screaming over the music. His mouth so close to my ear, I can smell his last cigarette, his beer and the sweet stale breath of his words.

'Come on,' he says.

Where?

'In here.' He pulls me into a small room, almost a hallway.

It's musty and has worn, possibly puke-stained carpet. It's so dark, compared to the star-flecked dance floor, that I trip in the shadows and wobble on my feet. He takes the chance to scoop me onto a futon wedged in the corner. My bare summer skin hits plastic.

Plastic? Oh that's clever, because you never know who is going to spill a seven-dollar shiraz on your prize couch.

His body sandwiched on top of mine feels good, heavy, sweaty. My neck strains, turning to see his gorgeous face. His dark hair blocks the square of light coming from the other door.

His mouth on mine. We are melting in this summer night. Past his ear, which I am biting, I can just make out a bathroom window, people talking, trees waving hello

His strong hands hold me to him. We are mouths kissing and

bodies stretching and backs arching, lips on necks and hands on arses, and sweat, and grinding, and music in our ears, and please don't ever let it stop. More, more, I want more! More vodka, more kisses. Oh bloody hell, this is good. I'm swooning at these kisses – kiss me, kiss me, devour me with your beautiful lips. Kiss me forever!

The promise of more. The thrill, oh the thrill, of jeans pressed hard against jeans. The excitement and fear of someone coming in as we push into each other, the thrill of not knowing him that well, all of this, is heaven.

Don't stop! Don't stop! His belt pushes into my waist.

Ow, the pain, the good, good pain of lust –

Ow! *Owww!*

Ah fuck, that's right, I've just given birth – I'm back with a baby in my arms.

Our baby, that rooftop boy's and mine.

You crazy kids! You've got two now, you silly fuckers.

But I remember – do you? Long, long ago, that other me – younger, whirling, dancing, setting the world on fire.

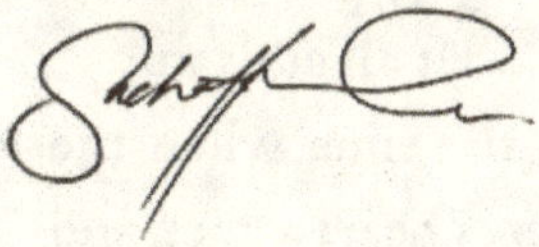

GENEVIEVE MORRIS

Dear General Physical, Mental and Emotional Health,
and Cholesterol and Blood Sugar Levels,

How have you been?

Firstly, can I just apologise for not being in contact with you on a more regular basis over the years? Please don't for a minute think that it's because I don't care about you or think of you often. That could never be the case. I mean, when Mum had her first heart attack at the age of thirty-eight, when I was only twelve, that's when I guess we really first met, wasn't it? And you've been a pretty big part of my life since then. It's just that things get in the way. Kids, work, social life, TV, Words with Friends . . . It all adds up.

Cholesterol, I bet you'll always remember the time when the four of us kids had our readings taken after Mum's heart attack and I got the highest score (7.6) even though I was only twelve and the youngest child. My joy was short-lived when you explained to me that it's better to get a reading closer to 4.5. Whatevs! It's currently at 5.6, FYI. I think it's probably only now that I'm a mum myself that I've become aware of how ill health can affect your children. And yet for so many years I've neglected to actually do anything about it.

Blood Sugar, you decided you'd like some attention too recently, and I was ready for you, since the rest of my family battles with type 2 diabetes. Jeez, you almost sucked me in, too, with your

6.2 reading (the normal range being between 3.6 and 6.0.) With the alcohol consumption, the Lindt chocolate, the Sara Lee apple pies with cream (I know, Cholesterol, but this bit isn't about you), I honestly don't know who I think I am when I'm under the spell of naughty consumption. It's like when Tim and I first got together almost nineteen years ago; in that first year we just ate and drank and rooted and smoked pot and ate and drank and rooted and ate hash cookies, and when I look back on photos from that time we got fairly large. My neck was as wide as my head. And nobody said anything like, 'Hey, you guys are porking up a bit, maybe you should ease up!' I probably would have told them to fuck off if they had, but my point is it can so easily happen. Well, Blood Sugar, I've lowered you from 6.2 to 5.4 now, so can we just agree to keep reminding each other, in a nice way, to think before we eat?

Mental Health, through bouts of depression and anger I would always catch up with you and various psychologists/psychiatrists, so I got to know you quite well, didn't I? It might seem like a bit of a mystery as to why we don't hang out more often, but can I be honest? You quite often really give me the shits. I find you high maintenance, you talk around in circles, you prevent me from *doing* by always forcing me to dwell on *thinking*. When I had my second child, Frankie, you'll recall I fell into a bit of a postnatal heap. I was lucky enough to be referred to a sensational psychologist who is a mother–baby specialist. That was four and a bit years ago and I've gone back to see her occasionally when needed, and one of the best strategies she has given me is to remember to *get moving*. Not sit in the shit – which no doubt you might prefer me to do – but to get physically active. What a revelation.

Which I guess is why you, General Physical Health, as the overseer of the whole unit, are owed the biggest apology. I'm forty-five years old, so seven years older than Mum was when she first became ill. I've never been a cigarette smoker, and that's probably been my saving grace. The fact that Mum was a smoker turned me off it, but I have smoked my fair share of marijuana in the past – and still do on the odd festive occasion. I like it. But the fact that I've started being more physical over recent years has helped in so many areas, and will hopefully mean I'm able to maintain a reasonable level of health as my kids and I grow older.

In January of this year (after months of agonising over will I or won't I?), I joined a mums' exercise group run by a personal trainer. They're called 'Booty Babes', which is why I'd been reluctant to join. I remember I pulled up so sore after the first session that I thought, I don't know if I'll be able to continue with this. But I did. It's now almost September and I can fucking jog! Not a really long distance or anything, but considering I couldn't even run for a tram in the past, this is big. My happiness levels are much higher, while my cholesterol and blood sugar levels are lower. I've also managed three sober months this year, which I find helpful (Febfast, Abstinence April and Dry July) and I'll need to do Sober September or Octsober to keep on feeling good. If I could be more moderate in the other months that could help too! But baby steps.

The reason I decided to write to you all in the first place was to let you know that Mum passed away two and a half weeks ago. She was seventy-four. High-grade lymphoma was what got her in the end. She had battled so many illnesses in her life: heart attacks, angina, breast cancer, diabetes, osteoporosis, depression and, of course, lymphoma. Some were unpreventable diseases, but had she had a better level of general and physical health, I believe the fight would have been a more evenly matched one.

This is why I make this promise to you, General Physical, Mental and Emotional Health and Cholesterol and Blood Sugar Levels, not to sacrifice our relationship any longer. We must keep in touch. We must make it a priority. If we don't, life will be shit. And

I don't want that, for myself, or for Tim or Nessie or Frankie. I want longevity, laughter and love. And I'm thankful that our training group is now called 'Mums in Motion', because I also want dignity.

Yours in reasonable health,
Genevieve xxx

Genevieve Morris

To my unfinished business

AILSA PIPER

To the girl still walking in Yamaji Country,

I was born at the bottom of the world, on the edge of a great ocean. Before my eyes could focus, I was taken to a place in the desert, where I grew strong out of the red dust that was my whole world.

My mother, she said I walked before I crawled, but I remember the earth up close at eye-level – stuffing fat fistfuls of it into my mouth, inhaling it into my lungs, making paste with the drool I dribbled into it.

I can't remember a first step, maybe because, as Mum said, I walked early. But in the silent red of the desert, under the still blue of the sky, I walked down gullies and along ant trails, past spinifex spikes that bit my flesh, and across creek beds of eternally dry sand.

My strides lengthened. My body strengthened. I walked, staking out territory I thought of as my own, unaware I was tracing lines that had been mapped for thousands of years.

I sang as I walked – songs I didn't know belonged to other people. Songs my grandmother taught me.

'Jerrenbarrah warrenah . . .'

Songs that belonged to that red earth.

It walked me through my childhood, until I had to go away to a school where we played on concrete and asphalt, and I made a friend who was blonde, like me. She was a town girl, but she was allowed to come to our home for holidays, where we'd float in the icy water of a house tank, drifting toward the spongy green moss that coated the corrugated iron walls, before kicking ourselves back into the centre again. We were in the sky, in the water, in our dreams.

'Jerrenbarrah warrenah. . . .'

Bubble-and-squeak in the frypan. Beady-eyed emus at the gate. Bushfires on the horizon meant women cutting corn beef sandwiches late into the night. Orange and blue silk shirts against black skin meant horse-breaking time.

Water-bag water, sweet like no other, spilling down my chest. Slurping roo-tail soup and spreading quandong jam. Featherfoots on the ridges. The dripping cool-house walls at midday and the silent void at night.

'Jerrenbarrah warrenah . . .'

I didn't know it could end. Like the desert, it would just continue.

Then I was taken away from the red, back to the edge of the great ocean, where I walked myself into adolescence, winding my way through its lush terrain. I listened to new songs, and, for the first time, to the sound of my own voice, and of my mother's and grandmother's. I didn't want to be different, so the desert songs went unsung.

I walked on into adulthood, falling in love with words from the top half of the world. I walked them into my brain, erasing the songs of the red earth and its silent sky, and closing the door my grandmother had opened.

That grandmother had travelled from a tiny moss-green island, all the way across the great ocean, to reach our desert at the bottom of the world. She learned a new language called Yamaji to ward off the loneliness she felt, and it was in Yamaji that she gossipped and sang.

It was only later, when I walked myself into a world called the theatre, that I understood she had an accent like no other, a blend of County Antrim and Yamaji. She said she dreamed in two languages. By the time she died, I was dreaming in languages from the top half of the world. The dominant hemisphere.

When my mother was dying, she insisted she was being sung to death, and wouldn't let go until she was visited by Pearl, a Yamaji woman who came as though conjured, and spoke words of comfort I wouldn't have understood. They joked together, and sang a line or two, and when Pearl left my mother was ready to take the walk from *is* to *is not*.

By then, I could have said *grazie*, *gracias*, *merci* or thank you to Pearl, but I had not one word of Yamaji to express my gratitude.

I've never returned to the red earth I mapped as a child, though in recent years I have let myself sing when I walk. I talk to myself, too. I do it in four languages, and I feel I'm a different person in each of them. Mostly I live and love in English, but I walk taller in French, I am surer in Spanish, and in Italian I just want to grin.

But none of those languages was formed from the land I call home, and I don't even know if that snatch of song I have carried is really the song I was given so long ago.

'*Jerrenbarrah warrenah . . .*'

I have unfinished business with the red earth and silent sky of Yamaji country, and with the girl who was left behind when I walked away.

I understand that those songs can never be fully mine, any more than French *chansons* or Spanish *canciones*. But I want to know who I will be when I form those sounds again; and more, much more, I want to know what I might hear, if I could listen to Yamaji being spoken and understand it again – just a little.

Perhaps if I could say 'thank you' in Yamaji, a conversation might begin. Perhaps if I could say 'sorry' in Yamaji, I might earn the right to retrace my steps down those ant-trails and gullies, and I might just find you, the girl out there walking, trying to come home.

Ailsa

Ailsa x

KATE MULVANY

To my unfinished business,

Hi. We've never met. At this stage, it's unlikely we ever will.

Sorry about that.

It's not for want of trying. I promise I've tried to set things on course for you and me. I've asked for directions from all sorts of people – medical, governmental and mystical – in order to get to you. Find you. Hold you. Meet you.

But the fact is, my darling . . . Wait. Would I call you 'darling'? I don't think so. I'm not really a 'darling' person. Maybe you're not either. Are you? Maybe 'sweetheart'? 'Buggalugs'? 'Bubski'? No. Maybe just your name. Whatever that would be – they say you know the name the moment you . . .

Anyway, the point is, whoever you are, I tried.

Let me explain things properly.

Once upon a time long, long ago in the '1960s' in the place where I live – which is a planet called 'Earth' – there was a war in a 'country' – that's a patch of land – called 'Vietnam'. Vietnam has very nice people living in it who are always smiling and make delicious food. A 'war' is like a big fight started by 'governments' – they're people in suits who make decisions for the rest of us. Anyway, these people in suits decided that they would have a war in Vietnam because . . .

Because . . .

I'll have to get back to you on that one.

Anyway, at that stage, in the 1960s, only 'men' – they're people with penises, one of which you may or may not have (don't tell me) – were allowed to fight. Nowadays they let 'women' – who are people with vaginas – fight too, which is really thoughtful of them.

(Oh, by the way, I'm going to use the words 'they' and 'them' a lot in this letter. You can make up your own mind about who 'they' and 'them' are. 'They' and 'them' do and say a lot of things, but don't get confused – 'they' and 'them' are not really worth worrying about most of the time.)

Anyway, when people are having a war, they often use 'guns' to hurt each other. Guns are metal things that project other metal things into people's stomachs and faces and bottoms and stuff. In Vietnam they used guns but they also used a 'spray' – that's like a lovely cool mist – to kill the trees so that the 'enemy' – don't worry, you won't ever have one of those – had nowhere to hide.

Anyway, my 'daddy' – you would have called him 'Granddad' or 'Poppa' or something like that – he was told he had to go to Vietnam to be in the war with the guns and the spray. And he went because they didn't give him a 'choice'. A choice is something everyone should have but a lot of people have them taken away for all kinds of funny reasons. Anyway, my dad – your Granddad or Poppa or whatever you want to call him – went to Vietnam and luckily didn't have any metal objects hit him in the belly, face or bottom. However, he was unfortunate enough to 'breathe' – breathing is this thing that humans do where they suck air in and out of their lungs – it keeps them alive. 'Alive' is something you're not, so don't worry too much about the breathing thing.

Anyway, Dad breathed in the spray and he brought it back to 'Australia' – that's the patch of land I'm writing from. He brought it back inside his body and he and 'Mum' – a mum is what I'd be to you – he and my mum 'made love', which is a wonderful occurrence when two people – sometimes more, but generally two – show each other how much they care for one another by doing all sorts of interesting and wacky things with their bodies. When two people make love – wow, I'm getting a bit teary – I never thought we'd actually have this conversation – but when two people make love, sometimes . . .

They make a miracle.

Now, 'miracle' is a word that's been stolen by the 'church' – a church is not a building like you might think, but a big corporation. But I want you to know that the real definition of a miracle has nothing to do with priests and altars and wine and water but is in reality something that happens everywhere, every minute, every day. Because every living thing in the universe is a miracle. The way we all got here is crazy – it shouldn't be possible – but it is. It is. There are miracles literally everywhere.

I wish you could see.

Anyway, Mum and Dad – your Grandma and Granddad – made love and – miraculously! – made me. Unfortunately, that spray that Dad breathed in Vietnam made its way through his body and into mine. The spray made my 'organs' – they're annoying musical instruments, but they're also things that pump blood around a human's body and keep us ticking – that spray made my organs very sick, and so the doctors – they're very overworked people who try their hardest to make poorly people feel better – had to take out most of my insides which makes it very hard for me to do certain things.

Like make you.

But that's the bad news. The good news is, in my mind, you still exist. The government and the war and the spray did not take you away from me. Because the possibility of you does not wane. I promise. Me and you – we're not finished. Otherwise they've won.

This is not a goodbye letter.

You and me, we're just biding our time. Waiting for the right temperature.

But because it's going to be quite tricky for us to ever actually meet, I want you to know what you might be in for when we do.

I hate balloons. Like really, really hate them. It's not the loud noise thing. It's the fact that they're gone so quickly. Their beautiful peaceful floaty life ends so abruptly and violently. It's a mortality thing. And so, if and when you happen, you won't have any balloons ever at your birthday parties. I just want to put that on the table straight away.

That said, I'm fine with bubbles and can do this really cool trick with my hands and soap and can make bubbles appear literally out of thin air. So that's a good trade-off.

Ankles don't run in the family, so don't expect to get any. Fine if you're a male. If you're a female, it will be frustrating to wear strappy heels. Sorry about that. Maths is also not a strong point.

I love reading books and will read you one every day, complete with awesome voices and props. I promise. I won't even skip pages like I know a lot of parents do. That's how much I love books.

I'm one of those people that posts cat videos. Sorry in advance.

I'm an actor and a playwright. That means sometimes I don't make much money. But for everything I can't afford to buy you, I will back it up with a network of crazy, wonderful, diverse, loving, brilliant artists who will be your family for the rest of your life. You will always be safe with them.

I will never take away your right to choose. No matter what. I'll be terribly opinionated about certain things that I think are best for you, but I will never ever fuck with your choices. You have to learn to make your own decisions. Just really try not to hurt anyone – including yourself.

I will say fuck a lot. It's a good word and covers a lot of bases. I don't mind if you say it too, but pick your moments.

Once I loved a man who found the world very, very sad. I thought he was going to be your dad and that maybe the possibility of you might make him better. It didn't. Sometimes love doesn't cure everything. Just so you know.

Of all the drugs, alcohol is the worst. Be careful with it.

Your grandparents are brilliant, eccentric, flawed, funny people. They've been through a lot. Ask them whatever you like. They'll probably have the answer.

I have no idea about God.

I love cuddles, the Muppets and spaghetti. Preferably all at once.

Sometimes I can be mean. I'll get cross at silly things and walk around like a huffy little duchess. I promise you, these moments are often short-lived, and I'm good at admitting I'm wrong. Unless I'm not.

Always insist on the best from your politicians. They're the ones that got us into this mess. So make sure they answer your questions.

I know now who I would like your dad to be and I will do my darnedest to make it so. Because he's wonderful and quite good-looking and terribly good with cats and I'd like you two to meet.

So . . . I will add to this list constantly until you come, because even writing to the possibility of you makes me smile. Makes me hope. Makes me dream. So wherever you are, whatever you are – my tiny cell of potential – my unborn, almost impossible possibility – I'm already proud of you. Maybe one day. Maybe one day. Maybe one day. Let's keep trying.

Love,
Mum

Mum x
(Kate Mulvany)

SALLY HEATH

Dear Writer,

Does our conversation ever end? I don't imagine so.

It starts in so many ways. I become obsessed with an idea and then hunt for a scribe who might get it as well. You become obsessed with an idea and hunt for a publisher. We both have half-ideas and worry at each other 'til something whole is formed.

Then comes the writing. Sometimes it comes together seamlessly, quickly, and is perfectly formed. Other times, no matter how much forethought, preparation and eagerness, the result is leaden, overwritten and breathless; not what either of us imagined.

But there it is. On a page. In an inbox. Waiting for feedback.

Of course, there are many pieces of writing submitted without any of those glorious preliminary discussions. What I start to read has no background story and your author history is an attached paragraph or the result of a Google search.

So I tread more gently, knowing nothing of you or the origins of the work.

Others are variations on versions that have been passed to and fro between us many times over. Inched on, developed by a queried word, a misunderstanding or a new thought.

Some are a self-contained thousand words; others necessarily spill across a hundred thousand words.

Each needs a response.

I prefer to do a first reading on hard copy and, because open-plan offices are distracting places, much of my evenings and weekends are spent reading your words.

My mother-in-law says her first vision of me was hunched over a manuscript in a car. I have missed hockey tournaments and vital milestones on the pony club circuit because I was immersed in your story or argument. Happily so.

But then I need to find words worthy of a reply. Just as I am stalling now, I know I often disappoint you.

Some responses are quick and brief. Submissions *are* often closed or publishing programs committed and full, but these are many times code for 'Did you even look up the organisation you sent your strangely shaped poem/family history/article on the same topic we published last week/250000 word biography of an obscure French dentist to?'

When you write articles that are good but just not that good, I try and suggest other outlets that might be grateful for them. I might hint at the problem by saying the topic has been well covered already. Or suggest that, while it is well crafted, it doesn't bring anything new to the issue. All writers should be readers and understand that the quality of what is being published is extremely high. And know what others have written before them.

Then there is the silence. That is usually when I am re-reading, getting second opinions, pondering and worrying on your work. Often there is a 3 a.m. rehearsal of the phone call or email I might compose. Somehow I can always read the notes I have written myself in the dark.

Sometimes you have ranged too wide and in the breadth of the piece lost momentum and direction. Other times you haven't had the nerve to not include every detail you have come across. You have lacked the courage to shut your notebook and write.

But to simply say 'it just doesn't work' isn't enough. Why the narky tone? Would it be better in the third person? Tell me more . . .

I am ever impressed and grateful that even when you are 'shocked' and 'disagree' with my queries, you still absorb and respond to critical suggestions. At final pages, when I risked, after so many years and versions, answering your 'And was there anything else?' with 'Yes, I am concerned about the digression in the middle of chapter thirteen', you kept your nerve and shaved down that section, making the press date three days later.

And you, award-winning author, who sent your piece of memoir with the added information that two other editors and an esteemed writer liked the piece very much, responded immediately to my suggestion of 'What about less of a shopping list and a bit more detail?' with 'Yes, I thought as much as well.'

And when I wrote a paragraph or two explaining why an extremely personal piece that covered a father's death and the loss of the family fortune lacked focus and didn't bring any of the characters to life, you thanked me for my 'close reading'.

My tiny feedback seems disproportionate to the works you send my way. But an untrained editor, such as I am, is only an intuitive one, so I am very aware my reactions are subjective and I have limited language to detail my thoughts.

I also know my reaction to a piece that transports me, that is so much more than what I was anticipating, can be equally poor. 'I love this!' says nothing. Not even 'job done'. Because even then, we will both massage words, phrases, look at the work in proofs, read it again once printed. Was there more I could have done along the way? Invariably, yes.

I know the satisfaction of a tied bow that says 'dealt with'. I have written to a mother-in-law of a previous decade to say, 'I'm sorry I never got to say goodbye.' And, even though it took almost twenty years, I've written and explained my actions to a sweet boy I was set to marry but then went to the registry office with another.

And with writing I know the elusive desire to create perfection unedited.

But maybe there are no tidy endings to writing and publishing. At its best, it is an exchange, always unfinished.

SARAH BLASKO

To my dearest, darling life,

You are mine. You are everything. I know now that you are my imperfect and unfinished work, but for so many years I thought that you were somehow a foregone conclusion. Even now, I still struggle to accept that you are not. But although we were somehow separated when I was a child, I now claim you back as my own, as my first love. You are my beginning and my end. My first and my last. You may not go on and on forever and continue after my death, and I may never fully understand you, but that does not make you any less significant to me. You are precious and you are all I have in this moment. From you joy, sorrow, suffering, hope and love spring forth, and I embrace you. Teach me. I am here.

It's taken me a painfully long time to be able to acknowledge you in this way. I was ashamed and didn't want to be a part of you. You see, I was taught what you were very clearly from the time I was born and before I had the chance to know for myself. I thought somehow I knew you from what others told me and so I built up a very limited picture of you. I didn't believe that I could discover you for myself and you were often neglected. I thought there was only one important reality and that it lay beyond you and beyond what I could see in you. I was told you would end very soon and what mattered was the next life and the spiritual world, not you or the physical world around me.

Even now I try so hard to love and cherish you, to know you and accept you, when all I want to do is diminish your importance, to run away from you and fantasise about there being something more, something other than you – my ever-constant life. I often reject you for your faults because I want to believe that I am different from you, that I am somehow not a part of you. I pretend that I don't relate to you, when you *are* me and I you. It sounds crazy that I could ever think of us as separate. But it's always been easier for me to think that I'm not from here, that I don't belong in this life, I belong to God. All that matters is what is to come in the *next* life. The afterlife. But if it does exist, what is that life to me if I have not tried to know you, my constant?

It is a blessing and a relief to now accept that you are unfinished, that you are imperfect, that I have this time to get to know you, to learn. I don't have to pretend I know everything and that I can attempt to know you for myself. For you, my life, are never going to be what I think you are and you will constantly defy my expectations and surpass my understanding. It turns out you are so much more than I ever gave you credit for. You are ever-changing, full of complexity, and I will never fully know you – but that is the wonder of you, my life. If I take time to gaze upon you, to ponder you, to look and touch and smell and taste, and continue to enquire until my final breath, I still won't fully understand you – but I will at least know something of you and be surprised by you.

I thought you were limited and merely a prelude to something far more important and that you were not full of mystery or even worth knowing. I thought you were mostly irrelevant and that the important things I needed to know about you were held in the Bible. But I am thankful that I am here now at this point of realisation and that I still have this time to revel in you just for what you are – nothing more. Not because of any need to find God in you, but because I realise that you are wonderful in yourself and I want to enjoy you. To delight in your complex beauty – to feel all your joy and sorrow, and to accept you at long last.

I thought I'd worked you out from the age of about ten years old when I gave myself to God. It seemed to me that God valued you, but only if you brought me to him. That everything worth knowing about you related to him. I saw you through his eyes rather than my own. I looked upon you, I observed you, I criticised you, but I really knew nothing of you even though I thought I did. I lived cut off from all the potential that you offered and I was afraid to step into the unknown. I chose to live in a state of concrete reality. I was told you were an in-between place that I would suffer through until I reached that haven where I truly belonged. That you were full of evil and imperfection and I shouldn't grow too accustomed to you, but keep my distance so as not to let you taint me. I was told that heaven was where I belonged, not here on earth with you. In heaven everything was perfect. There was no suffering, there were no tears, and if I could just hold on in this life then I would make it there.

The problem is, when I decided to hold on to this ideal of heaven, I neglected you. You dried up, and it's taken years to fill in your colours again. I was often led to believe that you were almost the antithesis of heaven and so I shied away from knowing you fully and inhabited a very limited sphere. They may have been right. You are not always beautiful, you can be ugly and cruel and full of evil, but you are mine. I didn't want to accept you because you were flawed when there was something awaiting me that was perfection. Why get too close to this life, when my real life would start in the next?

I distinctly remember at a church camp when I was twelve earnestly believing that Jesus was going to come back soon and that I wouldn't see thirty years of age and so you didn't matter so much. It was almost a relief; it was an escape. And this sense of you not mattering has lingered with me ever since and has often created an emptiness inside of me. When you feel you're going to lose something you detach, after all.

I must confess that for many years I used you as a place to inhabit like a waiting room. When I thought I didn't need you we drifted apart and I could never, until much later in life, understand that this disconnection from you was what caused me so much pain. When hard times arose, the feeling of emptiness was my inability to accept that this was you, right here in front of me. 'How could it be?' I questioned. 'This is you? It can't be you, this is not what I was told you were!' And so there were many times when I wanted you to be gone, I wanted you to be over, because it was too hard to accept you.

Sometimes I do hate you. You are a constant reminder of imperfection and I learned at a very young age to only love perfection and purity. That you are an unfinished business, a work in progress, has probably been the toughest thing I have had to learn and I struggle with this every day.

Oh my dear life, you are much more than I could have ever known. I wish I had realised earlier that all of your difficulties really do make the experience of you richer somehow. I can't even begin to thank you for being imperfect, for the overwhelming beauty I have experienced in the midst of all the heartbreak and loss you have brought.

And so I promise to adore you and be true to you for as long as I'm on this earth. And if there is another life after this, then I will love that too, but first I must finish this work before I can begin the next.

I will – even though sometimes I feel disconnected from you, I drift away, I feel alone, misunderstood, hurt, and I can no longer see all your potential and promise.

For what did I honestly think was more worthy than you?

You, my life, are thankfully not over yet, you are unfinished . . . And having only just begun to realise what you mean to me, I want to let you know that I'm not ready to lose you, not yet.

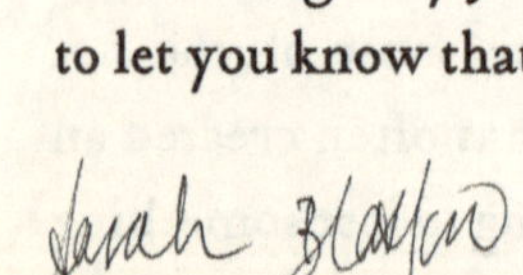

To the thing I yearn for

NELLY THOMAS

Dear D-Wayne,

Let's get one thing clear from the start – you have a ridiculous name. I never had the chance to tell you that, D-Wayne, in the almost five years we worked together, but I'm telling you now.

Wayne is a name. D-Wayne is a name with a superfluous consonant. The first of many mistakes your parents made with you, I'm sure.

The thing is, D-Wayne, you were my first. My first boss. You managed the only fast food outlet in my home town in the West Australian Wheatbelt. It was called Big Rooster. Guess who was the Big Rooster, D-Wayne? Yes, D-Wayne, it was me. I dressed in a rooster suit and entertained kids at their birthday parties.

D-Wayne, we'd never had birthday parties before you because the 'restaurant' in our shop consisted of a couple of tables and some discarded stuffing we couldn't get off the terracotta tiles. (Well, I say we 'couldn't' get it off, D-Wayne, but I'm sure if I'd got down on my knees and scrubbed it, I could have prized it free, but we both knew I wasn't that kind of girl, D-Wayne.) But you, D-Wayne, didn't let the lack of suitable space deter you! You had vision, and simply moved the parties – to the car park.

Sure it was 40-plus degrees most days.

Okay, the car park was made of bitumen.

It's true, we were on the Great Eastern Highway.

And yes, *there were cars coming in and out*.

But damn it, D-Wayne, you chalked off a square section in the corner and insisted that this magical powdery force field would protect the youngsters in our care. Chuck a snack pack and a can of Coke at them and voila – it's Whippersnapper Mardi Gras!

And yes, D-Wayne, I dressed in that rooster suit in 40-degree heat in that car park for you and I entertained those kids. Of course, all that came to an end one fateful day when a little boy put his hand inside my rooster suit, squeezed my breast and yelled, 'It's a girl, it's a girl!' Humiliating me was one thing, D-Wayne, but it was the '80s and you weren't about to risk a *do-gooder-lesbian bloody sexual harassment suit!* You'd seen *9 to 5*, D-Wayne, you knew how that little scenario ended.

Besides, that was the best job you'd ever had, D-Wayne! You were a manager, with a badge, and your own car park!

Oh, D-Wayne, remember your car park? In a stunning act of management, one day you waltzed into work and announced that you were creating a reserved car park. For yourself. It was to say 'MANAGER' on a plaque screwed to the curb, and no one else was to park there. None of us had a licence, and almost all the customers used the drive-through, but nonetheless, it was a brilliant idea, D-Wayne. You carved out a little piece of paradise, just for numero uno. With that one gesture, D-Wayne, you announced to the world: 'Today, I'm gonna be somebody.' And you were, D-Wayne, right up until the Colts lost the grand final and Mouse Hoban got dared to smear shit on your plaque. It didn't shine after that, did it, D-Wayne?

The thing is, D-Wayne, when it comes down to it, we just didn't get along. By which I mean, I had to work for you, and you were a bit of a cunt. Now, I don't use that word lightly – and I've waited a long time to say it – but if the stained Y-fronts fit, D-Wayne, you gotta wear them. To be fair to you, though, you were an improvement on the previous manager. You were just mean and incompetent; he spent most of his time trying to get a hand job behind the grease trap.

Some of your worst moments were probably just oversights. Like when you introduced the new uniforms. We went from a perfectly respectable blue skirt, white shirt and *kerchief* (your emphasis, not mine, D-Wayne), to a tight, yellow dress of see-through fabric with a tiny red apron. I was a size 16, D-Wayne. You had a morbidly obese wife – no judgement, D-Wayne, just some info – and obviously had a thing for the volumptuous (sic), but the world didn't, D-Wayne. Not then, not now. You didn't think of that, did you, D-Wayne?

Other times you were a combination of incompetent and cowardly. Like, remember when you'd miscalculate the stock, D-Wayne, and we'd run out of chicken and you'd make me front the angry mob? I was fourteen, D-Wayne.

'I'm sorry, sir, we don't have any chicken left today.'

'You're called Big *Rooster*!'

'I realise that.'

'What are you, just big? *Hahahahah.*'

Then there were the times you were just desperate to fuck me up. You'd make me try and sell out-of-date coleslaw, you'd get me to clean the toilets after footy teams had come through, and oh, then there was the time you made me sing about the new Hawaiian Pack over the PA to the tune of 'Stutter Rap':

Now hey there people won't you lend an ear,
I've got an Hawaiian Pack and I'm selling it here.
It was made in this town in WA,
With a chicken, pineapple and banana fritter today.
And it comes with chips,
And it tastes real good,
I'd eat it all day if I could.
Yeah, I'd eat it all day if I could.
Say what?
I'd eat it all day, if I could.

Would they like chips with that? No, they wouldn't, D-Wayne.

Of course, there *were* times you'd try and help me, D-Wayne. Like the pop quizzes, D-Wayne. Remember those? I was doing well at school, and you, D-Wayne, quite rightly, were worried I'd get too big for my boots. To help me out with this you'd fire questions at me at random times, just to prove I was actually stupid.

'Hey, Nelly, what's the capital of Ethiopia?'

'Addis Ababa, D-Wayne. It's the '80s, we just did a project on the famine.'

'Hey, Nelly, what's twelve times twelve?'

'144, D-Wayne. Now should I salt the chickens?'

'Hey, Nelly, who wrote *A Fortunate Life*?'

'AB Facey, D-Wayne. It's, like, the only book in the library, dude. There's a display cabinet for it.'

Then there was the time we threw down over the third decimal point of pi. You said it was 3.141. I said it was 3.142. You got a math textbook from Mrs Edgecombe that said it was 3.141. I explained that it depends how many decimal points you go to, and that the next number is 5, so in this instance you round *up* to 3.142. You told me to go and clean the deep fryer. 3.141 times.

It got to the point, D-Wayne, where I pissed you off so much by winning an English award at school, that you asked me to bring in my year twelve literature essays *so you could critique them*. I thought I had to, D-Wayne, so I did. You thought my essay on *Wuthering Heights* had some problems, D-Wayne, and you wrote, in big red ink, some helpful suggestions, like 'stupid sentence', 'wrong', 'you don't understand anything', and, my personal favourite, 'what's your point?'

Incidentally, D-Wayne, I did go on to university – the first person in my family to do so – and I even did honours in English. My thesis was called, *'Queerying Australian Cinema: Sense and sexuality in* The Adventures of Priscilla, Queen of the Desert*'*. Yes, D-Wayne, I realise *Priscilla* is a movie and not a book, but it was the '90s, D-Wayne, and everything was a text then. Oh, D-Wayne, you know Fouc-ault about these things.

Look, D-Wayne, I must go, but I can't leave without saying one thing. D-Wayne, I forgive you. I forgive you for the yellow uniform, the rooster suit, the Hawaiian Pack rap, the sneering comments and the pop quizzes. I even forgive you for not giving me the night off when The Angels came to town and Doc Neeson threw that guitar pic at Charise Italiano. (Am I ever gonna see his face again, D-Wayne? No way, D-Wayne, get fucked, fuck off). I forgive you for running out of chicken, for the car park and for taking a young girl and undermining her confidence at every opportunity.

I sincerely hope, D-Wayne, that today, a quarter of a century hence, you're happy, that your family is healthy (and possibly slenderer), and that if you happen to be dead, you've found that big personalised car park space in the sky.

Before I go, D-Wayne, I've yearned, all these years, to sort one thing out, and so, for the purposes of today's event, I did some research into pi. In fact, I contacted Dr Simon Cropper at Melbourne University. I don't know if you know him, D-Wayne, but he's pretty fuck'n good at maths. And guess what, D-Wayne? He has confirmed that the third decimal point of pi is, in fact, 3.142.

Yes, D-Wayne, I was right. *Say what?* Yep, 100 per cent right.

Yours sincerely,
Nelly Thomas

DANI VALENT

A letter to my eldest daughter, who is now nine, to be given to her when she turns fourteen, because I am hoping – yearning – that she won't be the kind of teenager I was.

Dear R,

I was horrible when I was your age. Rude. Careless. Selfish. Angry. I fought with my parents – your nonna and grandad, who we both know are lovely and reasonable. I fought with them about the usual stuff: late nights, boys, skirts, where it was okay to be, and who with. I guess it was hormones and growing up, but all I knew was that I wanted to kiss boys, take drugs, push anything solid and obstructive, find new ways to be naughty. I badly wanted all that: I felt like it would fit me, that it was the way to become myself. And I put myself in harm's way until harm started happening.

I barely considered my parents' feelings for five years. I saw them only as facilitators or blockers, not as people who felt and thought, though they kept sharing their thoughts and expressing their feelings, their 3 a.m. worries, their careful concerns. That made me impatient. It only touched me insofar as it prevented me from doing what I wanted.

I lied all the time, not so much to prevent conflict but really just to save time. There's a great trick that I hope you never learn: you say you're staying at Bec's house and Bec says she's staying at your house. And then you go to nightclubs with your fake IDs.

Fake ID? Oh, you just photocopy your birth certificate and white-out the year, then dye the paper and use a typewriter to put it back a year or three.

Typewriter? A clickety-clack thing. Like the one we threw out.

It wasn't even that much fun. Bec was much prettier and when she lit a cigarette she didn't set her hair on fire so she pashed the spunky guys with cars and I spoke to their awkward tram-ticketed friends.

And by the way, I will always text your friends' parents and that's how I will always catch you out. And you're grounded.

[Um, Michaela, Marieke? I'm not putting this letter in the time capsule today, okay? I think I need to work on it a bit before I seal it up for R.]

Anyway, ever since you were born I have wondered if part of your role will be to avenge my mother. Not that she would wish it. She's too nice.

But when you roll your eyes at me because I'm wearing 'the ugliest trousers in the world', or you complain that I never let you have fun, or you fume at me because I am trying to keep you safe, well, I feel like I deserve it and then some.

Sometimes I see you hate me for a little while and I almost like it. I appreciate it, anyway: the raw humanity of that drive to separate. It's awe-inspiring. But it drains me, too. Makes me sad. And sometimes I just feel like a bad mother unleashing a rude, angry girl on the world.

I vowed I wouldn't be like my parents. But when piercing love and panic makes me feel like they must have felt, at the very least I try hard not to let certain maddening phrases leave my lips. *It's not appropriate. Because I said so. This conversation is over. While you're under this roof . . .* But I've already heard myself say them and when you spit them back at me, that's when I most feel like a failure.

I was pretty sure I was going to be one of those cool mums. But I had to let go of that expectation when I arranged to pick up your older brother, my teenage stepson, from a party.

'You'll just text me from the car, right? Don't come in,' he said. 'Seriously?' I asked. 'What am I going to see in there?' 'Nothing, it's just inherently embarrassing when a parent comes inside.'

Ah, sweet, politic child of the divorced. It's not you, Dani, it's me. Even so, he checked twice to make sure I would stay in the car. I got the subtext too: I should keep my eyes forward and, please, no smileys or kisses in my 'I'm here' text message. I'm a parent, ergo I don't have a clue.

There's an incident from my teenage years that still chills me when I think about it. My mother and I were having one of our normal 'You're not going!' 'Yes I am!' discussions. It escalated somehow and I remember Mum came towards me, possibly in anger and hurt, but more probably in a kind of love that I couldn't accept just then.

I pushed her and she fell and I was so shocked to see her on the ground that I turned and left the house and walked up the steep hill away from it, her, every step a fight with gravity. I was even battling the elements. I hope you won't need to do that, R.

Mum wrote me a letter soon after that, a relinquishing of sorts that must have cost her a lot and hopefully let her off the hook a bit too. I remember one phrase from it, 'woman grown', and the power that I felt it gave me. And how sad it made me too.

R, I remember when you were eight and a half – passionate about ponies, Slurpees, piano and the Famous Five. I first smelled sweat on you and spotted a few advance-party pubes and I felt grief that you were changing into a creature that would pull away from me.

Around the same time you had a fight with your little sister. I was a frustrated witness to this particular sisterly embrace and I decided it was your fault so I tried to pull you off her. Your strong body twisted away from me and I realised that I couldn't really control you physically any more. I saw you realise it too. There was a kind of relief in that, and also fear.

I try to let you go a bit more each month, certainly each year. And each extra release is partly because I hope you will not push yourself hard away from me, the way that I did from my loving mother.

I hope that you won't be like me – that you'll be less hateful and contemptuous. But I do want you to feel some of what I did, and for you to latch onto the things you need to do to become yourself, to feel the world is welcoming and open for you and full of stuff you're desperate to do.

And maybe, just maybe, you'll do it with grace and gratitude, not just attitude. Perhaps you'll even pash the guy with the car.

Love,
Mum

dani xo

LINDA BULL

Dear Dad,

As I am writing this letter, you are cleaning my backyard and singing loudly in your best Bing Crosby voice, yelling out for more garbage bags, with your overalls completely unbuttoned, and telling me off for collecting so much junk.

I have been asked to write a letter about the thing I yearn for. Lots of things have come to mind, but you keep rising to the top.

I know it will embarrass the hell out of you. I can see you scratching your beautiful bald head and thinking – why me? Why the bloody hell don't you write about your mother or something more interesting? Why don't you write about the idea of yearning for a cleaner house or five minutes rest?

Perhaps most women would write about their mothers. No offence, Mum, you are an awesome force of a woman and if I get the opportunity again you'll be next, but quiet little Aussie Bull, your husband of fifty-odd years, has got me thinking today. That's the thing, Dad – you always make me think.

So here goes, a letter to you. Hopefully by the end you'll understand.

We've always been close, right from the very beginning. Was it because you got first dibs on my name? Vika got the exotic Tongan name and you chose Linda for me. I know it wasn't because it means beautiful in Spanish – although I'd like to think so. You got your inspiration from the TV ad for the electric blanket: 'Sleep wonderfully warm with Linda.' Thanks for that – the boys at school had a field day. You could have made up some story to make me feel better and more exotic, but that's not you. You don't lie and you never have. You just give it straight, whether you like it or not, honest as the day is long.

I've always loved my name, by the way – even the Bull bit. I decided on my wedding day to surprise you all and keep it. As you'll remember, it was not a popular choice with the in-laws. I just wanted to keep the name going for your sake. I told you it was because it was my identity, blah blah blah, but it was really for you. I remember your cheeky wink as I delivered the bad news to my new mother-in-law that I was sticking with Bull. Your advice, 'stick to your guns, love', made me more determined to do so.

It turned out to be good advice. Fast-forward twenty-three years. Do you remember sitting outside my shop every day with two cappuccinos and four dim sims to share, waiting to cheer me up with food as I rebuilt the wreckage of my marriage? I just wanted to be with you at that time as I unravelled. We've always been happy in each other's company. Or were you just using me as an excuse to eat four dim sims? We go well together, unlike the dim sim/cappuccino combination.

When I was little I just wanted to help you in the garden, your clumsy assistant helping build, rake and stoke the incinerator, or sit on your lap and watch Dave Allen. I think I got my smutty sense of humour then. Those days and the little things you did for me say a lot about you. No fuss or bother, just 'be there when it counts'.

Another bit of advice you have given me is 'work together'. It's simple but important. You are not a 'watch me' kind of guy, but you do lead by example, the way you run the family with Mum, or Colonel Grandma as I call her.

I wonder if you ever thought your only children would end up working together for over thirty years and counting. Singing as a career choice for not only one but both of your kids must have been challenging, especially earlier on, but your approach of 'just let them go and see what happens' has given us the freedom to stuff up and give it our best shot. Correct me if I'm wrong but I think no one has been more surprised than you that we're still performing. We don't always get it right, but we work together well and have tried for yours and Mum's sake.

You've worked hard all your life as far as I know and it has been no mean feat. It's been trying at times. I know you've often said, 'I could have been off playing golf all weekend,' but I've never ever seen you lift a golf club.

You have put everything into your successful marriage to Mum. The Doncaster boy and the Tongan chick. I wonder also if you thought you'd still be married to Mum after forty-eight years. Your saying 'you marry one Tongan, you marry the lot' says it all.

What was really going through your head as you sat through endless Sundays in Tongan church listening to a sermon in a language you didn't understand? If you were distracted and dreaming of sailing your homemade catamaran, I couldn't tell.

When you were pushed to the couch because of a lack of beds and too many Tongans over the years, you never seemed to mind. As long as you had a warm dog on your lap and a cold beer in your hand.

I've only heard you complain once and that was because your beautiful lawn was dug up to cook yet another *umu*. Yet there you were with Mum at the end of the day, shovel in hand, filling up the hole from the underground oven together.

With all of these things, if it were me, you wouldn't hear the end of it. I'd be thinking, I'm bored! I want to go home! I want my bed back! Bloody Tongans!

Time goes so quickly, like you always say. I do wonder how at forty-five years of age I have managed to get this far without too much damage done. Had I not been cradled in the arms of a loving family, things would have been different.

My favourite thing you have ever said over a family dinner, and it's a big favourite with the kids too, is 'just because there's snow on top, doesn't mean the fire's out inside.' I guess that was your way of saying you're never too old to be passionate, and to never give up trying – to enjoy life.

Try to see the good in people.

Try to be positive.

Try to be patient.

Try to smile.

To be fair and honest and respectful of others.

To live a life simply, without regrets.

You're a top bloke, Aussie Bull, and as your well-worn favourite t-shirt says:

'Old Guys Rule'!

Love you always,
Linda

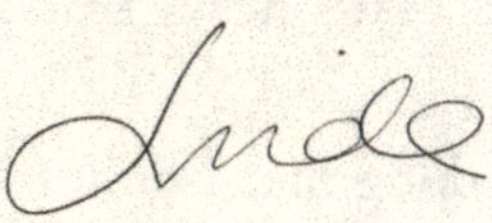

ELLA HOOPER

Dear Creativity,

Muse, magic, whatever name and shape you take – you know who you are.

We've had glory days and, man, I'm tempted to rhyme that with whorey days. Let's just say, days where we'd both rather have been somewhere else.

I thought I'd write you this letter re yearning as you two are intrinsically linked for me. I know you both so well, but probably don't stay in touch with you like I should. And that's not a true reflection of my deep feelings for you both.

Yearning was my first love. Where he was taking me, I didn't know, but he swept me off my earthbound feet and up into wild, rampant imaginings with him.

And he was sweet enough to set me up with my next big love, you, Creativity.

You came on strong and rocked my boat. I fell completely and thoroughly.

In my carefree teens I pretty much worshipped you.

But, although I've held you in such high esteem, I've neglected you too. Let you become an outer-circle friend. And that, for one who identifies – albeit humbly – as an artist, is just no good.

When I think about us in the old days, I see you, so buoyant, sitting in the bush in the isolated terrain of our youth, headstrong. Defiant.

You were cheerfully uninhibited but also very green. You had a lot of chutzpah. You led me boldly into parties and folk festival jam session circles; into art class debates with teachers and experiments in bad teenage poetry.

And although your range was very limited, they were great prolific times for you and me.

We really cut our teeth, all crooked and craggy as they were. I later got braces when I could afford it. An analogy, perhaps?

Maybe it's because of your initial buoyancy that I slipped into the habit of taking you for granted.

Maybe, too, it's because we were celebrated for what we assumed to be just a fraction of our future potential, that we didn't exactly sweat the process in the years that followed.

So, soon enough, when I was both busy and lazy being young, structures sprung up around you.

Boxes were built for you, rigid and inflexible, against your grain and against your nature.

I signed you up for things I'm not sure you were ready for. I bound you to partnerships, I signed you to record companies. I listened to the loud voices of others as opposed to yours and mine. Sometimes you howled, and sometimes you whispered, but I guess you just weren't developed enough to take the lead vocal in my song yet. And plus, you didn't speak the languages that were thrust upon you – the foreign languages of business and schedules.

All of a sudden at a tender age you were a commercial entity. And thus began our rocky patch.

In my distraction, with eyes and ears full of glitter and noise, I didn't fully appreciate you or what made you tick. I didn't feed you and yet expected you to grow.

So, understandably, you took your sabbaticals. And though they left me nervous and panicked with a loss of identity, I would change nothing about the set-up in your absence.

But, my old friend Creativity, I'm finally getting older and maybe even wiser. Saturn returned as our brutal counsellor and has enlightened me with much new information on what it is that you need, what you really want, and certainly what you don't!

So I wanted to send this letter to you now, and tell you that you've been on my mind, and in my heart. To let you know I need, love and respect you and that I yearn for our glory days.

You know I've yearned for a lot of things – I'm a grade-A yearn-er. Yearning was my first love, after all.

I've yearned high and wide and hard ever since I could grasp the concept of 'other', pulling all sorts of otherness to myself with a hearty emotional telekinesis.

It's you, Creativity, and your return to the quiet place at the core of me that I yearn for now. You can't be rushed and hurried; I now know you don't work like that. But I wanted to tell you I've made some preparations.

An outer-circle friend or mere workmate no more, I can now offer you a protected and respected place of respite, a new studio-workshop in my soul, and pride of place once more on the mantel of my mind.

I've disentangled us from contractual obligations; I've cut down 40 to 60 per cent on pleasing people with loud voices; I've given the routines that you found so stifling a shake-up. I've increased your variety of outlets and made sure some of them have nothing at all to do with boxes or platforms, and we can be completely private if you like. I know you once felt overexposed and then were shy in the wake of it.

I might even start doing yoga regularly, to keep the place clean for you, free of the stress-mess that used to clutter up some of your endeavours.

It's been at times a tough and dramatic developmental phase, my dear Creativity, and maybe I had to do this bit alone, but an upside is that all the offcuts from the recent renovations in here should give you quite a bit of new material to work with when you move into your new studio.

So how about it? A renewal of the lease agreement? A renewal of our vows? The hasty, happy teenage ones replaced by a firm, thought-out commitment, still as passionate as ever but focused now on the process and enjoyment, not results or the expectations of others.

I'll await your reply, my old friend.

By the way, how is your sweet sidekick Freedom doing? Some say she's your imaginary friend, just a 'concept', but when you're around and we're in fine form together, I can see her quite clearly, sitting there, winking at me . . .

ALEXANDRA SCHEPISI

Dear Time,

Where, oh where have you gone? We used to be so close. I had you in my diary all over the place. You used to hang with me, plan the future with me, let me dream, expand and relax. There was just so much of you but, year by year, you have really drifted away.

Why? What did I do? Have I offended you? Or have you just moved on? Found other people to love, to caress, to inspire?

God, I miss you. I miss you so much I'm aching. I want you back so bad I think my head might explode. Every part of me yearns for you. I have looked for you everywhere. Everywhere! Morning, noon and night, even in my dreams, I search for you. I keep flipping through my diary, scanning my iCalendar, looking within, without . . . I have tried yoga, tried to meditate, tried all sorts of things to reinvent you, re-imagine you, but I can't say it works for long.

I make phone calls in the car wherever possible as it's one of the only places I can get a snatch of you. I read on the train – a rare opportunity to sit still. Can't read in the car, can't talk on the phone on the train, so I make use of every tick of the clock. Every second I am *doing something*. Never an idle moment. I check my emails while eating breakfast in the shower, open my bills while waiting for the doctor, clean the kitchen while on Skype, and work in my sleep. I am doing my pelvic floor exercises as I write this letter to you now. There are no breaks; it's just a constant, high-speed treadmill of activity, and it never ends. I've even considered a catheter bag so I don't have to stop to go to the toilet.

All the while my list of things to do gets longer and longer. How does that work? It's because you've gone. I am forever cramming in as much as possible as the hours fly by; the days seem to get shorter and I swear there is one less day in the week. I don't understand the concept of a weekend as my week doesn't end. And tell me, what the hell is with a leap year? Why can't every year be a leap year?

I used to be able to sit still! To just sit and breathe. Be surprised by the moment every now and then. There used to be unplanned, unscheduled events in my life. I even got bored from time to time. Sometimes there was just too much of you and I guess I didn't appreciate you then. Stupid young thing. So naive. I look back and kick myself. If only I had so much of you in my life now. I have realised now that I took you for granted and I was foolish. Please forgive me – an ungrateful, silly thing who has seen the error of her ways and now realises your true value and beauty. I've changed. I need you back. I need you now more than ever.

I'm a wreck without you. Really. I don't sleep (you know I need eight hours), and I no longer swim – in fact I barely exercise at all any more. I don't see my friends. I have stopped having fun, other than in rare, scheduled, mini bursts of hilarity, which generally leave me feeling exhausted the next day and even more grief-stricken for your absence, wondering if there's an extra Sunday somewhere or if maybe today is the beginning of daylight saving. Daylight saving, where we just keep springing the clock forward to stretch the sunshine out that little bit more.

I feel so old without you! Maybe that's what age is – chasing after you. Desiring you, wanting you more than we can have you.

I no longer wear a watch as it was making me obsessed with you. I couldn't stop checking it and all it did was cause the anxiety to rise as I was constantly reminded of how little you are around these days.

I thought about booking a one-way airline ticket around the world, travelling west at a constant speed in pursuit of you, forever crossing backwards over the international dateline and never disembarking. Maybe then I'd find you, or at least a bit more of you. It's on my list.

Did I tell you I'm pregnant? Did anyone tell you? I would have but I've been a little busy with work six days and nights a week and relatives dying and my neighbours deciding to rip down their adjoining house and completely rebuild without telling me or applying for permits. As a result I haven't really had a chance. In fact, I've barely come to terms with it myself and I am due in a week and a day. Now *this* is a period of my life when I really need you. I have shed many a tear, wondering where you are and why you would leave me alone at such a time.

My husband yearns for you too. He tries to hide it but I know he does – all he does is work. The three of us would make such a sweet combo. We'd be so much happier and calmer. We'd actually be able to *talk*; to go out to dinner; to lie on the couch together like in the good old days, him teaching me about eighties music that his parents used to ride their exercise bikes to; maybe even choose a baby name.

Oh, the things I'd do with you if you came back to me! Old things, new things, wild things, even really dumb things. For a start I would plough my way through that fucking 'to do' list, now so long I could safely wrap all that asbestos in my backyard in it and remove it myself! Then what? Bring on the rest of my life!

I could go to a movie – actually in a cinema. I could ride my bike there and enjoy the breeze on my face, or even *stroll* there, through the cemetery, checking out old names, marvelling at the lives of those whom you left behind. I could repair those cracks in my house and replace the paint-splattered green sheet that has been my curtain for eight years with actual shutters, through which I could peer out at my neighbours as they wander by with you on their side as well. Better yet, I could sit out on the front porch in the afternoon sun and greet them with a lazy 'g'day' as I raised my G & T to them. G & T with cucumber, that is, cucumber that I would grow in my backyard. Then I could invite friends over and cook them a huge meal. No rush – I'd take all day, perhaps even reinvent the menu in the process, and I'd set the table with a tablecloth and flowers. The next morning I could sleep in – forever! After that I might consider visiting family, although I'd have to have a flip through some photo albums first to remind me what they look like and what their names are as it's been a while. I'd learn Italian, French and Spanish, and pick up that guitar that has been collecting dust under my bed for so long. I'd buy some clothes that fit me and don't have holes in them, then I'd indulge in some serious bodily grooming, and, hell – why not? – maybe even some pampering. While under the rigorous sweep of some oiled-up hands I would close my eyes and start dreaming of the kind of holiday I'd book when I got home. Apartment in Paris; house down the Great Ocean Road with a beach view where I could just sit and stare at the sea for hours; thermal pools in Iceland; the Trans-Siberian Railway; Alaska to roll with the bears; Mexico for some chilli, guns and ancient ruins; the Amazon to pick acai berries fresh from a tree and smear them on my face with indigenous tribes, high on homemade alcohol; mountain villages in Thailand; new suits in Vietnam; unknown foods in Laos. Oh! With you back I could take a whole year off and book a round-the-world trip!

And all of this before I have a baby. Shit, when is that?

Oh boy, where have you been? Where on earth did you disappear to? Why are you waiting so long to come back to me, torturing me, making me beg like this?

Please. Pleeeeeeeease Time. Come back. Come back and hold my hand. Stroke my face gently as I doze off to sleep at night. Let me know that you love me as much as I love you.

I don't want eternity – I just want you here, now. And I want you to stick around for a little while. I'm going to need you.

Your one and only,
Alex

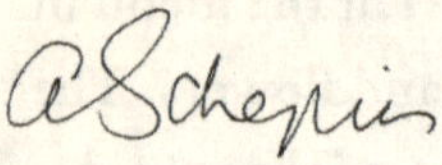

To the woman who changed my life

LUCAS STIBBARD

To the other participant in what was technically my second kiss,

Near the school oval where I scored ninety-five not out before retiring due to an unfortunate cricket ball/groin/lack of cup incident (you were there for that too) is the old adventure playground. Most of our grade used to play catch and kiss there at lunchtime. If I were more paranoid, I'd note that I never got kissed, but I'm just putting that down to being a faster runner than the others.

You may remember that in grade two I catered and officiated a marriage between Terry and Pania in that weird bunker thing near the driveway of the adventure playground. Nowadays I'd certainly choose a nicer setting for a wedding catered with crisps and undertaken by three very serious seven year olds. I don't know if you know but the P and C decided to take out the playground about five years ago because of the rusted metal and the needle-like splinters of old, dry wood. They thought an educational ecology area would be more useful.

The park across the road has changed too, and the toilet block where I first read the word 'cum' is a pile of rubble by now. Gone is the bandstand where every year as kids we'd experiment with mild S & M, giving ourselves candle wax burns at the Lions Club Carols by Candlelight. And sadly so too has the bench where you were the other party involved in what was technically my second kiss.

I doubt you even remember this but it has been a big influence on me, so I'll help you with the details that you didn't know or can't remember. We were in grade seven. Things were going okay for me. After six years of being the only kid so highly strung you could have played me like a Stradivarius, I was getting it together. Me, the kid who once heard two teachers behind me conferring about my nervous disposition, with the words 'neurosis' and 'ulcer' being bandied about freely. Admittedly I thought they were talking about Voltron characters . . .

Anyway, by grade seven my shit was about as together as the average twelve year old's. Everyone including you had forgotten about me feigning illness to avoid playing with the other kids at lunch and that incident in grade three. The simple life of mates and school was all I knew. Yep, by grade seven everything was rolling along quite nicely.

And then it all changed.

Well, to be accurate, you changed. It was amazing: one minute all us boys were teasing you about, well, being a girl. Then one of us, I have no idea who, noticed these extra straps under your uniform, and you started to walk around with your arms crossed all the time. It looked like you were shackling your chest – afraid that if let loose, your suddenly bumpy chest would lunge out threateningly at passers-by.

I am so sorry that you felt so self-conscious. I am sure that the attention of a pack of mildly pubescent boys didn't help. It was odd: suddenly, with no thought as to how to avoid girl germs, all the boys wanted to hang around with you – to, well, kiss you, I guess. That is what your average twelve-year-old sophisticate did, apparently. James Bond did it, and look how suave Roger Moore is. I am sorry, though, that we made what was probably already a fairly stressful time for you worse.

The year rolled on and, in one of those indecipherable moves made by educational bodies, we were all taught CPR. Thinking back on it, it was probably a pretty shrewd decision. Within five years, most of us would have smoked enough to lack the lung power to revive a wheezy toddler.

Every Friday for the last term of grade seven we spent an hour and a half having vaguely sexual experiences with inflatable mannequins. During these classes we got paired up. And I cannot describe to you the awful and aching embarrassment that I felt having to pash a mannequin in front of you. To your credit, you seemed to be entirely fine with this and, bless you, you chose not to belittle my poor lip skills with the plastic head and torso that we shared.

After a few weeks of this, we started to walk back to our classroom together after CPR and, bless you, you seemed to be genuinely interested in my thoughts and opinions on the future of skateboarding once we master anti-grav technology and you laughed at my lame jokes. It is only now, more than twenty years later, that I realise this behavior is called flirting.

Then as we arrived back outside the classroom you'd look at me expectantly. What did you want? I had no idea. I was far too busy waiting for you to ask me out.

That was how these things went, right? As a woman of the world, almost half a year older than myself, surely you knew how these things went?

I waited. You stared at me.

Nothing.

After months of practice, I could cock an eyebrow à la Roger Moore like nobody's business. I gave that a crack. Nothing. My rogue eyebrow was failing to have the same effect on you as Commander Bond's had on *Octopussy*.

A blind stab of desperation:

'So what would you say *if* I asked you out?'

'I'd say yes.'

At which point Mr Ford yelled at us both to stop flirting and get into the classroom.

That afternoon I sat and counted the minutes until the end of school like a rosary. The smell of fresh bread wafted from the Tip Top factory down the road and the sunlight danced on your hair. After school I decided to do the manly thing and walk you home. We got as far as the park when you stopped, grabbed me and kissed me. And this was not like the aforementioned incident in grade three.

Oh no, kissing Miss Jameison, our grade three teacher, had been carefully thought out. Fantasised about. And planned with a precision that would have put the Holden Stunt Team to shame. I'd walked to the front of the room, looked her in the eye and laid one on her. I recall seeing the shock on her face as I finished my lip-based declaration of love and then ran out of the classroom, checking my face in the toilet mirror downstairs for blushing or the spontaneous burst of hair on my chest or top lip.

Thankfully enough, Miss Jamieson never spoke of this again. In fact, I don't think anyone did, which until now hadn't struck me as odd but upon reflection seems uncharacteristic of pre-adolescents, so I guess she probably swore everyone to secrecy. Or everyone had a sudden and amazing moment of decency.

But our kiss in the park across the road from school, that fateful and bread-filled windy afternoon in grade seven, was a delightful surprise.

You stopped, grabbed me and kissed me. Even with all my eight-year-old ardour I didn't get kissed back by my grade three teacher. You, on the other hand, were a more than willing party to what I will always look on as technically my second kiss. A kiss that came out of nowhere and ambushed my face like a wet flannel. I went from wondering if Mum would be mad at me for being late home, to being kissed with abandon by a girl with trained attack breasts.

Then we strolled home together and kissed again at your door. I don't recall getting home. Mum grounded me for being late.

The next Monday morning, I saw you walking around holding

hands with Terry. And, in one heart-rending moment, you kissed, and I realised I didn't have what it takes to be an international man of mystery. And, let's face it, being a suburban boy of painful obviousness just doesn't cut it in the playground.

Like my crush and subsequent guerilla kiss with the world's hottest grade three teacher, my brief moment of lip-numbing passion with you was never spoken of again.

But, thank you. That afternoon changed my life; it ignited a love of those wonderful, awkward moments of negotiation in all of our lives, the breathless moments of electricity and anticipation that are a precursor to every great memory we have, and which are the basis of the romantic comedy work that has been the backbone of my work for, well, pretty much my entire career.

I hope wherever you are that you are just as amazing as my memories of you. And, again, thank you.

Thank you,
Lucas Stibbard

RICHARD FIDLER

Dear Khym,

I know you're not comfortable with this kind of thing. Your background is Singaporean, while my lot are Irish-Australian. You aren't really into drunken emotional declarations, all that 'I love you, mate' stuff in the pub. Too much drama.

Maybe I should spare you this discomfort; I could be a bit coy and write to another, more oblique feminine presence in my life, like the female USB socket on my laptop. Or I could direct this letter to my life companion of twenty-two years and the mother of our children.

So let's go with that then, shall we?

March 1991: I first see your face under circumstances that now strike me as creepily mail-order-bride-ish: in a casting agency book. My comedy group is making a low-rating sci-fi sitcom at the ABC in Melbourne and we get the idea that in the future all newsreaders will be Asian women. Ted Robinson, the EP, says your audition has just the right mix of authority and deadpan comic timing.

Three weeks later you're in the makeup chair at ABC Studios in Elsternwick, and you look every bit the Hong Kong newsreader that we want: authoritative, corporate, bulletproof in heavy makeup, ready for the day's shooting.

Then it's late afternoon and we're done for the day and I'm outside waiting for a cab. It's that moment in late spring in Melbourne when the weeks of rain dissipate and the weather turns dry and warm. And you emerge from the building.

You look completely different, like a superhero who's changed into her secret identity. The stage makeup is gone and I can see your features clearly. Your waist-length hair is down. You're wearing a vintage sundress and you turn your face up to the late afternoon sunshine and you smile gently and you're so lovely I can't breathe for a moment.

This, I understand, is the Thunderbolt. There's a scene in the first *Godfather* film where Michael Corleone is hiding out in a Sicilian village. He sees the woman Apollonia for the first time and the stone-cold gangster is struck dumb. The Thunderbolt.

I think about you all the following week.

On the set it's so hard to flirt with you. You're friendly but businesslike, and I worry I look too needy. *Look interested – but not needy,* I tell myself, and I get even more nervous.

Then my friend Tim grins and says, 'You can tell Richard is attracted to Khym because he keeps sitting next to her.'

I visit my parents the following Easter weekend and I wonder how I will ask you out on a date. The possibility of happiness with you hovers before my eyes for those four days like a shimmering orb and I wonder what will happen if I dare to touch it. Will it burn me?

So then:

First date and the full flood of romantic love.

You invite me into your apartment in St Kilda, and (this seems funny to me now) I get very excited when I scan your bookshelf.

I spot a row of Penguin Classics, black and spine-cracked: a copy of *Madame Bovary*, a lovely old edition of *The Tale of Genji*, a Gabriel García Márquez, a Milan Kundera, several earnest paperbacks on the New Hollywood cinema of the '70s. Elizabeth David's *French*

Provincial Cooking is dwarfed by a volume of erotic Japanese art, and I think: *I have to marry her now.*

January 1993: We are married in St Mark's Anglican Church, two blocks from our place in Fitzroy. The ceremony is conducted in 40-degree heat and filthy humidity.

We hold the wedding party at our garden apartment and the clammy air congeals at last into thick and heavy rain. The guests run outside to greet it and the party picks up speed and becomes a giddy, muddy frenzy. And you: wildly, insanely beautiful, and me: so happy.

Two difficult years in London. Then nine years in Sydney.

The tide of romantic love ebbs and withdraws, but it recedes into a larger, deeper body of water, and our truer, less idealised selves come more clearly into view.

I was slow to see the whole of you because you were so close. The man who lives right next to a mountain will take decades to grasp the totality of that mountain. Your presence in my life is so large and close I can only slowly glimpse its true outline, its shape and volume.

At first it was more than enough that you were interesting and beautiful with a serious bookshelf and an unshockable sense of humour. I think I was too naive to give much thought to whether you were a good and kind person. I probably just assumed it.

But you *are* a good and kind person. You're honest and never sneaky.

You always, *always* do what you'll say you'll do.

For all our shared tastes and interests, we have different temperaments.

Long before we met we developed our own defences against the inevitable sadnesses of life.

You are by nature and conviction a melancholic human being. I, however, am an optimist. I know this irritates you and you think I'm delusional. I think optimism and pessimism are two sides of the same coin, and they're both subjective misperceptions that arise from different temperamental inclinations.

Not you. You just think you're right. And fuck, that's infuriating and occasionally hilarious.

We've been playing a game of *Ha! See?* all our married lives. When something goes wrong in the world, when there's a disappointment somewhere, you'll turn to me: *Ha! See?*

December 2001: Our friends John and Prita have invited us over to their place in Bondi Junction for dinner.

On the way there I hear you dreamily wonder, 'Ohh . . . Prita's Indonesian. Maybe she'll make beef rendang.'

I say, 'Yeah, that'd be nice'.

Then after a moment, a slight tilt of the head and you mutter, 'Oh. Maybe she won't . . .'

And then, finally and poignantly, 'How sad . . .'

Of course when we arrive Prita says tentatively, 'I've made this Indonesian thing. Beef rendang? I hope you like it.'

I leap to my feet in triumph and jab a finger at you: *Ha! See?*

Sometimes the universe does reward those who dare to dream with beef rendang.

June 1999: We have a son. In 2003, a daughter.

And there's all that moving around. I count thirteen houses and apartments in four different cities in our time together. All those forgotten lounge rooms, kitchens and bedrooms where the key moments of our lives have played out.

And now, Brisbane. We never planned to live here, did we? We live in a modest bungalow in a Brady Bunch suburb. Our kids go to a good local school. I'm happier here and you seem to be happier too. But I wish I hadn't put you through all that moving. You need ongoing friendships and community. I understand that now.

You're not high maintenance. I'm thankful for that. You don't demand gifts and attention and nice remarks. You're not a needy puppy. You're more like the cat that just won't sit on your lap and wriggles out of your grasp, but is always there, nonetheless.

It's very hard for you to say 'I love you.'

Things have to be pretty awful for that to happen.

November 2011: You and I and the children sit down to dinner at home. It's my birthday, so you prepare a dinner of Vietnamese food to be cooked at the table.

There's a sudden burst of flame. My shirt catches fire.

I tear it off and run into the shower and I can see that all the skin on my right arm is blackened and ruined.

An ambulance comes, morphine is administered and I am taken to hospital. You're more distressed than I am.

I ring you from hospital the next day and you cry out those three words before you can stop yourself.

I remember them. I hope you meant them.

Three days after skin graft surgery, you're sitting next to my hospital bed and I'm struggling because the painkiller dosage isn't really cutting it today.

The donor site on my leg is buzzing and throbbing, and it takes all my concentration to manage it, to suppress the hyperventilating and the trembling in my arms and hands.

You clasp my left hand in both of yours. You close your eyes, and you inhale and exhale slowly. Within a minute my breathing falls into sync with yours, and the trembling stops. The pain fizzes out like a cheap firecracker. In another minute I'm asleep. I'm out for three hours.

I wake up and you're gone and I wonder if you hypnotised me like a chicken.

You've always had this otherworldly quality. There are so many Chinese ghost stories in your family.

April 1995: We're living in Sydney, in an apartment that had once been part of the old Darlinghurst Gaol.

We're washing the dishes and we're talking about the poltergeist that keeps pranking us: moving things about, opening deadlocked doors.

I'm completely at a loss because nothing like this has ever happened to me before, but you know what's required. You put down the tea towel, look up to the roof and say, emphatically, 'Look, you're welcome to stay. Just don't freak us out.'

After that there are no more open and closed doors and the mail stays where we've left it.

I wish you respected your own talents more. You can be too clever, too self-defeating, with your pessimism sometimes. But I've come to accept that it's wrong and foolish to try to change that, to 'fix' it by haranguing you. There are some Gordian knots that are best not cut with a sword.

You have nothing of the prude or the snob in you at all. I love that about you.

I love that you're immune to flattery. It never delights you to be told that you're beautiful (and by the way, you *are* beautiful). You rightly believe it's an overrated quality, and it's one reason you were never truly happy living in Sydney: a city that admires glossy surfaces and rewards aggressive self-promoters.

In fact you don't take any kind of compliment easily. You politely move the conversation elsewhere, but I can see what you're thinking: *Well, it's very kind of you to say that, but ultimately our arses sag and all of us die and become worm shit, don't we?*

May 1993: I take you on a holiday to Venice.

I thought you might be awestruck by the place: a medieval city constructed on a smattering of muddy plugs of land seems like a miracle to me. But you're underwhelmed by Venetian grandeur (which I think, and still think, is perverse) and you shrug at the folly of all that time and effort and cruelty. And nothing, nothing, annoys you more than mediocre, overpriced food. You're more likely to see perfection in a chair or a bowl of handmade noodles.

And now I come to the quality I most admire in you. (Are you paying attention, Khym? Because you tend to switch off a bit when people are saying nice things about you.)

I think that melancholic temperament, that distrust of sentiment, that disdain for bullshit, has made you an unusually wise and compassionate human being.

You complain sometimes that I don't listen to you, but have you noticed I rely on your good judgement all the time?

Let me hit the wayback machine one last time.

November 1992: We're in Dublin, shopping for wedding rings in a small jeweller's shop off Grafton Street. We settle on two identical *Claddagh* rings: each ring is a simple gold band with a heart held in place by two hands under a crown.

We follow the local tradition and wear them while engaged with the heart pointing out, and then when we get married, we turn the heart inwards.

Neither of us wear those rings now. Yours was a little loose fitting and it slipped off your finger one day in 1996 and was lost forever. Mine had to be cut from my finger in hospital last year.

January 2013 will be the twentieth anniversary of that muggy wedding in Fitzroy. We need new rings for the decades that remain to us.

I can't imagine life without you.

I feel untethered when you're not here.

I still take pleasure in the peace of your company and I'm still so fiercely attracted to you.

It *is* a good life. With you it is, anyway.

Ha! See?

Your husband,
Richard

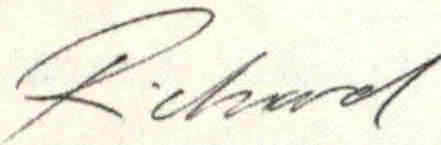

SCOTT SPARK

To the sisters I never had,

My parents always wanted a daughter. My suspicions were first raised on a childhood road trip to Hervey Bay. For in-car entertainment, they gave me a walkman and two cassette tapes: Madonna's *The Immaculate Collection* and Bette Midler's *Experience the Divine*. Eventually, when I was older, they more or less confessed: yes, they were pleased to have a son, but if they could have determined my sex, I would be a bona fide woman. At least they were honest.

No child wants their very existence to be a disappointment to their parents. I mean, if I could've been a woman – if I felt the urge strongly enough to *become* a woman – I would have. It's just that I've always been quite happy being a boy. And I'm not sure I'd really make a terribly good woman. (I know what you're thinking – that's not true – but it really is.)

It's not as though I didn't try, but all my early childhood attempts at playing the piano in my mum's shoes and jewellery were a disaster. Both my parents vetoed that direction. And personally I'm glad, because let's be honest, Liberace – remember him – was bullshit. I mean, he looked like a fucking nutcase.

When I was eighteen I told them I was dating a boy, and soon after that they talked about adoption (completely unrelated, I'm sure). It was the first time I'd ever heard them discuss such a thing, but there they were, in their early fifties, genuinely considering taking parenthood out for one final spin.

Now, you might think I would be hurt or offended by this. But more than anything, I was kind of excited by the prospect of finally having a sibling. Because one thing I'd always wanted more than anything else was a sister.

So, this letter today, to the woman who has changed my life, is dedicated to the sister I never had. (Not the girl my parents were supposed to adopt – I don't know where she is. Probably still living in a remote Chinese village somewhere.)

So, I've always wanted a sister. This was problematic when I was young, as I'd let girls in the neighbourhood believe I was in love with them when really I just wanted to hang out. Quite simply, they were better company than boys; they shared my dislike for sunshine and didn't want to beat me up. In my teenage years, this led to awkward, slightly disingenuous midnight make-out sessions underneath outdoor furniture to the soundtrack of The Mavis's 'Cry' (it's actually a surprisingly good song fourteen years later).

I've spent my entire life compensating for the sister I never had. In my own way, *I've* been adopting sisters. I remember when I was a misshapen twelve year old with an undercut, entering high school – I barely knew anyone at my new school and it took me quite a long time to make even a single friend. The very best thing about each day was hearing Helen Razer's voice on triple j. I'd never encountered anyone quite like her. And I wanted her to be my big sister. I loved how she so eloquently shifted between mannerly, intelligent observations to wrecking-ball commentary, all punctuated with obscenities. Some people said she didn't make any sense. She always made sense to me! I thought to myself, Here's someone who could really teach me a thing or two about the world.

But it wasn't Helen who saved me in those early days of high school – the lifeline came from a tall, sprightly girl named Lorelei Vashti. She belonged to an after-school choir, made up of mostly older, more daring, more worldly students, and she encouraged me to join too. We sang wonderfully strange choral arrangements of Edward Lear prose. I know what you're thinking – what a bunch of tossers. But you have to remember, we were too young to know and be horrified by the Manhattan Transfer, and this was way before *Glee* ruined choirs for everyone.

Almost everyone in my life who's given me the time of day when I needed someone to care has been a woman. Not everyone, but mostly.

Back in 2006, I'd recorded some genuinely woeful demos, and for some reason I had a copy on me when I was at work. My day job for a very long time now has been producing radio at the ABC. And this one day, a tiny, sort of Liza Minnelli-looking girl came in and sang on the radio. She sang Rufus Wainwright's song 'Want'. And I stopped her afterwards, said hello and handed her my shitty recordings (much to my mortification looking back on it).

Anyhow, a week later my phone rang, and this boisterous, knockabout voice said, 'Hi, it's Megan, Megan Washington – you gave me your songs, and I really like them, and I'm wondering if you'd play a gig with me sometime?' She said, 'I'm just figuring out what I'm doing with myself, and won't be ready for several months, but we should do something together next year.' A week passed, and then I received another call from Megan, and she said, 'I'm playing at Ric's tomorrow night – do you want to support the show?' From that night on, we've been exchanging songs, gigging, celebrating, commiserating, binging on miscellaneous YouTube videos, drinking and shopping together. And it all began with her caring enough to call.

When you encounter death for the first time, there's usually someone nearby who says, 'Call me anytime.' And, nine times out of ten, you don't call, because you think, What do they really know? Or you just don't want to bother them, because you're not sure what you need from them. A few years ago, when it became clear that my dad was in pretty bad shape and wasn't going to recover from the hundreds of tumours in his body, there was a friend who I called because she cared enough to say, 'Call me anytime.' Simone had lost her mum several months earlier and, at that moment, there really was no one else I could've spoken to. She was it, because she knew the ropes.

I don't know how your brain works, but I feel as though I can't speak honestly without being tangential, because for me the truth is either a one-sentence quip – darts of genius by Dorothy Parker or Oscar Wilde – or it's like a web or a nest. Things you collect, that you put together, and somehow it holds you. Or traps you.

So what am I trying to say? Obviously, I think there are plenty of redeeming qualities about dudes. Clearly, I think they're more than all right. But I'm not sure where I'd be if it weren't for all these adopted sisters in my life. Their book smarts, street smarts, wherewithal, taste, ingenuity and love. Not to mention their hugs and senses of physicality. As a fat child who grew into a gay teenager, I really despised my body. And chicks seem to understand that feeling.

In the same way my parents wanted a daughter, I wanted a sister. But if it wasn't for me being an only child, I might not have so doggedly befriended all these indispensable, wonderful chicks in my life.

I can't possibly name them all – and if I try, I'm bound to make some kind of embarrassing accidental omissions (and, with age, I'm learning to avoid accidental omissions wherever possible).

So: thank you to my parents for not adopting that Chinese village girl (and if politicians ever decide I'm fit to raise a child, I will make it up to her personally, I swear!), and boundless love to all my proxy sisters. Who knows what kind of mess I'd be without you?

Scott Spark

PAUL CURTIS

Dear interceding bitch,

The woman who changed my life? Ha – I seriously doubt it. There is no fucking way! Your empty husk of a soul is too dry and decrepit to have any impact on anyone or anything, to evoke even a modicum of change. Stranded at an intersection with no life, a dead end with no entrance, drowning all it touches in a gutter of effluence, the stench of which one should have seen staining the horizon a mile off.

No, this letter goes elsewhere, to someone of genuine effulgence. Far from those maddening clouds, the unfettered words in this letter are addressed to the golden ray of light that cuts through such gloom, evoking something much more salient. Enduring. Transformative.

In that sense, this letter becomes addressed to another.

To my dearest beloved: the woman who really did change my life.

Or, more, changed me into life. Charged me into life. Kinetic flurries ignited with every touch, setting forth a twisting trail of mutual captivation ever since and still to this day nearly twenty years later. She is more than that could ever be, so shut the fucking door and delete the house before the cold creeps in. Ranting and cursing, your rancour finds no hearth here. The warmth of this tale seeks its comfort in the arms of my true other.

I occasionally think what lingers in the past can only find form in story. Stories poised on the edge of personal testaments to what was and, without recital, may never be again. Stories once tangled in a lattice of mythic embellishment take up the slack of reality to honour a burgeoning and welcome fantasy.

What once upon a time seemed like a calm night lost in the distance, twilight drifted into night and a shift in tempo gave a brazen yawn as a call came in to bring the organ and make some noise. Lacking in any noticeable musical prowess, the keyboard I possessed in truth only allowed expressions of noise, so limited opportunities to do so were taken up with gusto. Before long I was piling in the back of a car and heading to whatever awaited, loaded with organ and gall. No idea of the web I had been drawn into, I was met with the freakish vision of a transplanted power station overtaken with the minions of the creative underworld. Through a dawning shroud of influenza, I suddenly felt lifted into otherness and all else swept away.

Standing riveted amid the industrial waste on the concrete precipice overlooking a huge gaping pit in front of me, not only out of fear of plummeting off or even impaling my foot but more caught in the radiance of her beauty below. The beacon of her white dress absorbed my attention amid the scrabbling feral creatures naked in the fetid water around her. Her raw heart dangled over her bust, sprinkling its bloody residue like some crimson aureola. When she emerged to the upper level, determined to put an end to those of us making the noise, I found recess in the dusty shadows, at once fixated by her presence and yet fearful of making myself known, navigating around anything capable of sending her ricocheting my way. Feet crunching on surrounding debris, I felt fear and excitement choke the back of my throat with the tremor of some future eruption.

The blood and light emanating from this strange pit: here was the signal for some genuine, pulsing change.

If you may recall, this tale I rigorously paint as our inaugural meeting was actually our second, the first being a blundered juncture amid the dingy confines of a crowded club foyer fleetingly brought together by an intermediary whose projections of excessive promise hoisted on me were met with a flatulent stare tainted with the smell of anything but roses. Fortunately, this second encounter didn't amount to an actual meeting either, as I clung to those enticing shadows to avoid further humiliation, thus dampening any possibility of future progress.

From that moment deeply entranced, after carefully picking my way through the rubble an actual rendezvous eventually came about later, albeit a more comical affair too ridiculous to embarrass the three or four persons involved here. Anyway, before we knew what was what and who was who, we were embroiled in a whirlwind of passion and pursuit twisting and turning in a dynamic embrace, pushing and pulling each other in any direction that came forth.

I hold on to that fantastical story as our locus of impact and now presented in this public scenario as both mythic testimony and declaration of ongoing love above and beyond anything capably achieved in this ragbag of words. But even more so I use this opportunity as a cathartic purging, hopefully expunging any trace of that maleficent wolf that attempted to cloak our rosy fantasy in its sooty misfortune.

So in reality this letter, as it can only be, is indubitably addressed to you, my love. The changes cast in the gold of what we have forged together.

To you, my sweetest meat, from one so ever changed.

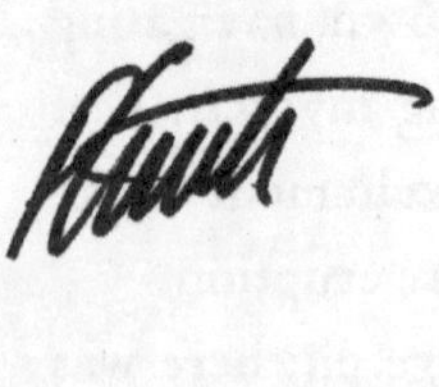

STUART GLOVER

Dear Mother,

The last time I wrote was when I was eleven in order to beg you to come and get me from holiday camp – mid-week – after I had accidently struck another boy in the face with a kayak paddle. But today I thought I should write again: write before it is too late. You are getting older and there are things to be said; things from our earliest days; things that happened but are never mentioned.

After consideration I decided that the best thing to do was to write a letter that you will probably never see, and read it aloud to a room full of strangers, and to students of mine, and maybe even an ex-girlfriend who might shift her feet knowingly. So let me start.

They say that if you can remember the late sixties you were never there. But I want to take you back to 25 April – Anzac Day – in a year when the Beatles were still a band. I had just been born, but barely so, and, to my disappointment, my arrival at the Mater Hospital was greeted as a calamity rather than as a joy.

My head lolled and I was purple – and not from the effort of being born but because my lungs were too small to function. I had come ten weeks early but at a time in history when this was still usually a death sentence. I should have been a Cancer but instead I was a Taurus.

You and I remained strangers. We didn't have time to meet at first. All I saw was your face as I was rushed away. You looked so sad and so fearful. When you are a baby, the doctors and the nurses forget themselves. They talk about your fate with a naive, unhelpful openness. I was shocked to overhear that I was likely to die. But in the meantime I was hurried to neonatal intensive care and placed in an incubator that seemed comically large for a two-pound baby. The nurses leaned over me and I was fitted with tubes.

Later, as the catheter went in, a priest arrived. You were elsewhere in the hospital, and Father, in the rush of things, was hardly there at all. So I was baptised alone, so that when my death would come I would be sinless and able to enter the house of God.

But I survived that day, and after an hour or so you joined me. I could see you – the other side of my bubble: So large, so beautiful, but so far away. But oddly the question of sin – or of blame, at least – was in the room. Was it me or was it you? No one knows for certain why babies come early: infection, bleeding, early foetal endocrine activation, placental disruption. An unhelpful friend said it was nerves.

I am not sure who should take the blame. But maybe you were angry? I would be. I know I was a replacement baby. I know that my sister had died just twelve months before. How you must have hoped that a new baby would wipe away that pain. My early arrival, my terrible state, my possible death, must have been unbearable. It must have been impossible to leave the hospital at night not knowing whether your baby would be there in the morning.

For my own part, I think I was unsure whether I was there at all. Whether I was alive or dead. The bubble is a strange place. It is impossible to feel anything there – or perhaps just best not to. Occasionally you or the nurses would hold me, but really I was too sick to be nursed or to be touched. Instead, mine was an odd, grim, floating world. The saddest photograph I know is of a baby monkey whose mother has died. Afterwards the poor thing was raised in a bubble. In the photo, it clings with whitened knuckles to some fur cut from another animal but its eyes are dead. For me, there were days when I was unsure whether I wanted to live at all.

After a fortnight or so – though it seemed longer in the timeless bubble – I began to feel stronger, I began to draw deep breaths. But then you did not come one day. And when you came next, you seemed distant and horribly sad.

I barely knew him, but it was a shock even for me that my father had died a couple of days before: a car accident, with a truck, near Marburg, on the road home from Toowoomba.

I was only thinking of myself at the time – of how distant you'd become, or how dead or frantic you sometimes seemed. They were awful days that became awful months. You were a young, middle-class woman in small-town Brisbane – just a shade too old to enjoy the education and benefits that feminism would bring within a decade. Now you were alone, without a husband, but with a three-year-old boy and a very sick baby. There is little that could have been worse.

A strict Freudian might say I had in fact enjoyed a catastrophic Oedipal victory over my father – that in a display of terrible power my very birth had vanquished him. I had my mother, although distraught, all to myself. But let's be honest, the whole thing left its mark on both of us. Yet we endured those days.

This is not the letter of a homesick eleven-year-old boy who wants an excuse to come home early from camp, nor is it even a long-delayed letter of adolescent complaint to you and my stepdad.

This is a letter from a baby, from a wordless time, from a self that never got to speak, but who knew that something had happened. Something terrible. Something that in some way coloured everything that happened afterwards.

Still, it is our story, and these are my words for you.

Stuart

KRAM

This is hard to write.

I really thought it would be easy – just write a sweet letter to the woman you love. No worries. But to be honest I've been procrastinating for days. I tried to start a few times, but kept on getting the shits with it.

So . . . I've decided it's best to keep it simple and rambling.

I love you. You drive me wild. You're so fucking sexy and hot. I mean, wow! Yeah! It's good to be alive! I was so lucky to meet you. This world is so big when it comes to that. Ships in the night are more common than shooting stars.

You have such beautiful eyes, and your kiss is so sweet and tender. You are a fantastic kisser! I love your pure heart of gold. I love that you dig what I do. And I love that I dig what you do. We support each other. We complement each other.

You like books. Lots of books. And art. I love your art. And old country music. And *Star Trek*, and *Doctor Who*, and *Anne of Green Gables*. Yes, *Anne of Green Gables*. We loved that TV series! And *Lord of the Rings*, of course.

And collecting English plates. And furniture. And Norwegian plates. And you like knives. Sharp knives. Last time we were at the airport they had to confiscate one of your knives from your bag.

You like axes – lamps – flowers – video games. I thought it was hot when you were a producer at a games company in Melbourne. Especially since in my '80s teenage heyday I was the Finley

Space Invaders champion . . .

You love your garden; cassettes; records; computers.

And oysters – I've seen you scoff a dozen oysters in a matter of minutes. And crab. Steak. Salad. Surfing. Kimchi.

And you love horses. And drinking stout. And jewellery – your dad's jewellery. And Lana Del Rey. You were so jealous that I got to meet her at Splendour. She was nice. Gave me a drag of her fag – had lipstick on it too – pink.

And fish. When I first saw you and your dad preparing and gutting and scaling and filleting freshly caught snapper, I was totally impressed. And a bit turned on. Sorry, I know it's weird, but I was. (By you, that is, not him.)

I always loved your fishing stories from when you were a kid. Like the time your dad took you out to Julian Rocks when you were seven and left you alone with a huge block of Cadbury Old Gold chocolate while he fished on the other side of the rocks in his boat. Or the time he put you in his backpack when you were a baby and went rock fishing at Tallow Beach after climbing over the rocks there to the headlands.

And you love old dresses from op shops. And new dresses from nice shops like Gorman. And coats. And cardigans – I must have bought you fifty cardigans. And the beach. And the earth. And the stars.

And on my birthday you got me a whole suitcase of blank cassettes for my 4 track. Stoked.

And you have many lovely shoes. And beautiful handbags – so many handbags. You even stole a goatskin bag from me that I thought was a man bag. I mean, as if you needed another handbag. How many beautiful handbags does a woman need?

And why is your car always so bloody messy? And why are all girls' cars so bloody messy? Especially creative girls? Why is the passenger seat (and this is the same for every pop star and famous actor chick I know as well, so it's not just some suburban bogan phenomenon) always covered in old cassette tapes and CDs and chip packets and bits of paper and used takeaway coffee cups and all your art stuff and shoes and other miscellaneous shit . . .

And you're clumsy like me. We're always stubbing our toes on the corner of the bed. It really hurts. Maybe that's why our kids say 'fucking hell' a lot, because we are always accidentally saying 'fucking hell' in excruciating pain.

You're complex. And simple. And gorgeous. And sweet. So sweet. And wonderful. It's wonderful being with you. Even if you bust my balls sometimes. It's okay. I don't mind.

And you're Norwegian. I love that. And you're cute. So cute. And smart.

Once I missed you so much when you were away working in San Francisco, I went through all your old photo albums and made a video of all the old photos of you in it. And I got really stoned every night and watched it over and over. It was during the 2006 World Cup, and the only time I left the house was to go down to the Railway Hotel in North Fitzroy for a chicken schnitzel.

I remember the first day we met. I came over to my mate's house to smoke some weed and hang out. You were his housemate and you were washing the dishes in your pyjamas. You were definitely the most beautiful girl I'd ever seen. Like an elf or a fairy. I'd never seen such a face before. And, oh my god, I couldn't stop looking at your bum – such a nice bum. Nice everything . . .

Inside I went, 'Whoa, who the fuck is that?!'

And your skin, so soft. And your lovely smile. I could tell straightaway you were a beautiful true person. Rare. Gorgeous. Deep.

And I liked your dog, Bernie. He was cute. I liked that he was a boy's dog. A cattle dog. Not a lap dog. And you liked that he liked me. We've still got him.

We stayed up talking all night and I smoked about forty cigarettes, and drank a lot of beers. We didn't kiss or anything: just talked.

The next day we walked to the pass and sat on a rock. More talking. Blah blah blah . . . The ocean is so beautiful, blah blah . . . How about the political situation in Tibet, blah blah . . . Triple j is cool – in Melbourne we have Triple R and PBS – blah blah . . . Just kiss her, for fuck's sake, you're a bloody rock star!

No, I'm not. I'm sixteen again. I'm looking down at the dirt and fiddling with this stick and delicately ripping gum leaves apart, one after another, so that the little centre stem remains. And my feet are making a hole in the dirt from my nervousness.

That night we went to the Carpark nightclub and got drunk. It was way too loud to talk much. I didn't like the music.

And then somehow I leaned over at the right angle and we kissed for the first time.

Then we went to my hotel room and had sex. After that I read to you in bed – Michael Jackson's autobiography. It was a really romantic day. A beautiful day.

It was weird for me, it took me some time to process. I was a cynical Melbourne indie music scene cool type, my band was one of the coolest and biggest in the country – we'd just won triple j's hottest 100, for fuck's sake. I'd only stayed in Byron a few extra days after the tour to hang out and meet some girls and take drugs and have a good time for a while before I went back to the city.

I wasn't supposed to fall for a sweet hippie chick. Not me.

I tried my best to be a bastard too. Sorry. And thanks. Thanks for hanging around with me. Thanks for loving me. Sorry I was a cunt. (Not all the time, just sometimes!)

After a while I got better at it. I was proud of you. So proud. I was proud of myself as well. Scored the beautiful girl! You rock, buddy!

Everyone liked you. The other rock stars loved you.

I loved you.

We became one of those couples at award shows. And at gigs. And at home.

We travelled heaps. You taught me how to cook. I taught you how to drive. You taught me how to snorkel. I taught you tennis. We played epic five-set hand-tennis matches on the beach. You looked so intense during those long rallies sweating in your bikini. I used to let you win. Then you started winning for real.

Then one beautiful night in Malibu, where we were staying with our Hollywood director friend and his family at the peak of our jet-setting Chateau Marmont LA days, I asked you to come down to Santa Monica beach.

We sat on the sand and I remember noticing how hideously huge and ugly the seagulls were over here. Then I started crying.

Later on, you said you thought I was going to say one of two things: 'I have cancer' or 'I want to break up with you.'

But no, it was simply: Will you marry me?

I revealed the ring . . .

Now I had been carrying the thing around with me all the way from Australia like Frodo Baggins and had secretly showed it to our friends Nic and Pia when I arrived in LA. They were sure you would say yes. And I showed it to our friends Mark and Susie as well – they were sure you'd say yes too. But as for me . . . Well . . .

No matter how confident a man may be – and no matter how much money he has made and has spent on a diamond ring, and no matter how far he has secretly carried it from one side of the world to the other, for this one and only special moment – he can never be sure of the answer to this question.

You said yes.

Then we immediately got stuck in a traffic jam on the Pacific Highway while driving home and the first song that came on the radio was 'Satisfaction' by the Rolling Stones.

Once we finally got home our friends took us out to dinner to celebrate, Malibu-style. They were lovely, it was beautiful, but nothing was as beautiful as you.

Another beautiful night in Malibu, again while staying with our Hollywood director friend and his family at the peak of our jet-setting Chateau Marmont LA days, you said you had something to tell me.

'We're going to have a baby! And I want to have it. Do you?'

No no no no no no no noooo. *Shit.* Not right now, babe, I mean, in a couple more years when we've settled down a bit, let's just think about it a bit longer, I mean, you know I love you but I thought you were on the pill, and, well, I . . .

Oh, okay.

No matter what a man says and thinks he believes about love and his relationship, and even if he's blissfully happy and in total love with his girl and wants to party on forever with her, it is, I believe, actually *this* moment at which he must look deep inside and ask himself: does he want to spend the rest of his life with this girl and does he truly and deeply love her – forever?

I said yes!

After that we had Lonnie. He's awesome. We love him. He's our beautiful son.

Then later on we had Elke. She's awesome as well. We love her. She's our beautiful daughter.

And their mum's name is Ree. You're beyond awesome. I really, really, really, really love you.

We've been together for sixteen years. You're as sexy as ever.

You changed my life.

You're my girl.

X

KÁRI GÍSLASON

A LETTER TO LADY CHATTERLEY

I was told to come straight away, that it was a matter of weeks. I've arrived, late, but I know you're still there, the same person I met twenty years ago. They tell me that you sleep in your room through most of the day, but that when you wake you're bright, as though the young Connie is back.

But they also say that you've changed your mind, and that you won't come out to see me.

I was a young man when I first read about you. And though I knew, of course, that I was only ever your reader, I somehow felt that I was your lover, too. Now, as I sit at my desk to write this letter to you, I find myself recalled to both roles: your lover and reader once more.

I am back to those moments when it was just you and me, and when there were no others to guard your room. That's what I want you to remember, as well – how we escaped and I suppose denied the world, because, in those days, that felt like the only way to remain wholly in it. How we were like Donne's lovers and that when the sun broke through the trees and warmed us, it warmed the whole world, too. That was the first rule of love: if you believed in your own universe, the universe believed in you. Clear the world away again, then, Connie, so that I can hold your hand and kiss you.

It's autumn, as it was when I left England and travelled the world without you. When I looked into the eyes of others, I saw the same sun – it was reflected as it is in yours – but the forest floor remained cold; theirs was a winter brightness, without the deepening warmth of the summer sun, which even below the horizon works its way back only for the sake of waking lovers.

Life has not left me with an empty case. But for a moment I've closed it a little so that I can see you as I did then. Before what, though? Have you thought about where you are going? Will you find the hidden places where I once found you, when you escaped the house, and walked and walked so that you wouldn't be able to see it? I can't stand the thought that you are trapped in the house again.

On my way back, as I was getting closer – felt in the sea air the coming coolness but also the dirt of England, of my childhood – I asked myself not only why but how you'd found me again after all these years. And with that thought came a companion, a faint promise that you'd followed me into every book I'd read since yours, just like Donne's sun finds the lovers no matter where they've gone.

I've so often returned to that day when you stood red-faced staring me down, telling me with your wide eyes that the world turns on a social axis, and that it was best to obey its rules. You were angry with me for staring back. But I've returned also to the pulse that felt another possibility, and that will always feel it wherever there is a body that unfolds ahead of the mind, even deceives the mind as the moon deceives the poets and steals their gaze away from the sun.

Like my friends, all serious young men who spent our nights alone, I believed only in the companionable silence of writing, and that my body was held to the world only by a pen. And yet that day I did stare back, and the body raced ahead of the pen. I opened and as quickly shut the book, but a shot had been fired through the woods, one that not only broke the silence and my faith in the solitude it guarded, but which also shot through the very journal in which I wrote and that I'd long kept in a pocket – my protection against sniper fire.

I believe you changed me, because you allowed me to take part in the changes that occurred in you. With you, I learned that there are promises only the body can make, and that only the body can accept – that my journal, my poems, letters such as the one that I write now, meant nothing without the body that carried them. I even made fun of Donne. When he said, *More than kisses, letters mingle souls*, I replied, In that case I'll live without the soul and take the kisses.

The bullet had passed through to the heart. You were right, and I wanted your body with me forever. The book and the journal had fallen open at the same time, at the same page. Your body fitted as the inner cast of my own.

And yet, Connie, you too were carried by words.

How did you prove to me that the body speaks, and that my body spoke most clearly when it entered the one I loved; that the body spoke for love, as poets do? It seemed to me that there was a paradox, a gap between the body and the fact that it needed to be written into novels, a riddle I've not solved yet and perhaps never will.

Is that why I've come back to you now, as your body fails and mine ages? Is it because I'm still asking the same questions? Why write at all, if the body is everything? Twenty years ago, my answer was that, even in love, solitude remains, a final unbreakable *I* that you sheltered from me as the grove was sheltered from the path, kept in reserve – but for what? Is it not, as it was for DH Lawrence, for the sake of words that we keep a space for ourselves? That in letters, not only souls mingle, but the entire world, too?

The annex by your room, the outer chamber where I was stopped, is so bleak that the sun merely lights grey to white. I wanted to push past your guards, insist that you see me. On the journey home, I listened too closely to a faint promise that said we would affect each other in the same way as we did when I was young. I listened until the sea whipped it into a certainty.

But on re-reading, I couldn't insist on that any more.

They say you don't come to the window often. But will you let me wait within sight of it for a day or two? Don't you want to breathe in these last moments of autumn? The woods seem so completely pure to me now, after these years away, the path turning to mud but the trees red, burning behind the fog: the final embers of October. That's how they stand before my mind's eye, drawing on their thin flames – an honour guard not only of how I once took refuge in books, but came to believe in them as well.

Will you come out, Lady Chatterley, as you did when I was twenty-one and you opened the book for the first time? Won't you come out while we're alive and not yet traded for souls? Come out, while the forest holds the sun.

Contributors

ROMY ASH's first novel is *Floundering*. In 2012 her work was anthologised in *The Best Australian Stories* and *The Best Australian Essays*.

EMILIE ZOEY BAKER is an award-winning poet, writer, performer, dancer, face-painter and MC. Only one of those things is a lie.

BEN BALL is the publishing director of the General Publishing department at Penguin Books Australia.

TOM BALLARD is a stand-up comedian and co-host of the triple j breakfast show. He belongs to a generation that has only ever really written actual letters by hand in a 'novelty primary school' context, so he apologises if what you've read is sub-standard, though he would like to remind you that he's been on television and so what he has to say is important.

From the successful creative and radio show partnership Hamish and Andy, **HAMISH BLAKE** is a nationally popular and versatile talent. His career is very much in tandem with his performing partner Andy Lee. After stepping out from university life and the demands of commerce degrees, they teamed up with their mates to create comedy/variety program *Radio Karate* for Channel 31. Rave reviews followed. Hamish and Andy's story reads as one accomplishment after another. From hosting student radio, the duo was swept up by Fox FM for

The Almost Midday Show, where their popularity soon promoted them to the drive slot on Fox in 2006 hosting their own show, *Hamish and Andy*. As a solo performer, Hamish made an appearance in ABC comedy series *TwentySomething*. He will also be co-starring in his first feature film, *Two Little Boys*, with Bret McKenzie (*Flight of the Concords*) , shot in New Zealand. Hamish has appeared on various Australian television series, including *Spicks and Specks*, *Thank God You're Here*, *Australia's Brainiest Comedian*, *The Librarians*, *The Panel*, *Rove*, *Talkin' 'bout Your Generation* and *The Footy Show*. He has also featured in the British version of *Thank God You're Here*. In 2008 he was a speaker for the negative team in the Melbourne International Comedy Festival's annual televised Great Debate.

ZOË FOSTER BLAKE is an author and columnist. You can find her nonsensical waffle weekly in *Sunday Style*, and each month in *Cosmopolitan*. She has a beauty blog called fruitybeauty, and too much brown sugar on her porridge.

I Awake is **SARAH BLASKO**'s fourth studio album. All three of her previous albums – *The Overture & the Underscore*, *What the Sea Wants, The Sea Will Have* and *As Day Follows Night* – have reached Platinum sales. Sarah has won two ARIAs for Best Female and Best Pop Album and also triple j's J Award for Australian Album of the Year. She has been nominated for a further fourteen ARIAs (including two for Album of the Year) and been shortlisted for two Australian Music Prizes and another J Award.

CANDY BOWERS is an award-winning writer, performer and hip-hop artist. The Director of *Black Honey Company,* Candy is currently touring her solo works *WHO'S THAT CHIK?* and *Australian Booty* across the country, debuting a brand-new hip-hop comedy show for kids, *MC Platypus and Queen Koala's Hip Hop Jamboree*, and writing a contemporary piece based on *Twelfth Night* with Queensland Theatre Company, entitled *Twelve*.

Acclaimed author, photographer and lifelong activist **BOB BROWN** rose to prominence when he led the campaign to save the Franklin River in the 1980s. After ten years in the Tasmanian parliament, Bob was elected to the senate in 1996 where he served for sixteen years. He was leader of the Australian Greens from 2005 to 2012, when he retired from the parliament to establish the Bob Brown Foundation.

CLAIRY BROWNE, lead singer of Clairy Browne & the Bangin' Rackettes, is a world-class diva to be reckoned with, femme prophet and self-professed arse lover.

Born of a Tongan mother and an Australian father, **LINDA BULL** has been singing with her sister Vika for as long as she can remember. For twenty-five years the glorious voices of Vika and Linda Bull have comprised one of the most distinctive, versatile and emotionally charged sounds on the Australian music landscape. Since their multi-platinum conquest of pop radio with the Black Sorrows in the late 1980s, the sisters have forged diverse pathways into soul, gospel, blues, country and the island music of their Tongan ancestry. Their rich solo vocals and instinctive harmonies have spawned eight albums of their own as well as illuminating studio and concert performances by Paul Kelly, Archie Roach, Renee Geyer, Kasey Chambers and many more. In 2005 Linda opened a quirky children's store, Hoochie Coochie, in the heart of North Fitzroy.

JENNIFER BYRNE is a senior journalist and broadcaster who has worked in all arms of the media: print, radio and television. Having done her cadetship at *The Age* and worked on UK's Fleet Street, she was a founding reporter with Channel Nine's *Sunday* program and spent some twelve years travelling the world for *60 Minutes* and as anchor for *Foreign Correspondent*. She was publishing director of Reed Books, won national awards as a magazine columnist and, since May 2006, has hosted *First Tuesday Book Club* and presented literary specials for ABC-TV.

PAUL CAPSIS is a multi-award-winning performer – a gifted singer, actor, writer and storyteller. His moving but humorous co-written solo theatre piece *Angela's Kitchen* earned Helpmann Awards for Best Actor and Best New Australian Work, and captured the hearts of both audiences and critics. Paul was delighted to be a part of the Men of Letters project.

LUCY CARTER is a radio and television journalist for ABC News and triple j news. She puns more often than she probably should. Mostly @lucethoughts.

KRISTY CHAMBERS is a registered nurse and non-fiction writer from Brisbane, Australia. Her first book, *Get Well Soon! My (Un)Brilliant Career as a Nurse*, was published by University of Queensland Press in 2012.

Actress, singer and, more recently, marriage celebrant, **JANE CLIFTON** is often asked if there is anything she can't do, to which she simply replies, 'Ballet and making money.' An arts graduate from Monash University's halcyon days of sex and demos and rock 'n' roll, Jane has carved out a four-decades-long show-business career. Her memoir *The Address Book* is her third book.

After graduating from acting at NIDA, **JEN CLOHER** decided to pursue a career in music. Her first album, *Dead Wood Falls*, was nominated for an ARIA for Best Female Artist. Her second album, *Hidden*

Hands, was named as one of the top ten releases of 2009 by *The Age*. Her third album, *In Blood Memory*, is out now! jencloher.com.

EVA COX, nee Eva Maria Hauser, was born in Vienna, less than a month before Hitler's anschluss made her stateless and soon a refugee. She therefore tries to create more civil societies so holocausts cannot happen again. An attempt to deny her three-year-old self a drum because she was a girl added a feminist perspective. A sociologist by trade, change attempts include the 1995 Boyer Lectures, academic teaching, research and writing, advocacy, media appearances and a multitude of political activism. Her daughter, partner and grandchildren, Asher and Reuben, and many friends keep her connected.

ANNABEL CRABB is the ABC's chief online political writer and host of the popular political cooking program *Kitchen Cabinet*. A still-at-large fugitive from the legal profession, Annabel began life as a journalist at *The Advertiser*, where she had a brief and high-risk gig as the kid who types in the Lotto numbers, before moving into politics. Since then she has worked as political correspondent, sketchwriter and UK correspondent for various titles at Fairfax, where she is currently a syndicated Sunday columnist. She won a Walkley Award for her 2009 essay on Malcolm Turnbull, and was Australia's 2011 Eisenhower Fellow. Annabel has appeared as a panellist on *Insiders*, *Gruen Nation* and *Randling*, is a mother of three and has written several books including 2010's *The Rise of the Ruddbot*.

PAUL CURTIS has participated in the music industry managing bands, promoting and booking tours, releasing records, designing posters and shirts, and even drawing strange pictures for the past twenty-plus years. He continues to manage Regurgitator twenty years down the track, and currently works with major art galleries curating music programs.

CHARLOTTE DAWSON is a television presenter, columnist, fashion and beauty expert, public speaker and MC. A former model, Charlotte is a judge on *Australia's Next Top Model* and appears regularly on the *Morning Show* and the *Today Show*.

EVA DE JONG-DULDIG is director of the Duldig Studio – a house museum and art gallery in Melbourne. A quarter-finalist at Wimbledon (1961–63), she was Champion of the Netherlands (1962) and played Federation Cup (1963).

ANTON ENUS has been working full time in broadcast news for thirty years, as a radio news reporter, press gallery journalist (Cape Town), current affairs producer and TV news presenter. He anchors *World News Australia* on SBS, a position he has held since 1999.

RICHARD FIDLER is the presenter of *Conversations with Richard Fidler* on ABC Radio across Australia. In another life he was a member of comedy trio the Doug Anthony Allstars.

GEORGIA FIELDS is an independent musician, songwriter, arranger, and producer based in Melbourne, Australia. Her debut self-titled album was released in 2010 to critical acclaim, being named ABC Radio National's 'Album of the Week'. Georgia is currently working on her second album, pioneering the genre 'disco pagan'. She is still nannying Isobel, who has recently learned to sing David Bowie's 'Moonage Daydream'.

ADAM GIBSON is a Sydney spoken-word performer, musician and writer. He has released two acclaimed albums and performs regularly with his band the Aerial Maps. The manuscript of his first novel was shortlisted for the *Australian*/Vogel award and and he has published three books of poetry. Aerial Maps' first album was named Best Spoken

Word Release 2005–2010 at the *Overland* Poetry Awards in 2010, and their second album has been hailed as 'an Australian classic'.

KÁRI GÍSLASON teaches creative writing and literary studies at Queensland University of Technology. His memoir *The Promise of Iceland* was published in 2011.

STUART GLOVER teaches writing at the University of Queensland. He publishes *Bumf* and writes creative non-fiction for a variety of small outfits. He was Founding Director of Brisbane Writers Festival.

Working as a comedian, presenter and writer, **CORINNE GRANT** is best known for her time on *Rove Live* and *The Glass House*. Her first book, *Lessons in Letting Go: Confessions of a Hoarder*, was released in 2010.

ROWENA GRANT-FROST is a Brisbane-based writer. Since 2008 she has written articles for *frankie* magazine.

ANDY GRIFFITHS is one of Australia's most popular children's writers. See andygriffiths.com.au if you'd like to know more, but don't bother if you don't.

SALLY HEATH is an executive publisher at Melbourne University Publishing. She edited the *Meanjin* journal for two years until March 2013 and before that worked as a journalist for twenty-five years.

THOMAS HENNING is currently eating a bag of marshmallows, which is making him ill. He is the co-director of the black lung theatre and whaling firm.

ANITA HEISS is an award-winning author of novels, non-fiction and poetry. She writes travel articles, eats chocolate and is an Indigenous

Literacy Day Ambassador. Her latest title is a memoir about identity titled *Am I Black Enough for You?* Anita lives in Sydney.

GERALDINE HICKEY has been described as a 'deceptively cheery dame who'll quietly take out your innards'. She is revered in the industry as a comedian's comedian. This was proven in 2011 and 2012 when she was shortlisted for the 'Piece of Wood' award at the Melbourne International Comedy Festival. A veteran of eight seasons of the Melbourne International Comedy Festival and a regular on the club and pub circuit around the country, her experience has grown her into the thinking crowd's crumpet. Last year Geraldine confirmed what it seems many of her fans already knew – she's come out of the closet. Her latest show, *Turns Out I Do Like Sun-Dried Tomatoes*, is a look back at the signs she may have missed to indicate she is totally gay.

Singer/songwriter **MISSY HIGGINS** has struck a profound chord with Australian music fans with her irresistible melodies, 'arrow through the heart' lyrics and a voice that clearly means it. Missy was thrust into the limelight after she won triple j Unearthed while she was still at high school. In 2005, Missy's acclaimed debut LP *The Sound Of White* spent seven weeks at number one and became the country's highest selling album of the year. *On a Clear Night* followed in 2007, also debuting at number one and giving Missy her first American hit, with the single 'Where I Stood' reaching gold sales stateside. Then after years of touring and seven ARIA Award wins, Missy quietly decided to take a break from music. She went off to uni for a while but her love for music eventually led her back to the studio, and in 2011 she set up in Nashville to record her first new songs in five years. Those recordings became Missy's third number-one album, *The Ol' Razzle Dazzle*, which, despite the five-year wait, became the most acclaimed work of Missy's extraordinary career. The break-up album with a difference, chronicling the much-loved singer's estrangement – and eventual rapprochement – with music making, spent over three months in the top ten after its mid-2012 release and became Missy's first release to make the Billboard Top 100 in America.

ELLA HOOPER is a singer-songwriter, presenter and op shop enthusiast who burst onto the airwaves and into public consciousness with a song she penned when she was fifteen. Spending most of her life so far entertaining the country as a feisty frontwoman of bands, she is now relishing shedding light on new Australian music via her various radio shows and the TV program *Radar*, as well as releasing her first solo record independently in 2013.

SACHA HORLER is one of Australia's most talented and well-respected actresses. Sacha is a multi-award-winning film actress, having made her feature debut in the critically acclaimed *Praise*. She went on to star in many more films including *My Mother Frank*, *Look Both Ways* and *My Year Without Sex*. Her numerous television credits include *Love My Way*, *CrashBurn*, *Secret Bridesmaids' Business*, *Rake*, *Offspring* and *Crownies*. In 2013 Sacha starred in the Broadway hit *Other Desert Cities* for the Melbourne Theatre Company. Her other theatre credits include performances in *God of Carnage*, *The Removalists*, *The Crucible*, *Pygmalion* and *Life After George* for the Sydney Theatre Company, and for Company B *Blue Murder*, *The Birthday Party* and *Hamlet*. In 1999, Sacha won an unprecedented two AFI Awards in the same year, Best Actress for her performance in *Praise* and Best Supporting Actress for *Soft Fruit*. Her role in *Praise* also saw her awarded the Film Critics Circle of Australia Award for Best Actress. She was again awarded an AFI Award for Best Supporting Actress for her performance in *Travelling Light* and has received a further four AFI Award nominations for her work in *My Year Without Sex*, *Secret Bridesmaids' Business*, *Grass Roots* and *Russian Doll*, as well as an Inside Film Award nomination for Best Actress for *My Year Without Sex*.

MERV HUGHES played fifty-three Tests, made 1032 runs and took 212 Test wickets. Since retirement Merv has been a bowling coach with a number of Victorian teams and a national selector. He makes his living by attending barbecues and telling tall stories. He has also written a number of books and hosted many tours to Test and One Day internationals around the world. His most recent book is *Merv Hughes' Best Sporting Insults*.

TRACEE HUTCHISON is a Melbourne-based broadcast journalist and author with twenty-five years experience in radio, television and print. A former triple j and Triple R announcer, she currently presents rolling news/current affairs coverage on ABC News Radio and Radio Australia across Australia, Asia and the Pacific, and writes commentary on a range of issues for the ABC website The Drum.

AMY INGRAM does stuff . . . She is an actor and sometimes director and producer. In 2008 she started the performance collective the Good Room alongside Daniel Evans, with whom she also directed the National Young Writers Festival. This year Amy has performed with La Boite Theatre Company, Queensland Theatre Company and the Good Room in their dance verbatim piece called *I Should Have Drunk More Champagne*. If you blink in the right spots during ABC-TV's *Mabo* and *Gods of What Street*, you might also catch her. In 2010 she won a Matilda Award for Best Emerging Artist.

TONI JORDAN is a Melbourne-based novelist. Her most recent book is *Nine Days*.

The kind of music that could make a bishop kick a hole in a stained-glass window: **MOJO JUJU** sings songs that sound like that night you can't quite remember, in that bar you swear you weren't at, with that girl you promise you've never met.

KRAM is best known as the singer/drummer in the ARIA award-winning rock band Spiderbait. In 1996 they became the first Australian Band to win triple j's Hottest 100 with the song 'Buy Me a Pony'.In 2004 they had their first Australian number-one single with 'Black Betty', with the song going triple platinum. In 2009 Kram released his debut solo album, *Mix Tape*, to critical acclaim, with the songs 'Silk Suits' and 'Good Love' used in film and television extensively in the US and the UK. In 2008 he was invited to the 2020 summit in Canberra by music legend and government minister Peter Garrett, and in 2010 he wrote and hosted his first television pilot, the live rock 'n' roll show *TTK*, with Tim Rogers and Tex Perkins as panellists, and guests Joel Edgerton and Myf Warhurst. In 2010 he formed the improvisation ensemble The Others with trumpeter James Morrison and pianist Paul Grabowsky, and in 2011 he joined other Australian artists as part of triple j's national tribute tour to Nick Cave, *Straight To You*, performing the songs 'Red Right Hand' and 'Henry Lee'. The Enmore Theatre show was filmed and broadcast on ABC-TV. He recently produced/co-wrote a kids album for Rhys Muldoon, *I'm Not Singing*, which was nominated for an ARIA, and he has made many television appearances on shows such as *Spicks and Specks*, *Good News Week* and *RocKwiz*. He's also co-hosted Jon Faine's *Conversation Hour* on ABC radio, and was once asked to write the car column for *Rolling Stone* magazine. Spiderbait completed their latest album in 2013 with producer Franc Tetaz in Los Angeles. Kram and his wife Ree have two kids, Lonnie and Elke.

ELMO KEEP is a writer at *The Awl*, *Meanjin*, *The Monthly*, Scribe and elsewhere. She lives in Ballarat, Victoria.

BENJAMIN LAW is a writer, columnist and journalist. His books are *The Family Law* (2010) and *Gaysia: Adventures in the Queer East* (2012). benjamin-law.com.

ADAM LIAW is a lawyer, cook, author and TV presenter.

WILLIAM MCINNES is an overweight middle-aged man with bad knees. He occasionally pretends to be somebody else on screen and also writes stuff.

KATE MCLENNAN is a Melbourne-based comedian, actress and writer. She has appeared on *It's a Date*, *Offspring* and *The Project*, and toured the country with her award-winning stage show *The Debutante Diaries*. She is currently developing her TV series, *Bleak*, with fellow writer Kate McCartney.

ROBERT MANNE is Professor of Politics at La Trobe University. He is the author or editor of twenty books and a regular contributor to *The Monthly*.

GEORGE MEGALOGENIS is an author, commentator and journalist. He has twenty-seven years' experience in the media, including over a decade in the federal parliamentary press gallery. He is a regular panellist on ABC-TV's *The Insiders*. He is the author of *Faultlines*, *The Longest Decade* and *Quarterly Essay 40: Trivial Pursuit – Leadership and the End of the Reform Era*. *The Australian Moment* is his latest book.

LAWRENCE MOONEY is a decorated comedian, having been awarded Best Comedy at Melbourne Fringe and Crikey.com.au's Best of the Fest at the Melbourne International Comedy Festival. His stand-up has led him onto the small screen in *Agony Uncles*, *Agony of Life* and *Problems* on ABC1. His own show, *Dirty Laundry Live*, started on ABC2 in 2013.

GENEVIEVE MORRIS has been an actor/improviser for twenty-two years on stage and screen. She's a mother of two, partner of one, and lives in the hills.

KATE MULVANY is an award-winning actor, playwright and screenwriter. She is also a cancer survivor and ambassador for several organisations representing the victims of Agent Orange.

RUBY J MURRAY is a writer. Her first novel, *Running Dogs* (Scribe 2012), follows the lives of a family living through the fall of the Suharto regime in Indonesia.

AMANDA PALMER is a performer, director, writer and musician who founded the internationally acclaimed punk cabaret band The Dresden Dolls. Amanda released her first solo album, *Who Killed Amanda Palmer*, in 2008, produced by Ben Folds and accompanied with the release of a fine art photography book on which she collaborated with esteemed author Neil Gaiman (who Palmer also recently married). She has fronted the Boston Pops at Symphony Hall, played venues from the Sydney Opera House to the Fuji Festival in Japan, and took on the acting role of the Emcee in a sold-out run of the Kander & Ebb musical *Cabaret* with Cambridge's American Repertory Theater in the fall of 2010. Amanda then self-released her second solo album, *Theatre Is Evil*, using crowdfunding, and gave a TED talk in 2013 called 'The Art of Asking'. She currently lives out of a suitcase and on her blog. Please visit her on The Internet, where she will invite you to sit down, pour you a virtual cup of tea, and give you a twitter cuddle.

SAM PANG is a presenter, writer, broadcaster and producer. Recently he has shared his views on life and relationships in the TV series *Agony Uncles* and *The Agony of Life* on ABC1, and for the past five years he has co-hosted SBS's coverage of the Eurovision Song Contest with Julia Zemiro. In 2010 he starred in the hugely popular *Santo, Sam and*

Ed's Cup Fever. Produced by Working Dog, the show was live and screened on SBS every night of the FIFA World Cup. This is the first letter he has written since he stopped writing to Santa Claus. Almost three years ago.

AILSA PIPER has spent her life in the theatre, working as a writer, director, teacher and actor. Her first book, *Sinning Across Spain*, told of her 1300-kilometre walk carrying the sins of others. She is also a voracious consumer of other people's poetry. She is currently working on a novel and a play. ailsapiper.com.

JULIE POSETTI is an award-winning and internationally published journalist and journalism educator who lectures in broadcast, multimedia and social journalism at the University of Wollongong (UOW). She is currently completing her PhD on 'The Twitterisation of Journalism' through UOW. A 25-year journalism veteran, she's been a national political correspondent, a regional news editor, a TV documentary reporter and a presenter on radio and television with the ABC. She's currently the Australia correspondent for the respected PBS website Mediashift, and she is also a social media trainer and consultant. Internationally published as a journalist and researcher, Posetti was a Walkley finalist in the investigative journalism category in 1996. She won the Australian Human Rights Award for Radio the same year, and in 2007 she received a Carrick Citation for excellence in teaching and learning in recognition of her innovative approach to journalism education. Her academic research centres on the intersection of journalism and social media, talkback radio, the ABC and media coverage of Muslims post-9/11. But her most important work is raising her four-year-old daughter.

LEIGH SALES anchors the ABC's prime-time current affairs program, *7.30*. She is the author of *Detainee 002* and *On Doubt*.

ZORA SANDERS is the editor of *Meanjin*. She previously edited the Melbourne Uni student magazine *Farrago* and occasionally even does a bit of writing, something she will have more time for once the fuzz finally lock her away.

ALEXANDRA SCHEPISI is an actor, a filmmaker and now a mum. She gave birth to her baby boy four days after reading her letter at the Women of Letters event in November 2012.

JILL SINGER is an award-winning journalist and author with extensive experience in the print and electronic media. She's worked at all levels behind and in front of the camera and microphone across Australia for both commercial and public broadcasters. Jill has produced and presented radio programs from remote rural locations, and designed, produced and presented national television news and current affairs programs. As well as winning awards for television broadcasts on architectural and medical issues, Jill has won the Walkley award for best television investigative journalist and twice won the Quill award for best television current affairs reporting. She currently lectures in journalism at RMIT and presents *Opportunities Australia* for the Australia Network.

Instead of siblings, **SCOTT SPARK** was kept company by two Great Danes and a piano. He began writing songs as a teenager and was unearthed by triple j in 2010, and shortly afterwards released his debut album, *Fail Like You Mean It*. He's since been awarded the Grant McLennan Memorial Fellowship and the inaugural Smoky Dawson Scholarship. His second album, *Muscle Memory*, was written between Australia and New York, and was recorded during a stint of sleeping on the floor in Los Angeles. He describes it as equal parts English Pub and Opera House.

TRACEY SPICER is one of the most versatile journalists in the country, currently anchoring at Sky News, broadcasting on Radio 2UE, and writing regular columns for thehoopla.com.au, the *Daily Telegraph* and *Sunday Telegraph*. She also does media and presentation training, and produces corporate videos through spicercommunications.biz.

LUCAS STIBBARD makes theatre and performance work. He is a founding member of The Escapists, a multi-disciplinary collective responsible for the critically acclaimed, multi-award winning anti-romantic comedy *Boy Girl Wall*, as well as *Elephant Gun* and *Attack of the Attacking Attackers!* The best thing to ever happen to him was meeting and eventually marrying fellow Escapist Neridah Waters.

SOFIJA STEFANOVIC recently wrote and directed a short film in which Thomas Henning plays a loser. She writes for print, TV and film. @sstefanovic

YUMI STYNES has been in radio and TV since she first landed a gig at the cable music station Channel [V] back in the year 2000. Since then she's made a couple of babies and several thousand people angry and continues to try to get people laughing every morning on a Sydney breakfast radio show on Mix106.5. Things she's learned after more than a decade in media: most people are inherently good, sport is tedious, and you can't please everyone.

MELANIE TAIT is the host and producer of ABC Radio National's *Now Hear This* storytelling series, author of one book (*Fat Chance: My Big Fat Gastric Band Adventure*) and writer of one play (*The Vegemite Tales*). She lives and works in Canberra.

NELLY THOMAS is a comedian who wrote a book and has done some other stuff, but nothing compares to her glory days as an under-13 State Regional Girl's BMX Champion.

DANI VALENT is an award-winning Melbourne writer, with a particular interest in food. She also spends a lot of time looking for lost jigsaw pieces and wondering what happened to all the hair elastics.

LORELEI VASHTI is a writer and book editor. She was a TV columnist for *The Age*'s *Green Guide* from 2010 to 2011 and is currently writing a book based on her popular blog, *Dress, Memory*, which will be published in 2014.

STEVE VIZARD is the father of five children, whose career path is less than certain. He has been an international commercial lawyer; the creator, producer and star of the landmark comedy series *Fast Forward*; a travelling underwear salesman for Holeproof; a Gold Logie-winning *Tonight Show* host (interviewing over two thousand guests from Audrey Hepburn and Bob Hope to Sir Peter Ustinov and Spike Milligan); the president of the National Gallery of Victoria; and the chairman of the Victorian Major Events Company (where he helped secure dozens of events for Australia, from the World Swimming Championships to exhibitions of Picasso and the Dutch masters). With Foxtel, he established thecomedychannel, and he founded one of Australia's largest production companies, Artist Services, producing over fifty shows from *Seachange* to the *Shaun Micallef Show*, and winning over two dozen Logie and AFI awards and an International Emmy. He has written for TV, radio and film as well as several books – his book, *Two Weeks in Lilliput*, a whimsical account of the constitutional convention at which he was an elected delegate, became a prescribed text on the English HSC syllabus. To the mirth of his children, he was named Father of the Year in 2001. He is currently dabbling in radio broadcasting.

SEJA VOGEL has played keyboards for such bands as Sekiden and Regurgitator, among others. In recent years she has embarked on a solo career under her own name and in her spare time she makes tiny nerdy felt replicas of instruments.

MEGAN WASHINGTON is an Australian musician and songwriter. She has won two Aria awards, for Best Female Artist and Breakthrough Artist, and the 2009 inaugural Vanda & Young Songwriting Competition.

JOHN WATERS is an actor/musician who arrived in Australia from England in 1968 on a two-year working holiday, and stayed.

LARISSA WATERS is the first Australian Greens Senator in Queensland. She is passionate about protecting our environment and public participation and accountability in government. She lives in Brisbane with her three-year-old daughter.

FRANK WOODLEY is master of physical comedy, whose man-child persona has been enjoyed by international audiences for over two decades. His most recent TV series, *Woodley*, is full of beautifully crafted visual humour mingled with sadness and a yearning for love.

QUAN YEOMANS has done a bit of meaningless stuff that he is mildly happy with. He couldn't really ask for a more privileged and easy existence and if he ever did, he would be just bitching out of turn. Quan hates bios because they sound awfully like eulogies for the undead. He's also the lead vocalist and guitarist for Regurgitator.

Acknowledgements

Enormous and inadequate thanks to the Women of Letters extended family. Galia and Alan Hardy, Lisa McGuire, Liam Pieper, David McCarthy, Lorelei Vashti, Gabi Barton, Lee Sandwith, Elaine Reyes, Kitty Robertson, Cousin Sondra Davoren, Nikki Lusk, Ronnie Scott, Auguste and Molly; we couldn't embark on nearly as many ridiculous adventures if you weren't all there to help us out. Thanks for giving up so many of your Sundays for us.

Thank you to those who have ensured that we have so many homes away from home – Fay Burstin, Joc Curran, the Red Rattler, the Basement and Avid Reader; and those who help us when we're away – Tarsha Hocking, Talia Cain, Nadine Cohen, Glenn Dickie, Vanessa Picken, James McGuire and Tim McGuire.

We're extraordinarily lucky to have Tara Nielsen on our team, who is possibly the only designer of her quality who only accepts payment in the form of the occasional dinner.

Thanks again to Ben Ball, Cate Blake and everyone at Penguin for creating these gorgeous books.

Our thanks to the Regal Ballroom for our beautiful home.

Thanks to everyone who buys a ticket to our shows, or shows up without one even when we've sold out, just in case.

And to Edgar's Mission, as always.